Mastering Eclipse Plug-in Development

Build modular applications on Eclipse by defining custom extension points and using OSGi services

Dr Alex Blewitt

open source
community experience distilled

BIRMINGHAM - MUMBAI

About the Author

Dr Alex Blewitt has been developing Java applications since version 1.0 was released in 1996, and has been using the Eclipse platform since its first release as part of the IBM WebSphere Studio product suite. He even migrated some plug-ins from VisualAge for Java to WebSphere Studio / Eclipse as part of his PhD in Automated Verification of Design Patterns. He got involved in the open source community as a tester when Eclipse 2.1 was being released for Mac OS X, and then subsequently as an editor for EclipseZone, including being a finalist for Eclipse Ambassador in 2007.

More recently, Alex has been writing for InfoQ, covering generic Java, specifically Eclipse and OSGi subjects. He was the keynote speaker at the *OSGi Community Event 2011* on the past, present, and future of OSGi. The coverage of both new releases of the Eclipse platform as well as its projects and video interviews with some of the Eclipse project leads can be found on the InfoQ home page; for this, he won the Eclipse Top Contributor award in 2012.

Alex currently works for an investment bank in London. He also has a number of apps on the App Store through Bandlem Limited.

Alex blogs at `http://alblue.bandlem.com` and tweets via Twitter as `@alblue` regularly and is the author of *Eclipse 4 Plug-in Development by Example Beginner's Guide, Packt Publishing*.

Acknowledgments

I'd like to thank my wife, Amy, who has been behind me for over 15 years, supporting me during the development of this and other books. Behind every man is a great woman, and I wouldn't be where I am today if it were not for her.

I'd also like to thank my parents, Derek and Ann, for introducing me to technology at an early age with a ZX81 and setting me on a path and career that would take me across the globe, even though the name of my first company could have been better chosen.

Special thanks are due to Ann Ford, Carla Guillen, Jeff MAURY, and Peter Rice, who provided detailed feedback about every chapter and the exercises therein. Without their diligence and attention, this book would contain many more errors than I would like. Thanks are also due to the Packt Publishing editing team, especially Dennis John, who was very patient with my rewrites. I'd also like to thank Sam Wood for keeping the book on the straight and narrow as well as Susmita Panda and Binny Babu, who were involved through the production process.

During the later stages of the book, I was also fortunate enough to receive some good feedback and advice from Lars Vogel and Ian Bull, both of whom are heavily involved in the Eclipse platform. I am especially grateful for Lars Vogel's website, `www.vogella.com`, which has been an invaluable resource over the years.

To Sam, Holly, and all the Akeley Wood Code Clubbers, this is just the start of your journey through life. Aim high, work hard, and do what you love.

Finally, I'd like to thank OD, DJ, and JC for their support in making this book possible.

About the Reviewers

Carla Guillen has a Master's degree in Computational Science and Engineering and is working at the Leibniz Supercomputing Centre of the Bavarian Academy of Sciences and Humanities. She is currently pursuing a PhD in monitoring performance of supercomputers in the field of Computer Architecture Organization. As part of the annual courses offered at the Leibniz Supercomputing Centre, she has been teaching a course on the use of the Eclipse IDE with the CDT and Photran plug-in for the past 4 years.

Jeff MAURY is currently working as the technical lead for the Java team at SYSPERTEC, a French ISV offering mainframe integration tools. He is also a PMC member for the Apache MINA project.

Prior to SYSPERTEC, he co-founded a French ISV called SCORT in 1996, which was the precursor of the application server concept and offered J2EE-based integration tools.

He started his career in 1988 at MARBEN, a French integration company specializing in telecommunication protocols. At MARBEN, he started as a software developer and finished as an X.400 team technical lead and Internet division strategist.

I would like to dedicate my work to Jean-Pierre Ansart, my mentor, and would also like to thank my wife, Julia, for her patience and my three sons, Robinson, Paul, and Ugo.

Peter Rice is a retired professor of Mathematics and has been active in IT consulting for the past 20 years. He is a certified trainer for IBM and Microsoft, and has worked through independent training vendors offering courses in programming languages (Java, C, C++, Perl, and so on), advanced systems (Eclipse, Eclipse Plug-in Development, Rich Client Platform, and Java EE), and various other technologies. He has also been consulted with on many projects and is currently working with Trail Management Systems on the development of a new generation of business management software.

www.PacktPub.com

Support files, eBooks, discount offers, and more

You might want to visit www.PacktPub.com for support files and downloads related to your book.

Did you know that Packt offers eBook versions of every book published, with PDF and ePub files available? You can upgrade to the eBook version at www.PacktPub.com and as a print book customer, you are entitled to a discount on the eBook copy. Get in touch with us at service@packtpub.com for more details.

At www.PacktPub.com, you can also read a collection of free technical articles, sign up for a range of free newsletters and receive exclusive discounts and offers on Packt books and eBooks.

http://PacktLib.PacktPub.com

Do you need instant solutions to your IT questions? PacktLib is Packt's online digital book library. Here, you can access, read and search across Packt's entire library of books.

Why subscribe?

- Fully searchable across every book published by Packt
- Copy and paste, print and bookmark content
- On demand and accessible via web browser

Free access for Packt account holders

If you have an account with Packt at www.PacktPub.com, you can use this to access PacktLib today and view nine entirely free books. Simply use your login credentials for immediate access.

Table of Contents

Preface

The Eclipse platform provides an extensible system for building plug-ins and applications in a modular fashion. While other books discuss the general mechanism to create plug-ins, this book dives deeper into the underlying mechanisms, including how to create plug-ins that have their own extension points and how to use OSGi services within an Eclipse application. It is expected that you are familiar with Eclipse plug-in development already and you understand the content covered in *Eclipse 4 Plug-in Development by Example Beginner's Guide, Packt Publishing*. By the end of this book, you will know how to write extensible plug-ins for both Eclipse extensions as well as standalone OSGi frameworks and provide end-to-end delivery of Eclipse applications with help and update sites.

What this book covers

Chapter 1, Plugging in to JFace and the Common Navigator Framework, demonstrates how to create JFace wizards and how to integrate content into the Common Navigator Framework, which is then used by Package Explorer to provide a tree view of the project's contents.

Chapter 2, Creating Custom Extension Points, shows how the Eclipse extension registry can be used to create an extensible plug-in that allows other plug-ins to contribute functionalities and how it can be used outside of an OSGi or Eclipse runtime.

Chapter 3, Using OSGi Services to Dynamically Wire Applications, introduces OSGi services as a means to extend an application's functionality. This chapter shows how these services can be configured declaratively with Declarative Services or Blueprint and how they can be configured using Config Admin along with the new changes in OSGi R6.

Chapter 4, Using the Gogo Shell and Commands, discusses how to use the Gogo shell embedded in Eclipse 4 and how to extend it by creating custom commands in Gogo script and Java.

Chapter 5, Native Code and Fragment Bundles, demonstrates how to load native code into an OSGi or Eclipse application and how fragment bundles can be used to extend the capabilities of the framework or existing OSGi bundles.

Chapter 6, Understanding ClassLoaders, goes into detail as to how the key concepts of a Java ClassLoader work and how they are used in an OSGi runtime. It also explains how non-OSGi workarounds, such as the Thread Context ClassLoader and ServiceLoader, can be used in an OSGi framework, along with presenting upgrade strategies for non-OSGi JARs.

Chapter 7, Designing Modular Applications, discusses modular design patterns such as the whiteboard pattern and extender pattern along with 18 best practices, including how to use semantic versioning and tools that can automate version number management.

Chapter 8, Event-driven Applications with EventAdmin, introduces the OSGi EventAdmin service and how E4 uses events under the covers to provide an interactive workspace, along with 7 steps for designing event-driven applications.

Chapter 9, Deploying and Updating with P2, shows how to create and manage P2 repositories (update sites) along with creating custom touchpoints and categories.

Chapter 10, User Assistance in Eclipse, demonstrates how to write help documentation for an Eclipse- or RCP-based product along with cheat sheets and running a public facing help server.

What you need for this book

To run the exercises in this book, you will need a computer with an up-to-date operating system (running Windows, Linux, or Mac OS X). Java also needs to be installed; the book's exercises were tested against JDK 1.7, but newer versions of Java should also work. The exercises were written and tested against both Eclipse Standard 4.4 (Luna) as well as 4.3 (Kepler). The principles should work for future versions of Eclipse as well, but note that each release of Eclipse has a migration guide in the *Platform Plug-in Developer Guide* help topic that will list any incompatibilities. This help information is also available online at `http://help.eclipse.org/` for the current release.

The exercises are available on the Packt website as well as on GitHub at `https://github.com/alblue/com.packtpub.e4.advanced/`. Using the GitHub code will require a Git installation such as EGit for Eclipse (available from the Eclipse Marketplace) or a standalone Git client from `http://git-scm.com/`.

Who this book is for

This book is aimed at existing Eclipse plug-in developers who know the basics of plug-in development but want to learn some of the techniques in greater detail.

Developers wishing to write extensible plug-ins will find the advice in chapters 1 and 2 useful to integrate with some parts of the Eclipse framework that they may not have previously used.

Those that are unfamiliar with OSGi services or don't know how to integrate into Eclipse will find chapter 3 a good introduction, which is usually not covered in other Eclipse plug-in development books. Those wishing to extend the Gogo shell will find the information in chapter 4 beneficial, and chapter 5 will benefit those who need help in including native code dependencies. Developers who need to include non-OSGi JARs will find the techniques discussed in chapter 6 to be useful.

For those who are looking for advice on how to structure modular applications, the practices in chapters 7 and 8 will be beneficial.

Finally, for developers responsible for providing products, chapters 9 and 10 show how to customize and publish P2 repositories as well as provide user assistance (help) for applications.

Conventions

In this book, you will find a number of styles of text that distinguish between different kinds of information. Here are some examples of these styles, and an explanation of their meaning.

Code words in text, database table names, folder names, filenames, file extensions, pathnames, dummy URLs, user input, and Twitter handles are shown as follows: "A cursor need to be closed to free the resource the object holds by calling the `close()` method."

A block of code is set as follows:

```
public void deleted(String pid) {
  System.out.println("Removing echo server with pid " + pid);
  EchoServer removed = echoServers.remove(pid);
  if (removed != null) {
    removed.stop();
  }
}
```

When we wish to draw your attention to a particular part of a code block, the relevant lines or items are set in bold:

```
            </goals>
        </execution>
        <execution>
            <id>baseline</id>
            <phase>package</phase>
            <goals>
              <goal>baseline</goal>
            </goals>
        </execution>
      </executions>
    </plugin>
```

Any command-line input or output is written as follows:

```
$ mvn install
$ mvn versions:set -DnewVersion=1.0.1
... make changes to Java files ...
$ mvn package
```

New terms and **important words** are shown in bold. Words that you see on the screen, in menus or dialog boxes for example, appear in the text like this: "Clicking on **Reset** (to scan the directory) followed by **Finish** will set up the baseline."

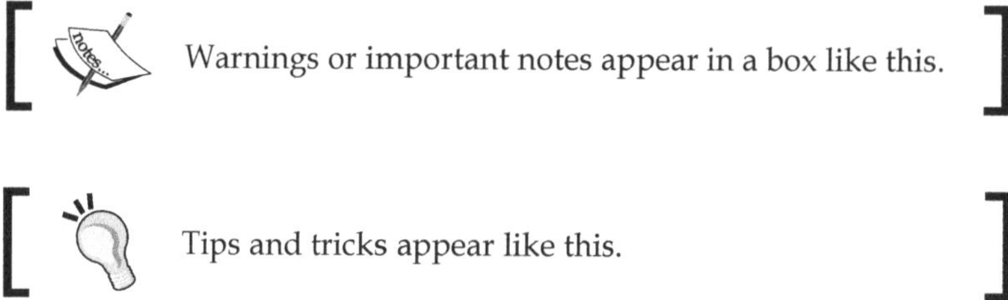

Warnings or important notes appear in a box like this.

Tips and tricks appear like this.

Reader feedback

Feedback from our readers is always welcome. Let us know what you think about this book—what you liked or may have disliked. Reader feedback is important for us to develop titles that you really get the most out of.

To send us general feedback, simply send an e-mail to `feedback@packtpub.com`, and mention the book title via the subject of your message.

If there is a topic that you have expertise in and you are interested in either writing or contributing to a book, see our author guide on `www.packtpub.com/authors`.

Customer support

Now that you are the proud owner of a Packt book, we have a number of things to help you to get the most from your purchase.

Downloading the example code

You can download the example code files for all Packt books you have purchased from your account at `http://www.packtpub.com`. If you purchased this book elsewhere, you can visit `http://www.packtpub.com/support` and register to have the files e-mailed directly to you. Alternatively, the code is available on GitHub at the book's repository `https://github.com/alblue/com.packtpub.e4.advanced/`.

Errata

Although we have taken every care to ensure the accuracy of our content, mistakes do happen. If you find a mistake in one of our books—maybe a mistake in the text or the code—we would be grateful if you would report this to us. By doing so, you can save other readers from frustration and help us improve subsequent versions of this book. If you find any errata, please report them by visiting `http://www.packtpub.com/submit-errata`, selecting your book, clicking on the **errata submission form** link, and entering the details of your errata. Once your errata are verified, your submission will be accepted and the errata will be uploaded on our website, or added to any list of existing errata, under the Errata section of that title. Any existing errata can be viewed by selecting your title from `http://www.packtpub.com/support`.

Piracy

Piracy of copyright material on the Internet is an ongoing problem across all media. At Packt, we take the protection of our copyright and licenses very seriously. If you come across any illegal copies of our works, in any form, on the Internet, please provide us with the location address or website name immediately so that we can pursue a remedy.

Please contact us at `copyright@packtpub.com` with a link to the suspected pirated material.

We appreciate your help in protecting our authors, and our ability to bring you valuable content.

Questions

You can contact us at `questions@packtpub.com` if you are having a problem with any aspect of the book, and we will do our best to address it.

1
Plugging in to JFace and the Common Navigator Framework

JFace is the set of widgets that comprise the Eclipse user interface, and it builds on top of the **Standard Widget Toolkit** (**SWT**). JFace also provides a number of standard higher-level tools that can provide interaction with users, such as wizards and standard navigator plug-ins.

In this chapter, we will create a news feed reader using a JFace wizard, and then we will contribute it to the **common navigator** so that it shows up in views such as the **Package Explorer** view.

JFace wizards

Whenever a new project or file is created in Eclipse, the standard JFace wizard is used. For example, the following screenshots show the wizards to create a new **Plug-in Project** or Java **Class**:

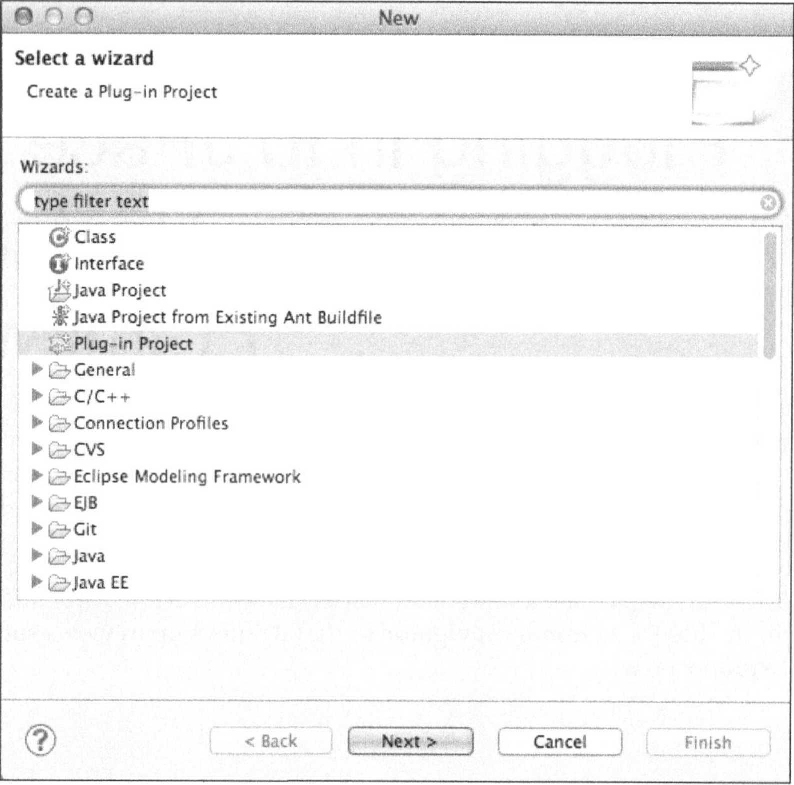

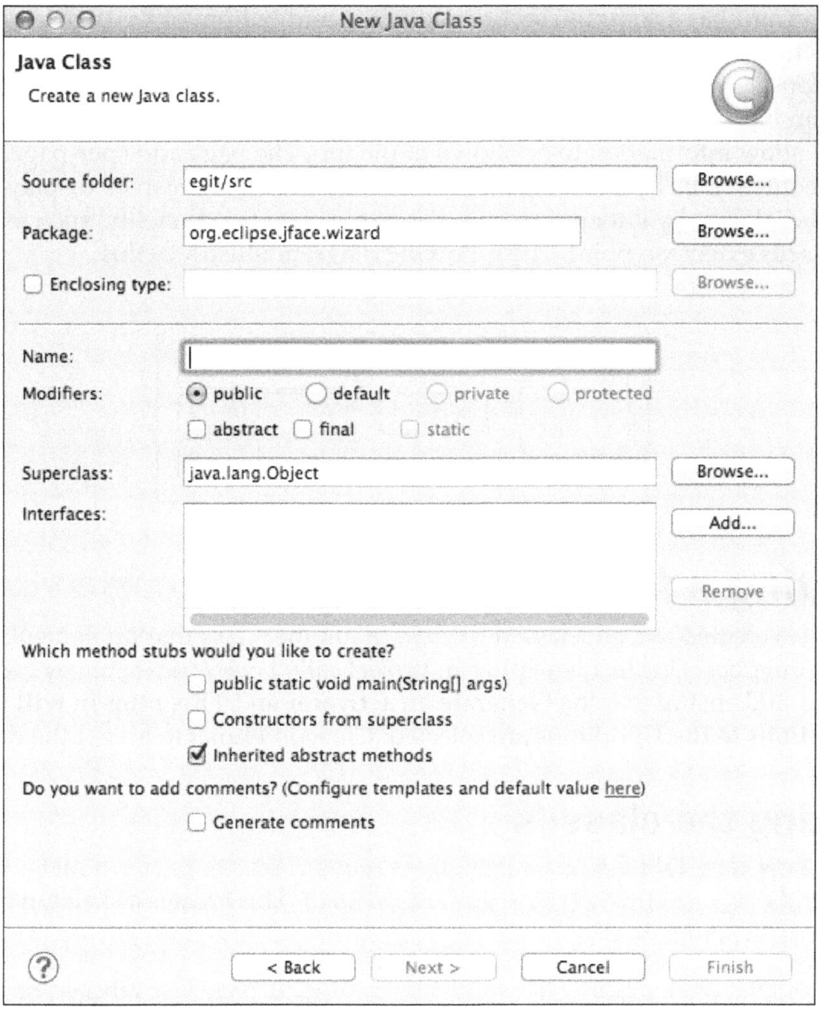
New Java Class
Java Class
Create a new Java class.
Source folder:
egit/src
Browse...
Package:
org.eclipse.jface.wizard
Browse...
Enclosing type:
Browse...
Name:
Modifiers:
public
default
private
protected
abstract
final
static
Superclass:
java.lang.Object
Browse...
Interfaces:
Add...
Remove
Which method stubs would you like to create?
public static void main(String[] args)
Constructors from superclass
Inherited abstract methods
Do you want to add comments? (Configure templates and default value here)
Generate comments
< Back
Next >
Cancel
Finish

A JFace wizard has a common section at the top and bottom of the dialog, which provides the title/icon and transition buttons along with an optional help link. Each wizard consists of one or more linked **pages** that define the visible **content area** and the **button bar**. The **window title** is shared across all pages; the **page title** and **page message** allow information to be shown at the top. The page adds per-page content into the content area by exposing a **page control**. The wizard can be displayed with a **wizard dialog** or by integrating with the workbench functionality, such as the **newWizards** extension point. The following diagram illustrates this:

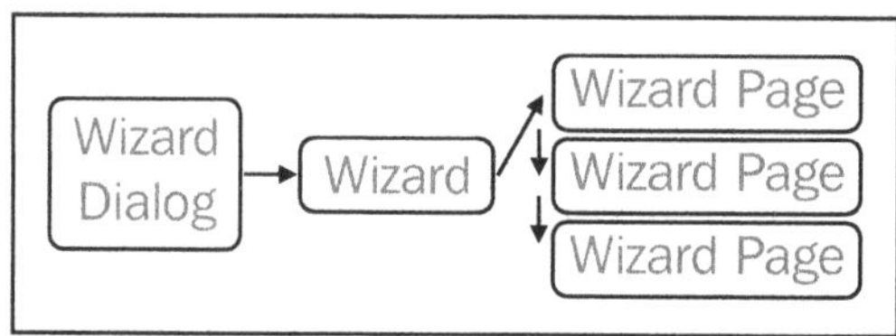

Creating a feeds wizard

A wizard is created as a subclass of `Wizard` or another class that implements the **IWizard** interface. Create a new plug-in project called `com.packtpub.e4.advanced.feeds.ui` and ensure that the **Generate an activator** and **This plug-in will make contributions to the UI** options are selected. Click on **Finish** to accept the defaults.

Creating the classes

Create a new class called `com.packtpub.e4.advanced.feeds.ui.NewFeedWizard` that extends `org.eclipse.jface.wizard.Wizard`. This creates a skeleton file with a `performFinish` method.

To add content, one or more pages must be created. A page is a subclass of `WizardPage` or another class that implements the `IWizardPage` interface. Pages are typically added within the constructor or `addPages` methods of the owning wizard.

Create a new class called `com.packtpub.e4.advanced.feeds.ui.NewFeedPage` that extends `org.eclipse.jface.wizard.WizardPage`. The default implementation will be missing a constructor; create a default constructor that passes the string `"NewFeedPage"` to the superclass' constructor.

The code should now look like the following code snippet:

```
package com.packtpub.e4.advanced.feeds.ui;
import org.eclipse.jface.wizard.Wizard;
public class NewFeedWizard extends Wizard {
  public boolean performFinish() {
    return false;
  }
}
package com.packtpub.e4.advanced.feeds.ui;
import org.eclipse.jface.wizard.WizardPage;
import org.eclipse.swt.widgets.Composite;
public class NewFeedPage extends WizardPage {
  protected NewFeedPage() {
    super("NewFeedPage");
  }
  public void createControl(Composite parent) {
  }
}
```

Adding pages to the wizard

The wizard has an `addPages` method that is called when it is about to be shown. This allows one or more pages to be added to allow the wizard to do work. For simple wizards, a single page is often enough; but for complex wizards, it may make sense to break it down into two or more individual pages. A multipage wizard typically steps through its pages in order, but more complex transitions can be achieved if necessary.

Create a new instance of `NewFeedPage` and assign it to an instance variable called `newFeedPage`. Create an `addPages` method that calls `addPage` with `newFeedPage` as an argument, as shown in the following code:

```
private NewFeedPage newFeedPage = new NewFeedPage();
public void addPages() {
  addPage(newFeedPage);
}
```

Adding content to the page

Each page has an associated content area, which is populated through the `createControl` method on the `page` class. This is given a `Composite` object to add widgets; a typical wizard page starts off with exactly the same stanza as other container methods by creating a new `Composite`, setting it as the control on the page and making it incomplete. The code is as follows:

```
public void createControl(Composite parent) {
  Composite page = new Composite(parent,SWT.NONE);
  setControl(page);
  setPageComplete(false);
}
```

Pages are typically set up as data gathering devices, and the logic is delegated to the wizard to decide what action to take. In this case, a feed has a simple URL and a title, so the page will store these as two instance variables and set up UI widgets to save the content.

Downloading the example code

You can download the example code files for all Packt books you have purchased from your account at `http://www.packtpub.com`. If you purchased this book elsewhere, you can visit `http://www.packtpub.com/support` and register to have the files e-mailed directly to you.

The code can also be downloaded from the book's GitHub repository at `https://github.com/alblue/com.packtpub.e4.advanced/`.

One of the easiest ways to get data out of the page is to persist references to the SWT `Text` boxes that are used to input content and then provide accessors to access the data. To guard against failure, accessor methods need to test for `null` and check that the widget hasn't been disposed. The code is as follows:

```
private Text descriptionText;
private Text urlText;
public String getDescription() {
  return getTextFrom(descriptionText);
}
private String getTextFrom(Text text) {
  return text==null || text.isDisposed() ? null : text.getText();
}
public String getURL() {
  return getTextFrom(urlText);
}
```

This allows the parent wizard to access the data entered by the user once the page is complete. The process of getting the data is typically performed within the `performFinish` method, where the resulting operation can be displayed.

The page's user interface is built in the `createControl` method. This is typically organized with a `GridLayout`, although this isn't a requirement. The user interface for wizards tend to offer a grid of `Label` and `Text` widgets, so it could look like the following code snippet:

```
page.setLayout(new GridLayout(2, false));
page.setLayoutData(new GridData(GridData.FILL_BOTH));
Label urlLabel = new Label(page, SWT.NONE);
urlLabel.setText("Feed URL:");
urlText = new Text(page, SWT.BORDER);
urlText.setLayoutData(new GridData(GridData.FILL_HORIZONTAL));
Label descriptionLabel = new Label(page, SWT.NONE);
descriptionLabel.setText("Feed description:");
descriptionText = new Text(page, SWT.BORDER);
descriptionText.setLayoutData(
  new GridData(GridData.FILL_HORIZONTAL));
```

The **Finish** button on the wizard is enabled when the page is marked as complete. Each wizard knows what information is required to finish; when it is finished, it should call `setPageComplete(true)`. This can be arranged in the `NewFeedPage` class by listening to text entry changes on the feed description and URL and setting the page to be complete when both have non-empty values:

```
private class CompleteListener implements KeyListener {
  public void keyPressed(KeyEvent e) {
  }
  public void keyReleased(KeyEvent e) {
    boolean hasDescription =
     !"".equals(getTextFrom(descriptionText));
    boolean hasUrl = !"".equals(getTextFrom(urlText));
    setPageComplete(hasDescription && hasUrl);
  }
}
public void createControl(Composite parent) {
  …
  CompleteListener listener = new CompleteListener();
  urlText.addKeyListener(listener);
  descriptionText.addKeyListener(listener);
}
```

Now, whenever a key is pressed and there is text present in both the description and URL fields, the **Finish** button will be enabled; if text is removed from either field, it will be disabled.

Testing the wizard

To test whether the wizard works as expected before it is integrated into an Eclipse application, a small standalone test script can be created. Although bad practice, it is possible to add a `main` method to `NewFeedWizard` to allow it to display the wizard in a standalone fashion.

Wizards are displayed with the JFace `WizardDialog`. This takes a `Shell` and the `Wizard` instance; so a simple test can be run using the following snippet of code:

```
public static void main(String[] args) {
  Display display = new Display();
  Shell shell = new Shell(display);
  new WizardDialog(shell, new NewFeedWizard()).open();
  display.dispose();
}
```

Now, if the wizard is run, a standalone shell will be displayed and the fields and checks can be tested for correct behavior. A more complex set of tests can be set up with a UI test framework such as **SWTBot**.

For more information about SWTBot, see chapter 9 of the book *Eclipse 4 Plug-in Development by Example Beginner's Guide, Packt Publishing*, or visit the SWTBot home page at `http://eclipse.org/swtbot/`.

Adding titles and images

If the wizard is shown as is, the title area will be empty. Typically, a user will need to know what information to put in and what is required in order to complete the dialog. Each page can contribute information specific to that step. In the case of a multipage wizard where there are several distinct stages, each page can contribute its own information.

In the case of the new feed page, the title and message can be informational. The constructor is a good place to set the initial title and message. The code to perform this operation is as follows:

```
protected NewFeedPage() {
  super("NewFeedPage");
  setTitle("Add New Feed");
  setMessage("Please enter a URL and description for a news feed");
}
```

When feed information is entered, the message can be replaced to indicate that a description or URL is required. To clear the message, invoke `setMessage(null)`. To add an error message, invoke `setMessage` and pass in one of the constants from `IMessageProvider`, as shown:

```
public void keyReleased(KeyEvent e) {
  boolean hasDescription
   = !"".equals(getTextFrom(descriptionText));
  boolean hasUrl = !"".equals(getTextFrom(urlText))
  if (!hasDescription) {
    setMessage("Please enter a description"
      IMessageProvider.ERROR);
  }
  if (!hasUrl) {
    setMessage("Please enter a URL", IMessageProvider.ERROR);
  }
  if (hasDescription && hasUrl) {
    setMessage(null);
  }
  setPageComplete(hasDescription && hasUrl);
}
```

To display an image on the wizard as a whole, the page can have an image of size 75 x 58 pixels. This can be set from an image descriptor in the constructor:

```
setImageDescriptor(
 ImageDescriptor.createFromFile(
  NewFeedPage.class, "/icons/full/wizban/newfeed_wiz.png"));
```

Now, running the wizard will display an icon at the top-right corner (if it doesn't, check that `build.properties` includes the `icons/` directory in the `bin.includes` property):

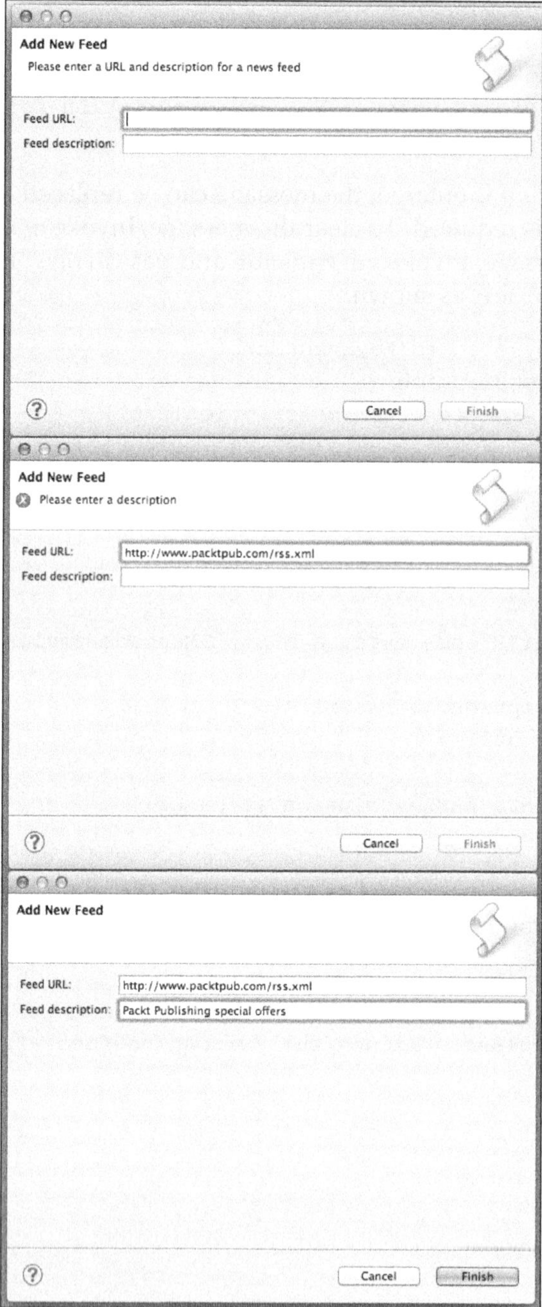

Due to Eclipse bug 439695, Eclipse 4.4.0 may be unable to load the `IMessageProvider.ERROR` image. If the red cross is seen as a small red dot, this can be ignored; it will work when running as an Eclipse plug-in. This bug is fixed in Eclipse 4.4.1 and above, and does not occur in Eclipse 4.3.

Use this to add a feed file of `http://www.packtpub.com/rss.xml` with a description of **Packt Publishing special offers**.

Adding help

To add help, the wizard needs to declare that help is available. During the construction of the wizard or in the `addPages` method, a call to the parent's `setHelpAvailable` method with a `true` parameter has to be invoked.

Help is delegated to each page by calling a `performHelp` method. This allows context-sensitive help to be delivered for the specific page displayed, and it also helps to get the state of the page or its previous page states. The code is as follows:

```
// Add to the NewFeedWizard class
public void addPages() {
  addPage(new NewFeedPage());
  setHelpAvailable(true);
}
// Add to the NewFeedPage class
public void performHelp() {
  MessageDialog.openInformation(getShell(),
    "Help for Add New Feed",
    "You can add your feeds into this as an RSS or Atom feed, "
  + "and optionally specify an additional description "
  + "which will be used as the feed title.");
}
```

Executing the preceding code will show a **Help** button on the bottom of the dialog; when clicked, it will show a help dialog with some text as shown in the following screenshot:

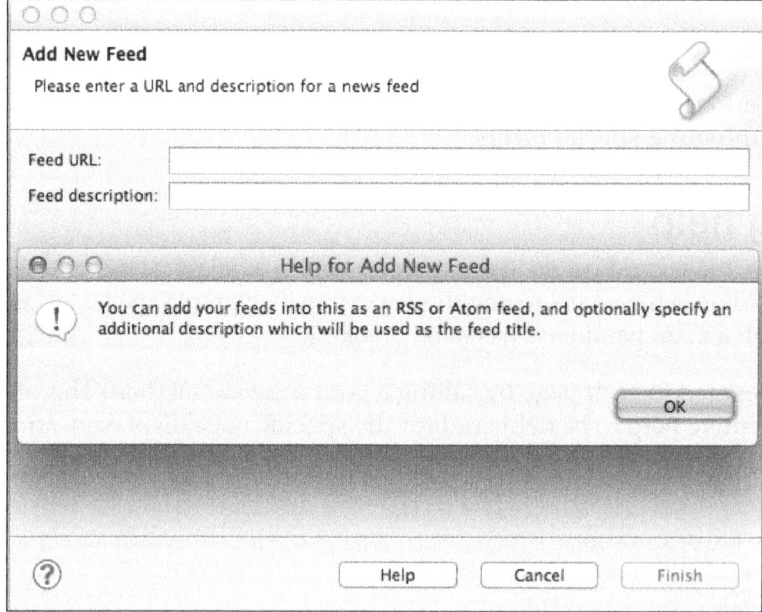

Finishing the wizard

When the user clicks on the **Finish** button on the wizard, the corresponding `performFinish` method is called. This allows the wizard to acquire data from the underlying pages and perform whatever action is required.

In this case, a `Properties` file called `news.feeds` can be created underneath a project called `bookmarks` in the workspace. This will require that `org.eclipse.core.resources` is added to the plug-in's dependencies.

> For more information about creating resources and projects, see chapter 6 of *Eclipse 4 Plug-in Development by Example Beginner's Guide, Packt Publishing,* or visit the Eclipse help documentation at `http://help.eclipse.org`.

First, acquire or create a project called `bookmarks` and then acquire or create a file called `news.feeds`. The underlying content will be stored in the `Properties` file as a list of `key=value` pairs, where `key` is the URL and `value` is the description.

To simplify access to `ResourcesPlugin`, create a helper method in `NewFeedWizard` that will obtain an `IFile` from a project as follows:

```
private IFile getFile(String project, String name,
 IProgressMonitor monitor) throws CoreException {
  IWorkspace workspace = ResourcesPlugin.getWorkspace();
  IProject bookmarks = workspace.getRoot().getProject(project);
  if (!bookmarks.exists()) {
    bookmarks.create(monitor);
  }
  if (!bookmarks.isOpen()) {
    bookmarks.open(monitor);
  }
  return bookmarks.getFile(name);
}
```

To access the feeds from the resources, create two `public static final` variables that define the name of the project and the name of the bookmarks file:

```
public static final String FEEDS_FILE = "news.feeds";
public static final String FEEDS_PROJECT = "bookmarks";
```

These can be used to create a helper method to add a single feed on the resource by reading the contents of the file (creating it if it doesn't exist), adding the feed, and then saving the new contents of the file:

```
private synchronized void addFeed(String url, String description)
 throws CoreException, IOException {
  Properties feeds = new Properties();
  IFile file = getFile(FEEDS_PROJECT, FEEDS_FILE, null);
  if (file.exists()) {
    feeds.load(file.getContents());
  }
  feeds.setProperty(url, description);
  ByteArrayOutputStream baos = new ByteArrayOutputStream();
  feeds.store(baos, null);
  ByteArrayInputStream bais =
   new ByteArrayInputStream(baos.toByteArray());
  if (file.exists()) {
    file.setContents(bais, true, false, null);
  } else {
    file.create(bais, true, null);
  }
}
```

Finally, to hook this method in with the `performFinish` method being called, pull the `description` and `url` fields from `NewFeedPage` and then pass them to the `addFeed` method. Since an exception may be raised, surround them with a `try/catch` block that returns `true` or `false` (as appropriate):

```
public boolean performFinish() {
  String url = newFeedPage.getURL();
  String description = newFeedPage.getDescription();
  try {
    if (url != null && description != null) {
      addFeed(url, description);
    }
    return true;
  } catch (Exception e) {
    newFeedPage.setMessage(e.toString(), IMessageProvider.ERROR);
    return false;
  }
}
```

Running the wizard from the test harness won't have an effect, since the workspace won't be open. It is thus necessary to contribute this to the new wizard's mechanism in Eclipse, which is done in the next section.

Adding the FeedWizard to the newWizards extension point

To integrate the wizard into Eclipse, it should be added to the `newWizards` extension point provided by the `org.eclipse.ui` plug-in.

There is a minor modification required in the wizard to make it fit in with the new wizard extension point: implementing the `INewWizard` interface. This adds an additional method, `init`, that provides the current selection at the time of calling. This allows the wizard to detect whether (for example) a string URL is selected and, if so, fills the dialog with that information. The modification is shown in the following code snippet:

```
public class NewFeedWizard extends Wizard implements INewWizard {
  public void init(IWorkbench workbench,
   IStructuredSelection selection) {
  }
  ...
}
```

Add the following extension, along with a 16 x 16 icon, to the `plugin.xml` file:

```
<plugin>
  <extension point="org.eclipse.ui.newWizards">
    <category name="Feeds"
      id="com.packtpub.e4.advanced.feeds.ui.category"/>
    <wizard name="New Feed"
      class="com.packtpub.e4.advanced.feeds.ui.NewFeedWizard"
      category="com.packtpub.e4.advanced.feeds.ui.category"
      icon="icons/full/etool16/newfeed_wiz.gif"
      id="com.packtpub.e4.advanced.feeds.ui.newFeedWizard"/>
  </extension>
</plugin>
```

Now, the Eclipse application can be run and a **Feeds** category will be added to the **New** dialog situated under **File**.

Icon sizes, along with naming conventions, can be found on the Eclipse wiki at `http://wiki.eclipse.org/User_Interface_Guidelines`.

Adding a progress monitor

The wizard container can have a progress bar for long-running operations and can be used to display the progress, including optional cancellation, if the job requires it.

To acquire a progress monitor, the wizard's container can be used to invoke `RunnableWithProgress`, which is an interface that has a `run` method with an `IProgressMonitor` argument. The `addFeed` method can be moved into an anonymous inner class, which allows the wizard to display the progress of the operation without blocking the UI. The code is as follows:

```
public boolean performFinish() {
  final String url = newFeedPage.getURL();
  final String description = newFeedPage.getDescription();
  try {
    boolean fork = false;
    boolean cancel = true;
    getContainer().run(fork, cancel, new IRunnableWithProgress() {
      public void run(IProgressMonitor monitor)
       throws InvocationTargetException, InterruptedException {
        try {
          if (url != null && description != null) {
            addFeed(url, description, monitor);
```

```
            }
          } catch (Exception e) {
            throw new InvocationTargetException(e);
          }
        }
      });
      return true;
    } catch (InvocationTargetException e) {
      newFeedPage.setMessage(e.getTargetException().toString(),
       IMessageProvider.ERROR);
      return false;
    } catch (InterruptedException e) {
      return true;
    }
  }
```

The `fork` argument passed to the `run` method indicates whether the job should run in the path of the `performFinish` method or if it should run in a new thread. If a new thread is chosen, the `run` method will return hiding any errors that may be generated from the result of the `addFeed` call. The `cancel` argument provides an option to cancel the job if run in the same thread.

The `addFeed` method can be modified (as shown in the following code snippet) to interact with the progress monitor after converting it to a `SubMonitor` and passing it to the child tasks as appropriate. Regularly checking whether the monitor is cancelled will give the user the best experience if they decide to cancel the job.

```
private synchronized void addFeed(String url, String description,
 IProgressMonitor monitor) throws CoreException, IOException {
  SubMonitor subMonitor = SubMonitor.convert(monitor, 2);
  if(subMonitor.isCanceled())
    return;
  Properties feeds = new Properties();
  IFile file = getFile(FEEDS_PROJECT, FEEDS_FILE, subMonitor);
  subMonitor.worked(1);
  if (file.exists()) {
    feeds.load(file.getContents());
  }
  if(subMonitor.isCanceled())
    return;
  feeds.setProperty(url, description);
  ByteArrayOutputStream baos = new ByteArrayOutputStream();
```

```
    feeds.save(baos, null);
    ByteArrayInputStream bais =
     new ByteArrayInputStream(baos.toByteArray());
    if(subMonitor.isCanceled())
      return;
    if (file.exists()) {
      file.setContents(bais, true, false, subMonitor);
    } else {
      file.create(bais, true, subMonitor);
    }
    subMonitor.worked(1);
    if (monitor != null) {
      monitor.done();
    }
  }
```

If the wizard is shown now, the cancellation button and progress bars are not shown. In order to ensure that the wizard shows them, the `addPages` method must also declare that the progress monitor is required, as shown in the following code snippet:

```
public void addPages() {
  addPage(newFeedPage);
  setHelpAvailable(true);
  setNeedsProgressMonitor(true);
}
```

Showing a preview

When feed information is added, the **Finish** button is automatically enabled. However, the user may be interested in verifying whether they have entered the correct URL. Adding an additional **Preview** page allows the user to confirm that the right details have been entered.

To do this, create a new class called `NewFeedPreviewPage` that extends `WizardPage`. Implement it using a constructor similar to the `NewFeedPage` and with a `createControl` method that instantiates a `Browser` widget. Since loading a URL will be an asynchronous operation, the browser can be pre-filled with a `Loading...` text message that will be briefly visible before the page is loaded. The code is as follows:

```
public class NewFeedPreviewPage extends WizardPage {
  private Browser browser;
  protected NewFeedPreviewPage() {
```

```
    super("NewFeedPreviewPage");
    setTitle("Preview of Feed");
    setMessage("A preview of the provided URL is shown below");
    setImageDescriptor(
     ImageDescriptor.createFromFile(NewFeedPreviewPage.class,
       "/icons/full/wizban/newfeed_wiz.png"));
  }
  public void createControl(Composite parent) {
    Composite page = new Composite(parent, SWT.NONE);
    setControl(page);
    page.setLayout(new FillLayout());
    browser = new Browser(page, SWT.NONE);
    browser.setText("Loading...");
  }
}
```

To have the browser show the correct URL when it is shown, override the `setVisible` method. This only needs to be done if the page is visible and also if the browser widget is not `null` and not disposed.

To find out what the value of the URL should be, the previous wizard page needs to be acquired. Although it is possible to store these as `static` variables and use Java to pass references, the parent `Wizard` already has a list of these pages and can return them by name. Use this to acquire the `NewFeedPage` from the list of pages, from which the URL can be acquired. The resulting `setVisible` method then looks like the following code snippet:

```
public void setVisible(boolean visible) {
  if (visible && browser != null && !browser.isDisposed()) {
    NewFeedPage newFeedPage = (NewFeedPage)
     (getWizard().getPage("NewFeedPage"));
    String url = newFeedPage.getURL();
    browser.setUrl(url);
  }
  super.setVisible(visible);
}
```

The final step is to integrate this into the wizard itself. The only change that is needed here is to add a field to store a reference to the preview page and pass it in the `addPages` method, as shown in the following code:

```
private NewFeedPreviewPage newFeedPreviewPage
 = new NewFeedPreviewPage();
public void addPages() {
```

```
        addPage(newFeedPage);
        addPage(newFeedPreviewPage);
        ...
    }
```

Now, when the wizard is invoked, both the **Next** and **Finish** buttons are enabled once the fields have been completed. Clicking on the **Finish** button as before will add the feed, but the **Next** button will take the user to a page that has a preview of the page.

Common navigator

The **common navigator** is a JFace `TreeView` component that has extension points for displaying arbitrary types of objects. Instead of having to write content and label providers for all sorts of different objects, the common navigator provides a tree view that allows plug-ins to contribute different renderers based on the type of object in the tree.

The common navigator is used by the **Project Explorer** view in Eclipse and is used to show the graphics and labels for the packages, classes, and their methods and fields, as shown in the following screenshot. It is also used in the enterprise Java plug-in to provide Servlet and context-related information.

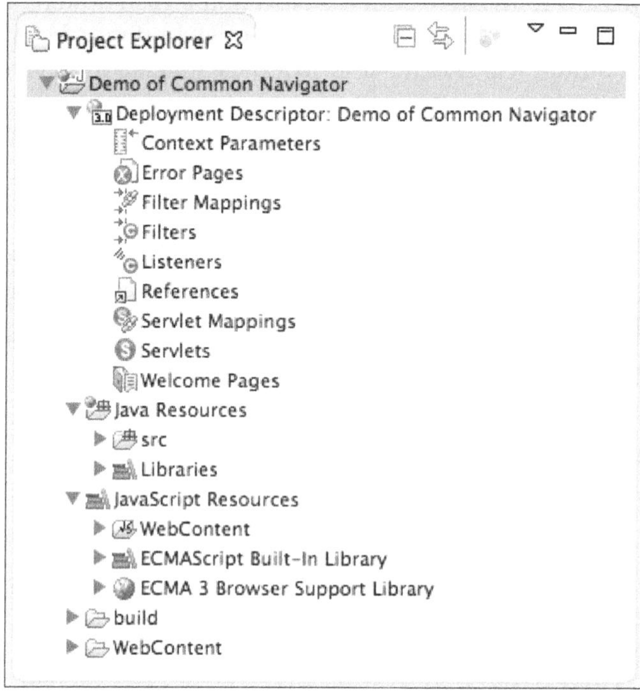

None of the resources shown in the screenshot of the **Project Explorer** view exist as individual files on disk. Instead, the **Project Explorer** view presents a virtual view of the `web.xml` contents. The `J2EEContentProvider` and `J2EELabelProvider` nodes are used to expand the available content set and generate the top-level node, along with references to the underlying source files.

Note that, as of Eclipse 4.4, the common navigator is an Eclipse 3.x plug-in, and as such, works with the Eclipse 3.x compatibility layer. `CommonViewer` provides a JFace `TreeViewer` subclass that may be suitable in standalone E4 applications. However, it resides in the same plug-in as the `CommonNavigator` class that has dependencies on the Eclipse 3.x layer, and therefore may not be used in pure E4 applications.

Creating a content and label provider

The common navigator allows plug-ins to register a JFace `ContentProvider` and `LabelProvider` instance for components in the tree. These are then used to provide the nodes in the common navigator tree.

For more information about content providers and label providers, see chapter 3 of *Eclipse 4 Plug-in Development by Example Beginner's Guide, Packt Publishing*, or other tutorials on the Internet.

To provide a content view of the feed's properties file, create the following classes:

- `Feed` (a data object that contains a name and URL)
- `FeedLabelProvider` (implements `ILabelProvider`)
- `FeedContentProvider` (implements `ITreeContentProvider`)

The `FeedLabelProvider` class needs to show the name of the feed as the label; implement the `getText` method as follows:

```
public String getText(Object element) {
  if (element instanceof Feed) {
    return ((Feed) element).getName();
  } else {
    return null;
  }
}
```

Optionally, an image can be returned from the `getImage` method. One of the default images from the Eclipse platform could be used (for example, `IMG_OBJ_FILE` from the workbench's shared images). This is not required in order to implement a label provider.

The `FeedContentProvider` class will be used to convert an `IResource` object into an array of `Feed` objects. Since the `IResource` content can be loaded via a URI, it can easily be converted into a `Properties` object, as shown in the following code:

```
private static final Object[] NO_CHILDREN = new Object[0];
public Object[] getChildren(Object parentElement) {
  Object[] result = NO_CHILDREN;
  if (parentElement instanceof IResource) {
    IResource resource = (IResource) parentElement;
    if (resource.getName().endsWith(".feeds")) {
      try {
```

```
          Properties properties = new Properties();
          InputStream stream = resource.getLocationURI()
           .toURL().openStream();
          properties.load(stream);
          stream.close();
          result = new Object[properties.size()];
          int i = 0;
          Iterator it = properties.entrySet().iterator();
          while (it.hasNext()) {
            Map.Entry<String, String> entry =
             (Entry<String, String>) it.next();
            result[i++] = new Feed(entry.getValue(),
            entry.getKey());
          }
        } catch (Exception e) {
          return NO_CHILDREN;
        }
      }
    }
    return result;
  }
```

The `getElements` method is not invoked when `ITreeContentProvider` is used; but conventionally, it can be used to provide compatibility with other processes if necessary.

Integrating into Common Navigator

The providers are registered with a `navigatorContent` element from the extension point `org.eclipse.ui.navigator.navigatorContent`. This defines a unique ID, a name, an icon, and whether it is active by default or not. This can be created using the plug-in editor or by adding the configuration directly to the `plugin.xml` file, as shown:

```
<extension point="org.eclipse.ui.navigator.navigatorContent">
  <navigatorContent activeByDefault="true"
   contentProvider=
    "com.packtpub.e4.advanced.feeds.ui.FeedContentProvider"
   labelProvider=
    "com.packtpub.e4.advanced.feeds.ui.FeedLabelProvider"
   id="com.packtpub.e4.advanced.feeds.ui.feedNavigatorContent"
```

```
    name="Feed Navigator Content">
  </navigatorContent>
</extension>
```

Running the preceding code will cause the following error to be displayed in the error log:

```
Missing attribute: triggerPoints
```

The `navigatorContent` extension, needs to be told when this particular instance should be activated. In this case, when an `IResource` is selected with an extension of `.feeds`, this navigator should be enabled. The configuration is as follows:

```
<navigatorContent ...>
  <triggerPoints>
    <and>
      <instanceof value="org.eclipse.core.resources.IResource"/>
      <test forcePluginActivation="true"
        property="org.eclipse.core.resources.extension"
        value="feeds"/>
    </and>
  </triggerPoints>
</navigatorContent>
```

Adding the preceding code to the `plugin.xml` file fixes the error. There is an additional element, `possibleChildren`, which is used to assist in invoking the correct `getParent` method of an element:

```
<possibleChildren>
  <or>
    <instanceof value="com.packtpub.e4.advanced.feeds.ui.Feed"/>
  </or>
</possibleChildren>
```

The purpose of doing this is to tell the common navigator that when a `Feed` instance is selected, it can defer to the `FeedContentProvider` to determine the parent of a `Feed`. In the current implementation, this does not change, since the `getParent` method of the `FeedContentProvider` returns `null`.

Running the Eclipse instance at this point will fail to display any content in the **Project Explorer** view. To do that, the content navigator extensions need to be bound to the right viewer by its ID.

Binding content navigators to views

To prevent every content navigator extension from being applied to every view, individual bindings allow specific providers to be bound to specific views. This is not stored in the `commonNavigator` extension point, as this can be a many-to-many relationship. Instead, a new extension point, `org.eclipse.ui.navigator.viewer`, and a nested `viewerContentBinding` point are used:

```
<extension point="org.eclipse.ui.navigator.viewer">
  <viewerContentBinding
   viewerId="org.eclipse.ui.navigator.ProjectExplorer">
    <includes>
      <contentExtension pattern=
        "com.packtpub.e4.advanced.feeds.ui.feedNavigatorContent"/>
    </includes>
  </viewerContentBinding>
</extension>
```

The `viewerId` declares the view for which the binding is appropriate.

A list of `viewerId` values can be found from the **Host OSGi Console** by executing the following command:

```
osgi> pt -v org.eclipse.ui.views | grep id
```

This provides a full list of IDs contained within the declarations of the extension point `org.eclipse.ui.views`. Note that not all of the IDs may be views, and most of them won't be subtypes of the `CommonNavigator` view.

The pattern defined in the content extension can be a specific name (such as the one used in the example previously) or it can be a regular expression, such as `com.packtpub.*`, to match all extensions in a given namespace.

Running the application now will show a list of the individual feed elements underneath `news.feeds`, as shown in the following screenshot:

Adding commands to the common navigator

Adding a command to the common navigator is the same as other commands; a `command` and `handler` are required, followed by a `menuContribution` that targets the appropriate location URI.

To add a command to show the feed in a web browser, create a `ShowFeedInBrowserHandler` class that uses the platform's ability to show a web page. In order to show a web page, get hold of the `PlatformUI` browser support, which offers the opportunity to create a browser and open a URL. The code is as follows:

```
public class ShowFeedInBrowserHandler extends AbstractHandler {
  public Object execute(ExecutionEvent event)
   throws ExecutionException {
    ISelection sel = HandlerUtil.getCurrentSelection(event);
    if (sel instanceof IStructuredSelection) {
      Iterator<?> it = ((IStructuredSelection)sel).iterator();
      while (it.hasNext()) {
        Object object = it.next();
        if (object instanceof Feed) {
          String url = ((Feed) object).getUrl();
          try {
            PlatformUI.getWorkbench().getBrowserSupport()
             .createBrowser(url).openURL(new URL(url));
          } catch (Exception e) {
            StatusManager.getManager().handle(
             new Status(Status.ERROR,Activator.PLUGIN_ID,
              "Could not open browser for " + url, e),
              StatusManager.LOG | StatusManager.SHOW);
          }
        }
      }
    }
    return null;
  }
}
```

If the selection is an `IStructuredSelection`, its elements will be processed; for each selected `Feed`, a browser will be opened. The `StatusManager` class is used to report an error to the workbench if there is a problem.

The command will need to be registered in the `plugin.xml` file as follows:

```
<extension point="org.eclipse.ui.commands">
  <command name="Show Feed in Browser"
   description="Shows the selected feed in browser"
   id="com.packtpub.e4.advanced.feeds.ui.ShowFeedInBrowserCommand"
    defaultHandler=
   "com.packtpub.e4.advanced.feeds.ui.ShowFeedInBrowserHandler"/>
</extension>
```

To use this in a pop-up menu, it can be added as a `menuContribution` (which is also done in the `plugin.xml` file). To ensure that the menu is only shown if the element selected is a `Feed` instance, the standard pattern for iterating over the current selection is used, as illustrated in the following code snippet:

```
<extension point="org.eclipse.ui.menus">
  <menuContribution allPopups="false" locationURI=
   "popup:org.eclipse.ui.navigator.ProjectExplorer#PopupMenu">
    <command style="push" commandId=
     "com.packtpub.e4.advanced.feeds.ui.ShowFeedInBrowserCommand">
      <visibleWhen checkEnabled="false">
        <with variable="selection">
          <iterate ifEmpty="false" operator="or">
            <adapt type="com.packtpub.e4.advanced.feeds.ui.Feed"/>
          </iterate>
        </with>
      </visibleWhen>
    </command>
  </menuContribution>
</extension>
```

For more information about handlers and selections, see chapter 3 of *Eclipse 4 Plug-in Development by Example Beginner's Guide, Packt Publishing*, or other tutorials on the Internet.

Now, when the application is run, the **Show Feed in Browser** menu will be shown when the feed is selected in the common navigator, as illustrated in the following screenshot:

Reacting to updates

If the file changes, then currently the viewer does not refresh. This is problematic because additions or removals to the `news.feeds` file do not result in changes in the UI.

To solve this problem, ensure that the content provider implements `IResourceChangeListener` (as shown in the following code snippet), and that when initialized, it is registered with the workspace. Any resource changes will then be delivered, which can be used to update the viewer.

```
public class FeedContentProvider implements
 ITreeContentProvider, IResourceChangeListener {
  private Viewer viewer;
  public void dispose() {
    viewer = null;
    ResourcesPlugin.getWorkspace().
     removeResourceChangeListener(this);
  }
  public void inputChanged(Viewer v, Object old, Object noo) {
    this.viewer = viewer;
    ResourcesPlugin.getWorkspace()
     .addResourceChangeListener(this,
      IResourceChangeEvent.POST_CHANGE);
  }
  public void resourceChanged(IResourceChangeEvent event) {
    if (viewer != null) {
      viewer.refresh();
    }
  }
}
```

Now when changes occur on the underling resource, the viewer will be automatically updated.

Optimizing the viewer updates

Updating the viewer whenever any resource changes is not very efficient. In addition, if a resource change is invoked outside of the UI thread, then the refresh operation will cause an **Invalid Thread Access** error message to be generated.

To fix this, the following two steps need to be performed:

- Invoke the `refresh` method from inside a `UIJob` class or via the `UISynchronizer` class
- Pass the changed resource to the `refresh` method

To run the `refresh` method inside a `UIJob` class, replace the call with the following code:

```
new UIJob("RefreshingFeeds") {
  public IStatus runInUIThread(IProgressMonitor monitor) {
    if(viewer != null) {
      viewer.refresh();
    }
    return Status.OK_STATUS;
  }
}.schedule();
```

This will ensure the operation works correctly, regardless of how the resource change occurs.

To ensure that the viewer is only refreshed on resources that really need it, `IResourceDeltaVisitor` is required. This has a `visit` method which includes an `IResourceDelta` object that includes the changed resources.

An inner class, `FeedsRefresher`, that implements `IResourceDeltaVisitor` can be used to walk the change for files matching a `.feeds` extension. This ensures that the display is only updated/refreshed when a corresponding `.feeds` file is updated, instead of every file. By returning `true` from the `visit` method, the `delta` is recursively walked so that files at any level can be found. The code is as follows:

```
private class FeedsRefresher implements IResourceDeltaVisitor {
  public boolean visit(IResourceDelta delta) throws CoreException{
    final IResource resource = delta.getResource();
    if (resource != null &&
     "feeds".equals(resource.getFileExtension())) {
      new UIJob("RefreshingFeeds") {
        public IStatus runInUIThread(IProgressMonitor monitor) {
```

```
          if(viewer != null) {
            viewer.refresh();
          }
          return Status.OK_STATUS;
        }
      }.schedule();
    }
    return true;
  }
}
```

This is hooked into the feed content provider by replacing the `resourceChanged` method with the following code:

```
public void resourceChanged(IResourceChangeEvent event) {
  if (viewer != null) {
    try {
      FeedsRefresher feedsChanged = new FeedsRefresher();
      event.getDelta().accept(feedsChanged);
    } catch (CoreException e) {
    }
  }
}
```

Although the generic viewer only has a `refresh` method to refresh the entire view, `StructuredViewer` has a `refresh` method that takes a specific object to refresh. This allows the visit to be optimized further, as shown in the following code snippet:

```
new UIJob("RefreshingFeeds") {
  public IStatus runInUIThread(IProgressMonitor monitor) {
    if(viewer != null) {
      ((StructuredViewer)viewer).refresh(resource);
    }
    return Status.OK_STATUS;
  }
}.schedule();
```

Linking selection changes

There is an option in Eclipse-based views: **Link editor with selection**. This allows a view to drive the selection in an editor, such as the **Outline** view's ability to select the appropriate method in a Java source file.

This can be added into the common navigator using a `linkHelper`. To add this, open the `plugin.xml` file and add the following to link the editor whenever a `Feed` instance is selected:

```
<extension point="org.eclipse.ui.navigator.linkHelper">
  <linkHelper
   class="com.packtpub.e4.advanced.feeds.ui.FeedLinkHelper"
   id="com.packtpub.e4.advanced.feeds.ui.FeedLinkHelper">
    <editorInputEnablement>
      <instanceof value="org.eclipse.ui.IFileEditorInput"/>
    </editorInputEnablement>
    <selectionEnablement>
      <instanceof value="com.packtpub.e4.advanced.feeds.ui.Feed"/>
    </selectionEnablement>
  </linkHelper>
</extension>
```

This will set up a call to the `FeedLinkHelper` class that will be notified whenever the selected editor is a plain file or the object is of type `Feed`.

To ensure that `linkHelper` is configured for the navigator, it is necessary to add it in to the `includes` element of the `viewerContentBinding` point created previously, as shown in the following code:

```
<extension point="org.eclipse.ui.navigator.viewer">
  <viewerContentBinding
   viewerId="org.eclipse.ui.navigator.ProjectExplorer">
    <includes>
      <contentExtension pattern=
       "com.packtpub.e4.advanced.feeds.ui.feedNavigatorContent"/>
      <contentExtension pattern=
       "com.packtpub.e4.advanced.feeds.ui.FeedLinkHelper"/>
    </includes>
  </viewerContentBinding>
</extension>
```

`FeedLinkHelper` needs to implement the interface `org.eclipse.ui.navigator.ILinkHelper`, which defines the two methods `findSelection` and `activateEditor` to convert an editor to a selection and vice versa.

Opening an editor

To open an editor and set the selection correctly, it will be necessary to include two more bundles to the project: `org.eclipse.jface.text` (for the `TextSelection` class) and `org.eclipse.ui.ide` (for the `IDE` class). This will tie the bundle into explicit availability of the IDE, but it can be marked as optional (because if there is no IDE, then there are no editors). It may also require `org.eclipse.ui.navigator` to be added to include referenced class files.

To implement the `activateEditor` method, it is necessary to find where the entry is inside the properties file and then set the selection appropriately. Since there is no easy way to do this, the contents of the file will be read instead (with a `BufferedInputStream` instance) while searching for the bytes that make up the selected item. Because there is a hardcoded name of `bookmarks` and a feed of `news.feeds`, this can be used to acquire the file content; though for real applications, the `Feed` object should know its parent and be able to provide that dynamically. The following code snippet shows how to set the selection appropriately:

```
public class FeedLinkHelper implements ILinkHelper {
  public void activateEditor(IWorkbenchPage page,
   IStructuredSelection selection) {
    Object object = selection.getFirstElement();
    if (object instanceof Feed) {
      Feed feed = ((Feed) object);
      byte[] line = (feed.getUrl().replace(":", "\\:") + "="
       + feed.getName()).getBytes();
      IProject bookmarks = ResourcesPlugin.getWorkspace()
       .getRoot().getProject(NewFeedWizard.FEEDS_PROJECT);
      if (bookmarks.exists() && bookmarks.isOpen()) {
        IFile feeds = bookmarks.getFile(NewFeedWizard.FEEDS_FILE);
        if (feeds.exists()) {
          try {
            TextSelection textSelection = findContent(line,feeds);
            if (textSelection != null) {
              setSelection(page, feeds, textSelection);
            }
          } catch (Exception e) {
            // Ignore
          }
        }
      }
    }
  }
  …
}
```

Finding the line

To find the content of the line, it is necessary to get the contents of the file and then perform a pass-through looking for the sequence of bytes. If the bytes are found, the start point is recorded and is used to return a `TextSelection`. If they are not found, then return a `null`, which indicates that the value shouldn't be set. This is illustrated in the following code snippet:

```
private TextSelection findContent(byte[] content, IFile file)
 throws CoreException, IOException {
  int len = content.length;
  int start = -1;
  InputStream in = new BufferedInputStream(file.getContents());
  int pos = 0;
  while (start == -1) {
    int b = in.read();
    if (b == -1)
      break;
    if (b == content[0]) {
      in.mark(len);
      boolean found = true;
      for (int i = 1; i < content.length && found; i++) {
        found &= in.read() == content[i];
      }
      if (found) {
        start = pos;
      }
      in.reset();
    }
    pos++;
  }
  if (start != -1) {
    return new TextSelection(start, len);
  } else {
    return null;
  }
}
```

This takes advantage of the fact that `BufferedInputStream` will perform the `mark` operation on the underlying content stream and allow backtracking to occur. Because this is only triggered when the first character of the input is seen, it is not too inefficient. To further optimize it, the content could be checked for the start of a new line.

Setting the selection

Once the appropriate selection has been identified, it can be opened in an editor through the `IDE` class. This provides an `openEditor` method that can be used to open an editor at a particular point, from which the selection service can be used to set the text selection on the file. The code is as follows:

```
private void setSelection(IWorkbenchPage page, IFile feeds,
 TextSelection textSelection) throws PartInitException {
  IEditorPart editor = IDE.openEditor(page, feeds, false);
  editor.getEditorSite()
   .getSelectionProvider().setSelection(textSelection);
}
```

Now when the element is selected in the project navigator, the corresponding `news.feeds` resource will be opened as long as **Link editor with selection** is enabled.

The corresponding direction, linking the editor with the selection in the viewer, is much less practical. The problem is that the generic text editor won't fire the method until the document is opened, and then there are limited ways in which the cursor position can be detected from the document. More complex editors, such as the Java editor, provide a means to model the document and understand where the cursor is in relation to the methods and fields. This information is used to update the outline and other views.

Summary

In this chapter, we covered how to create a dialog wizard with an optional page and have that drive an entry in the **New Wizard** dialog. This was used to create a feeds bookmark, which was then subsequently used to drive a set of fields in a common navigator—showing how the children of a resource can be updated.

In the next chapter, we will look at how Eclipse manages its extension points, and we will learn how to plug in to existing extension points as well as define custom extension points.

2

Creating Custom Extension Points

Eclipse is extended through the use of **extension points** and the **extension registry**. The registry manages a list of extension points and a list of extensions. Although it is commonly used in OSGi runtimes such as Eclipse, the **extension** registry can be used outside of an OSGi runtime as well.

Extensions and extension points

The first thing to understand in the registry is the terminology. An **extension** is a contributed functionality that is often found in the `plugin.xml` file as an `<extension>` element. The extension itself provides some configuration or customization that can be processed appropriately. An extension is like a USB device, such as a mouse or keyboard. For example, the new feed wizard was added as an extension in the previous chapter:

```
<extension point="org.eclipse.ui.newWizards">
  <category name="Feeds"
            id="com.packtpub.e4.advanced.feeds.ui.category"/>
</extension>
```

An **extension point** defines the contract of an extension, along with any required arguments or attributes that an extension must provide. An extension point is like a USB hub that allows extensions (USB devices) to be plugged in. For example, the `newWizards` extension point is defined in the `plugin.xml` file of the `org.eclipse.ui` plug-in as follows:

```
<extension-point id="newWizards" name="%ExtPoint.newWizards"
schema="schema/newWizards.exsd"/>
```

This refers to an XML schema document that defines the extension content, as shown in the following snippet:

```
<?xml version='1.0' encoding='UTF-8'?>
<!-- Schema file written by PDE -->
<schema targetNamespace="org.eclipse.ui"
 xmlns="http://www.w3.org/2001/XMLSchema">
  <annotation>
    <appInfo>
      <meta.schema plugin="org.eclipse.ui" id="newWizards"
       name="Creation Wizards"/>
    </appInfo>
  </annotation>
  <element name="extension">
    <complexType>
      <choice minOccurs="0" maxOccurs="unbounded">
        <element ref="category"/>
        ...
      </choice>
    </complexType>
  </element>
  <element name="category">
    <complexType>
      <attribute name="id" type="string" use="required"/>
      <attribute name="name" type="string" use="required"/>
    </complexType>
  </element>
  ...
</schema>
```

The schema defines the point for the `org.eclipse.ui.newWizards` extension (the ID is the concatenation of the values of `meta.schema plugin` and `id`). It declares that the extension has a category, which has required `id` and `name` attributes.

The schema also allows the PDE to verify whether elements are missing when editing a `plugin.xml` file, or provide code completion to insert required or optional elements.

Fortunately, PDE comes with good support to build this schema via a graphical user interface, so the XML can remain hidden.

Creating an extension point

To demonstrate the process of creating a new extension point in Eclipse, a feed parser will be created. This takes a `Feed` instance (which contains a URL) and returns an array of `FeedItem` instances. Extensions can be contributed to provide different feed parsers; this allows a `MockFeedParser` instance to be initially created that can then be substituted for other implementations in future.

Executable extension points tend to have a `class` attribute, whose class typically implements a particular interface. An `IFeedParser` interface will be created to represent the abstract API of all feed parsers; extensions that provide a feed parser will be expected to implement this interface.

Creating an IFeedParser interface

Since the feed parser could be used outside of a UI, it makes sense to create a new plug-in project called `com.packtpub.e4.advanced.feeds` and to refactor the `Feed` instance from the UI package (created in *Chapter 1, Plugging in to JFace and the Common Navigator Framework*) into this package as well.

When you refactor the `Feed` class, ensure that **Update fully qualified names in non-Java text files** option is selected, or remember to refactor the name in the fully qualified names in the `plugin.xml` file, since the class name is used in several places in enablement tests.

Note that you will also need to ensure that the `com.packtpub.e4.advanced.feeds` package is exported from the plug-in (from the **Runtime** tab of the manifest editor) and the package is imported by the `com.packtpub.e4.advanced.feeds.ui` plug-in (from the **Dependencies** tab of the manifest editor).

One this is done, an interface `IFeedParser` will be created to parse a feed, as shown in the following code snippet:

```
import java.util.List;
public interface IFeedParser {
  public List<FeedItem> parseFeed(Feed feed);
}
```

The intent is that this will return a list of items parsed from the feed. To do this, a `FeedItem` class will be needed as well. Each `FeedItem` instance will have an associated parent `Feed`, along with some other metadata.

It would be possible to create a mutable `FeedItem` instance with getter/setter pairs for each attribute. However, this leads to the possibility that a feed might be inadvertently mutated after it has been constructed.

A second approach is to use the constructor to add all arguments. Unfortunately, this prevents evolution of the class; as new parameters are added, more constructors need to be created with the values in place.

A better solution is to use the **builder pattern**, which allows a separate object to assemble the instance. This way, the object can be created but not mutated after it is returned. Visit `http://en.wikipedia.org/wiki/Builder_pattern` for more information.

To instantiate a `FeedItem` class, an inner `Builder` class will be used. This has access to the private fields of the `FeedItem` class, but permits the object to be returned without a means of mutating it afterwards:

```
package com.packtpub.e4.advanced.feeds;
import java.util.Date;
public class FeedItem {
  // FeedItem fields
  private Date date;
  private Feed feed;
  private FeedItem(Feed feed) {
    this.feed = feed;
  }
  public Date getDate() {
    return date;
  }
  public Feed getFeed() {
    return feed;
  }
  // FeedItem.Builder class
  public static class Builder {
    private FeedItem item;
    public Builder(Feed feed) {
      item = new FeedItem(feed);
    }
    public FeedItem build() {
      if(item.date == null) {
        item.date = new Date();
```

```
        }
        return item;
      }
      public Builder setDate(Date date) {
        item.date = date;
        return this;
      }
    }
  }
```

The preceding example shows how the builder pattern is used, in this case, for two fields: a parent `feed` and `date`. To extend the `FeedItem` class, add accessors in the builder to set other elements such as the following:

- Title
- URL
- HTML

A `FeedItem` class can now be instantiated using the following code:

```
new FeedItem.Builder(feed).setDate(new Date()).build();
```

Note that the builder pattern is fairly common in Java, as is the literate programming style used; by returning instances of `Builder` at the end of each setter method, this allows chaining of method calls into a single expression. The `build` method can also perform any necessary validation to verify that all mandatory fields have been assigned and any optional fields are assigned default values if necessary.

Creating a MockFeedParser class

To provide some feed data that can be used by a parser without having to make a network connection, a `MockFeedParser` class can be created. This will take a `Feed` instance and return a set of hardcoded `FeedItems`, allowing further testing to be done.

Because this class isn't intended to be directly visible to downstream users, put the class in a different package, `com.packtpub.e4.advanced.feeds.internal`. This way, the package will be hidden by the OSGi runtime and so dependent classes won't be able to see or instantiate it. The following code illustrates the creation of the `MockFeedParser` class:

By default, PDE and the Maven `maven-bundle-plugin` hide packages with `internal` in their name. This allows the public API to be separated from the internal implementation details to downstream clients.

```
public class MockFeedParser implements IFeedParser {
  public List<FeedItem> parseFeed(Feed feed) {
    List<FeedItem> items = new ArrayList<FeedItem>(3);
    items.add(new FeedItem.Builder(feed).setTitle("1st").build());
    items.add(new FeedItem.Builder(feed).setTitle("2nd").build());
    items.add(new FeedItem.Builder(feed).setTitle("3rd").build());
    return items;
  }
}
```

The mock can be populated with more data, such as an HTML body or different dates, if these are desired.

Creating the extension point schema

The extension point for the feed will be called `feedParser`, and it will use the `IFeedParser` interface.

To create an extension point, open up the plug-in's manifest by double-clicking on the `plugin.xml` or `MANIFEST.MF` files, or by navigating to **Plug-in tools | Open Manifest** from the project. Switch to the **Extension Points** tab, click on **Add**, and enter `feedParser` for both the ID and the name in the dialog that shows up. This is shown in the following screenshot:

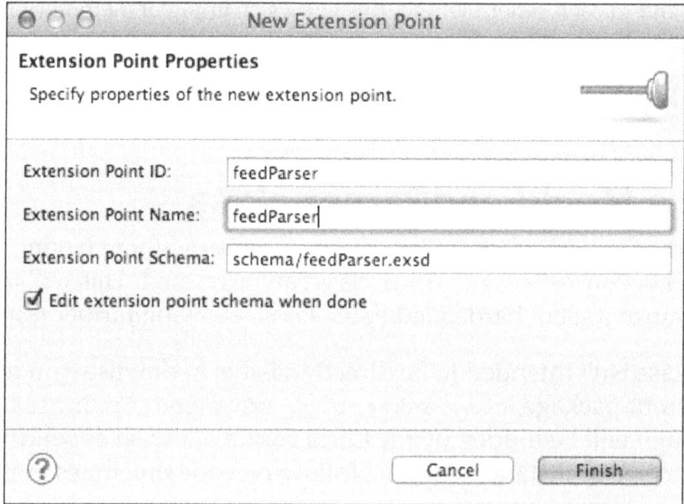

After clicking on **Finish**, the schema editor will be shown:

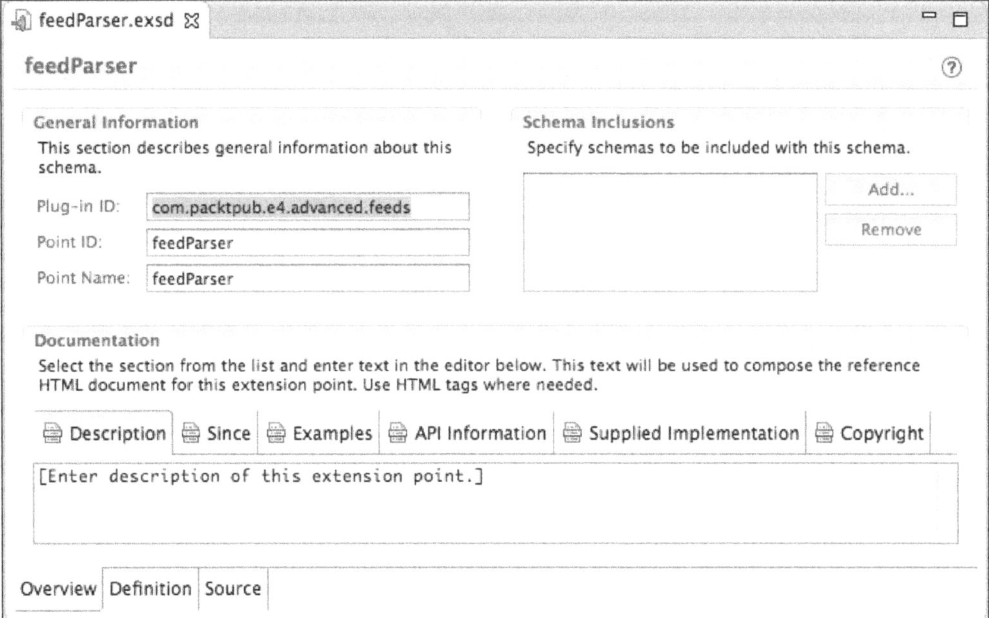

The **Description**, **Since**, **Examples**, **API Information**, **Supplied Implementation**, and **Copyright** are all text-based fields that are used to generate the documentation and can be left blank. However, this documentation will be shown to users in the future and is used to generate the information as seen in the Eclipse help center and at `http://help.eclipse.org`.

Switching to the **Definition** tab allows the contents of the extension point to be modified. Select the **extension** element, click on the **New Element** button to its right, and give it the name `feedParser`. This will be the name of the XML element that is expected by clients. To give it an attribute value, ensure **feedParser** is selected, click on **New Attribute**, and give it the name `class`. Its type will be **java** and it will be **required**; use the **Browse...** button next to the **Implements** textbox to select the `IFeedParser` created earlier.

The resulting schema definition will now look something like what is shown in the following screenshot:

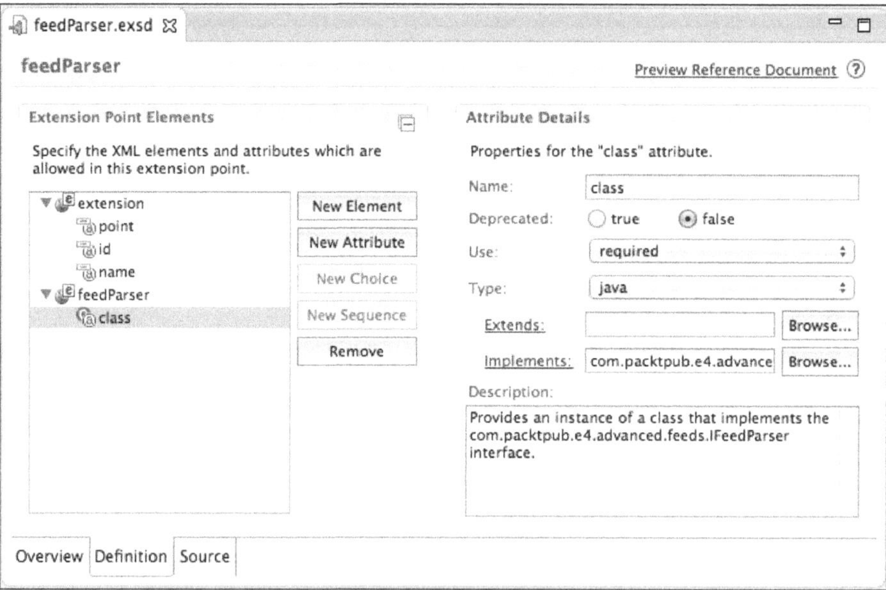

Under the covers, the extension is represented in two different files. The first is the `plugin.xml` file, which includes the following:

```
<?xml version="1.0" encoding="UTF-8"?>
<?eclipse version="3.4"?>
<plugin>
  <extension-point id="feedParser" name="feedParser"
   schema="schema/feedParser.exsd"/>
</plugin>
```

The schema reference points to the schema definition, which was created by the UI previously.

> Note that the `build.properties` file should be updated to include the `schema` directory in the binary output; otherwise, implementors of the plug-in won't be able to verify whether the `feedParser` element is correctly provided or not.

The schema is not necessary for the extension mechanism to work; it is mainly used by PDE when allowing the element to be created in the `plugin.xml` file. However, it has value in communicating documentation to other users of the extension point in both its intent and its requirements, and so providing the schema is considered best practice.

There are other values that can be defined on the extension point. For example, each element has one of the following values:

- **Name**: This is the name that will be used for the element or attribute. This must be a valid XML name for elements and attributes.
- **Deprecated**: This is `false` by default, but can be changed to `true`. This is used to indicate to clients that an extension point should no longer be used; it is often combined with the description to suggest an alternative or replacement function.
- **Translatable**: If an attribute has a value that can be translated (such as a label or another human-readable string), then this value should be `true`. If so, the value in the `plugin.xml` may be a percent string such as `%description`, and the value will be pulled out automatically from the localized `plugin.properties` file by Eclipse when the extension point is loaded.
- **Description**: This is a human-readable description that can be shown by PDE or converted into a help document that indicates how the point should be used.
- **Use**: The value for this can be `optional`, `required`, or `default`. If an attribute is marked as `optional`, then it does not need to be present. If an attribute is marked as `required`, then it must be present. If it is marked as `default`, then a default value box is shown that allows the default value to be defined, which is used when the attribute is missing.
- **Type**: This is the attribute type. The attribute value can be of one of the following types:
    - **Boolean**: This specifies that the attribute can have the value `true` or `false`.
    - **String**: This specifies that the attribute value can be a string. Strings may be translatable, and they can have **restrictions** that are preset values that the string can take (such as `North`, `South`, `East`, and `West` or `UP` and `DOWN`).
    - **Java**: This specifies that the attribute must be a type that either extends the specified class or implements the specified interface.
    - **Resource**: This specifies that the attribute can have a resource type.
    - **Identifier**: This specifies that the attribute might reference another ID in another schema document using an XPath-like expression of the form `org.eclipse.jdt.ui.javaDocWizard/@point`, where `org.eclipse.jdt.ui` is the plug-in namespace, `javaDocWizard` is an extension, and `@point` is the attribute `point` within that element.

There is a **DTD approximation** that is used to show an approximate Document Type Definition of the children. If an element has no children, then it will show `EMPTY`; for a text element, it will show `(#PCDATA)`.

PCDATA, which stands for Parsed Character Data, is used in HTML and originally came from SGML.

In addition, elements can be repeated. The schema editor permits a **sequence** of elements (in other words, a list) or a **choice** of items (one of a set). These are known as **compositors** and can be switched between using the **Type** drop-down. Compositors have a minimum value and a maximum value; if the minimum is zero, then it is effectively optional. The maximum value, if specified, allows a fixed number to be specified (for example `months=12`); but if the **unbounded** option is checked, then the compositor can have any number of child elements.

Typically, an extension point will permit more than one element to be added. To enable this, it is necessary to add a `Sequence` element underneath the `extension` element. The sequence is necessary to permit more than one element to be provided.

In the PDE schema editor, click on the **extension** element and choose **New Sequence**. The minimum value should be `1` and the sequence should be **unbounded**; these are the typical defaults, as shown in the following screenshot:

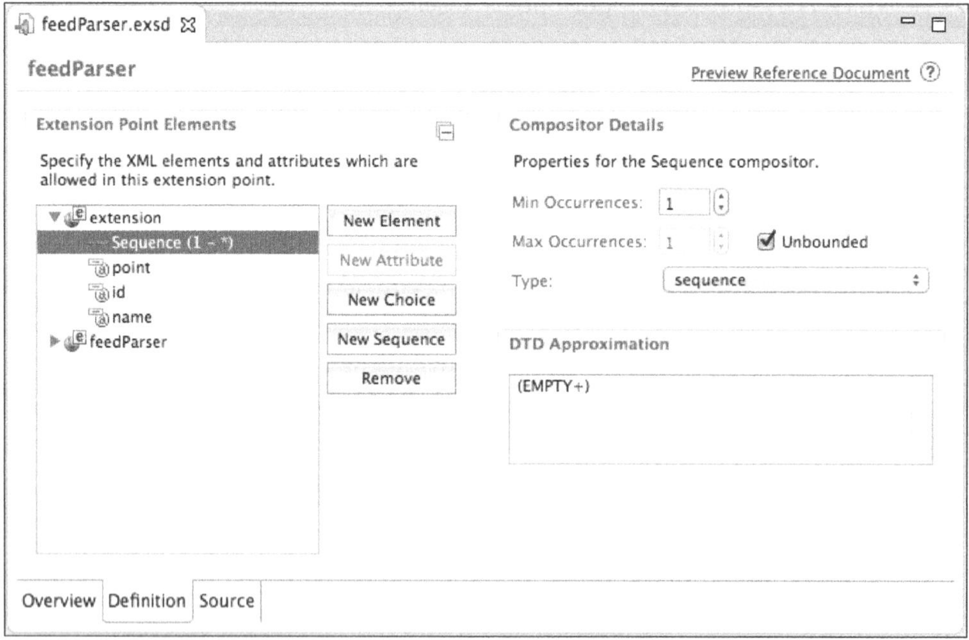

To add the `feedParser` point to the extension, drag-and-drop the **feedParser** element underneath the **Sequence** element, as shown in the following screenshot:

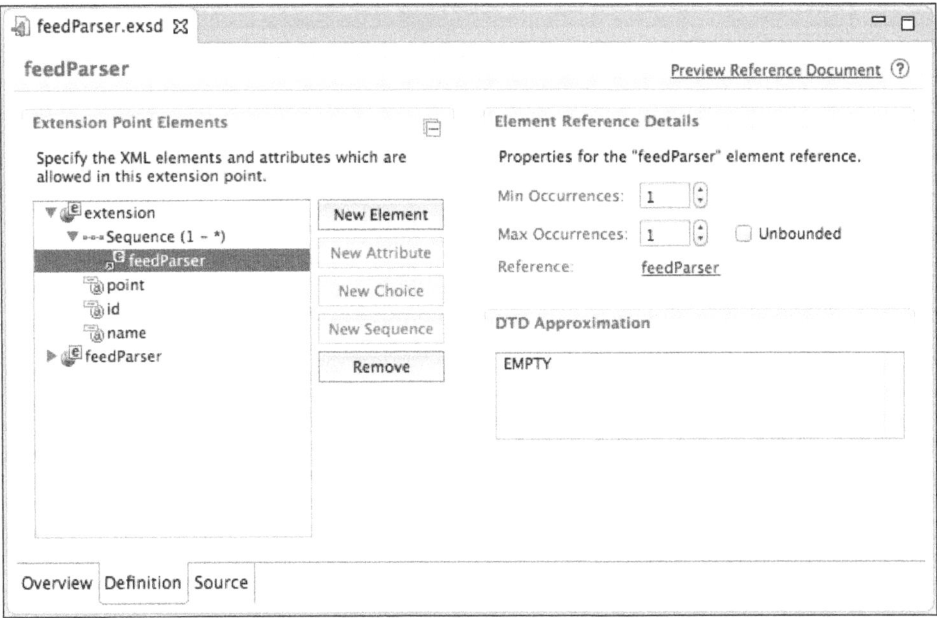

The `feedParser.esxd` schema should be similar to the following:

```
<?xml version='1.0' encoding='UTF-8'?>
<!-- Schema file written by PDE -->
<schema targetNamespace="com.packtpub.e4.advanced.feeds"
 xmlns="http://www.w3.org/2001/XMLSchema">
  <annotation>
    <appinfo>
      <meta.schema plugin="com.packtpub.e4.advanced.feeds"
       id="feedParser" name="feedParser"/>
    </appinfo>
    <documentation>…</documentation>
  </annotation>
  <element name="extension">
    <annotation>
      <appinfo>
        <meta.element />
     </appinfo>
    </annotation>
    <complexType>
      <sequence minOccurs="1" maxOccurs="unbounded">
        <element ref="feedParser"/>
```

```
        </sequence>
        <attribute name="point" type="string" use="required"/>
        <attribute name="id" type="string" use="required"/>
        <attribute name="name" type="string"/>
      </complexType>
    </element>
    <element name="feedParser">
      <complexType>
        <attribute name="class" type="string" use="required">
          <annotation>
            <documentation>…</documentation>
            <appinfo>
              <meta.attribute kind="java"
         basedOn=":com.packtpub.e4.advanced.feeds.IFeedParser"/>
            </appinfo>
          </annotation>
        </attribute>
      </complexType>
    </element>
  </schema>
```

Now the schema definition is complete.

Using the extension point

As with other extensions, they are added to a plug-in's `plugin.xml` file. It's not uncommon for a plug-in to define both the extension point and an extension in the same file.

Note that defining an extension point in the same file as an extension means that there is no way of removing that extension from the platform if that extension point is used elsewhere. Providing a plug-in that defines the extension point and then separate plug-ins for the extensions allows the extensions to be individually removed from the platform.

To add `MockFeedParser` to the `plugin.xml` file, add the following:

```
<extension point="com.packtpub.e4.advanced.feeds.feedParser">
  <feedParser class=
   "com.packtpub.e4.advanced.feeds.internal.MockFeedParser"/>
</extension>
```

In order to provide an easy way for clients to obtain a list of feed parsers, a class `FeedParserFactory` will be created in the `feeds` plug-in. This class will be used to provide a list of `IFeedParser` instances without having a specific API dependency on the extension registry itself. The code is as follows:

```
package com.packtpub.e4.advanced.feeds;
public class FeedParserFactory {
  private static FeedParserFactory DEFAULT;
  public static FeedParserFactory getDefault() {
    if (DEFAULT == null) {
      DEFAULT = new FeedParserFactory();
    }
    return DEFAULT;
  }
}
```

The registry is managed with an `IExtensionRegistry` interface, which can be accessed via the `org.eclipse.equinox.registry` bundle. It is possible to dynamically register extension elements, but the most common practice is to read the extensions that exist in the runtime. To do this, add the `org.eclipse.equinox.registry` bundle to the list of imported bundles in the manifest as follows:

```
Require-Bundle: org.eclipse.equinox.registry
```

The extension registry manages a set of extension points, which are identified with an ID—typically consisting of the contributing bundle ID and the specific ID of the extension point. From the preceding definition, the values will be `com.packtpub.e4.advanced.feeds` and `feedParser`, respectively. Add the following to the `FeedParserFactory` class:

```
public List<IFeedParser> getFeedParsers() {
  List<IFeedParser> parsers = new ArrayList<IFeedParser>();
  IExtensionRegistry registry = RegistryFactory.getRegistry();
  IExtensionPoint extensionPoint = registry.getExtensionPoint(
    "com.packtpub.e4.advanced.feeds", "feedParser");
  … // continued below
  return parsers;
}
```

> `IExtensionPoint` represents the extension point definition itself. This might return `null` if there is no such extension point, so it should be checked before use. In previous versions of Eclipse, the identifiers used to be stored as a single string, such as `com.packtpub.e4.advanced.feeds.feedParser`. However, this resulted in many thousands of strings that took up a lot of space in the PermGen area of the JVM. By splitting them into two separate strings, many extensions in the same plug-in share the same namespace, which results in just a single entry in the PermGen area. Note that PermGen has been removed in the latest JVM versions.

If the preceding code returns a non-null value, it can be interrogated further. The most common call is `getConfigurationElements`, which allows the extensions to be parsed. This gives a tree-like view of the content of the extension, mapping closely to the structure of the entries in the `plugin.xml` file:

```
if (extensionPoint != null) {
  IConfigurationElement[] elements =
    extensionPoint.getConfigurationElements();
  for (int i = 0; i < elements.length; i++) {
    IConfigurationElement element = elements[i];
    … // continued below
  }
}
```

If the extension point contained only textual information (for example, Mylyn's use of the registry to store URLs such as `http://bugs.eclipse.org` to report Eclipse bugs), then the element could be interrogated to return the actual textual value. In the `feedParser` example, the attribute containing the class name is the one of interest.

In this case, the extension point defines a class to be instantiated. To do this, there is a method called `createExecutableExtension` that takes an attribute name and then instantiates a class using that name from the appropriate bundle. In effect, this is similar to `class.forName(extension.getAttribute("class"))`, but uses the correct `ClassLoader`.

> Although it might be tempting to think that using `Class.forName()` would work on the returned class name, this doesn't work in the case where the class comes from outside the current plug-in. Since each bundle has its own `ClassLoader` and the plug-in that uses the extension is almost always not the bundle that provides the extension, it would not work in most cases.

Since it's possible that the extension has a semantic error, or that the plug-in might not be loaded successfully, the instantiation of the class should `try` and `catch` `CoreException`. If an error occurs, then the extension won't be useful; the runtime might choose to log the error (for further diagnostics) if appropriate. Don't forget to check whether the returned instance is of the correct type using `instanceof`; this will also look for `null`.

The object is instantiated with a zero-argument constructor and returned to the caller, shown as follows:

```
try {
  Object parser = element.createExecutableExtension("class");
```

```
      if (parser instanceof IFeedParser) {
        parsers.add((IFeedParser) parser);
      }
    } catch (CoreException e) {
      // ignore or log as appropriate
    }
```

Caching extension points

Should the return values of the extension be cached? It depends on what the use case is likely to be. If they are only going to be used transiently, then there might be no point in creating them each time. On the other hand, if they are cached, then additional code will need to be created to register listeners to note when the plug-ins are uninstalled.

The extension registry does a reasonable job of caching and returning values from the calls, so these can be assumed to be fast. However, for the instantiated objects, if identity is important, then it might be necessary to arrange some kind of cache of the executable extensions.

If the return result is cached, then any new plug-ins that are subsequently installed might not be seen.

The extension registry also has listener support; calling `addListener` on the registry will provide a way of picking up changes to a specific extension point. This can be used to update any caches when changes occur.

Integrating the extension with the content and label providers

Having defined an extension point with a `FeedItem` provider, the next step is to integrate it with the `FeedLabelProvider` and the `FeedContentProvider` classes created in the previous chapter. Integrating it into the `FeedLabelProvider` class is really simple because this is just an addition of a couple of lines:

```
public String getText(Object element) {
  if (element instanceof Feed) {
    return ((Feed) element).getName();
  } else if (element instanceof FeedItem) {
    return ((FeedItem)element).getTitle();
  } else {
    return null;
  }
}
```

When a `FeedItem` element is seen in the tree, its title will be used as the label.

Integrating with the `FeedContentProvider` class is the next step. To start off, declare that all `Feed` elements have children and the parent of the `FeedItem` element is `Feed` itself:

```
public Object getParent(Object element) {
  if(element instanceof FeedItem) {
    return ((FeedItem) element).getFeed();
  }
  return null;
}
public boolean hasChildren(Object element) {
  if(element instanceof Feed) {
    return true;
  }
  return false;
}
```

To parse the feed URL, perform the following steps:

1. Acquire the `IFeedParser` list (which comes from the extension registry).
2. Iterate through the list and attempt to acquire the `FeedItem` list.
3. If the value is non-null, return.

The code will be similar to the following:

```
public Object[] getChildren(Object parentElement) {
  Object[] result = NO_CHILDREN;
  if (parentElement instanceof IResource) {
    ...
  } else if (parentElement instanceof Feed) {
    Feed feed = (Feed)parentElement;
    FeedParserFactory factory = FeedParserFactory.getDefault();
    List<IFeedParser> parsers = factory.getFeedParsers();
    for (IFeedParser parser : parsers) {
      List<FeedItem> items = parser.parseFeed(feed);
      if(items != null && !items.isEmpty()) {
        return items.toArray();
      }
    }
  }
}
```

This pattern allows the `FeedParserFactory` class to return items in the order of preference such that the first parser that handles the feed can return a value.

Run the Eclipse application, create a feed (the URL and title won't matter at this point), and then drill down into the feeds and then into a single feed. The test data that was used in the `MockFeedParser` class should be shown in the list, as shown in the following screenshot:

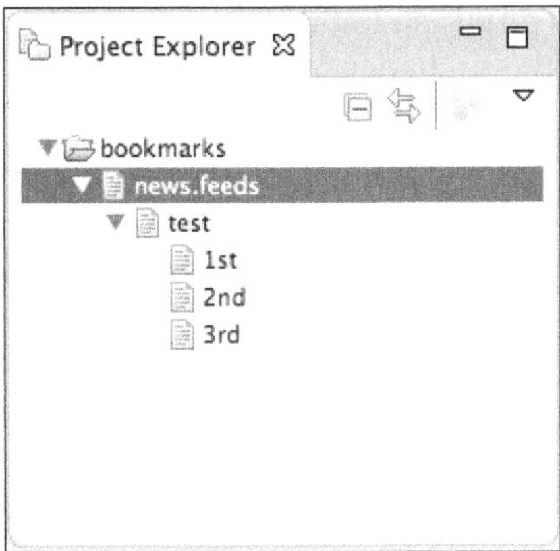

Showing a feed in the browser

Now that feeds are showing as individual elements in the content provider, the `ShowFeedInBrowserHandler` class can be copied and modified to allow individual `FeedItem` entries to be added. Refer to the *Adding commands to the common navigator* section in *Chapter 1, Plugging in to JFace and the Common Navigator Framework*.

Copy the `ShowFeedInBrowserHandler` class to `ShowFeedItemInBrowserHandler`. The only change that's needed is the change from `Feed` to `FeedItem` in the `instanceof` test and subsequent cast:

```
public class ShowFeedItemInBrowserHandler extends AbstractHandler{
  public Object execute(ExecutionEvent event) throws
   ExecutionException {
    ISelection selection = HandlerUtil.getCurrentSelection(event);
    if (selection instanceof IStructuredSelection) {
      Iterator<?> it = ((IStructuredSelection) selection)
       .iterator();
```

```
        while (it.hasNext()) {
          Object object = (Object) it.next();
          // if (object instanceof Feed) {
          //  String url = ((Feed) object).getUrl();
          if (object instanceof FeedItem) {
            String url = ((FeedItem) object).getUrl();
          ...
```

It will also be necessary to duplicate both the handler and command entries in the `plugin.xml` file, along with the change to the feed item. This is shown in the following:

```
<extension point="org.eclipse.ui.commands">
  <command description="Shows the selected feed item in browser"
   defaultHandler=
  "com.packtpub.e4.advanced.feeds.ui.ShowFeedItemInBrowserHandler"
   id=
  "com.packtpub.e4.advanced.feeds.ui.ShowFeedItemInBrowserCommand"
   name="Show Feed Item in Browser"/>
</extension>
```

Enabling the menu item is necessary to show the command associated with any selected `FeedItem` instances as follows:

```
<extension point="org.eclipse.ui.menus">
  <menuContribution allPopups="false" locationURI=
   "popup:org.eclipse.ui.navigator.ProjectExplorer#PopupMenu">
    <command style="push" commandId=
 "com.packtpub.e4.advanced.feeds.ui.ShowFeedItemInBrowserCommand">
      <visibleWhen checkEnabled="false">
        <with variable="selection">
          <iterate ifEmpty="false" operator="or">
            <adapt type=
             "com.packtpub.e4.advanced.feeds.FeedItem"/>
          </iterate>
        </with>
      </visibleWhen>
    </command>
  </menuContribution>
</extension>
```

If the application is run, then a `MalformedURLException` will be generated, since the `MockFeedParser` doesn't have any URLs set on it. Modify it as follows:

```
items.add(new FeedItem.Builder(feed).setTitle("AlBlue's Blog").
  setUrl("http://alblue.bandlem.com").build());
items.add(new FeedItem.Builder(feed).setTitle("Packt Publishing").
```

```
    setUrl("http://www.packtpub.com").build());
  items.add(new FeedItem.Builder(feed).setTitle("Source Code").
    setUrl("https://github.com/alblue/com.packtpub.e4.advanced").
    build());
```

Now running the application will show the URLs when selected, as shown in the following screenshot:

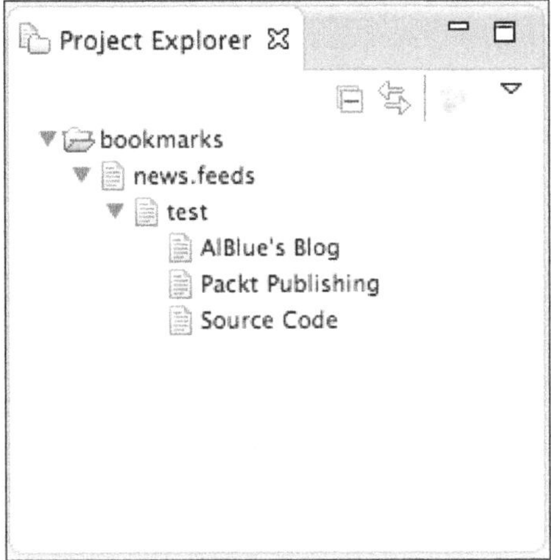

Implementing a real feed parser

The `MockFeedParser` can be replaced with an implementation to parse RSS feeds. This requires parsing some simple XML to understand the feed reference.

An **RSS** feed looks like:

```
<rss version="2.0">
  <channel>
    <title>Eclipse Example Feed</title>
    <description>Descriptive feed information</description>
    <link>http://eclipse.org/</link>
    <item>
      <title>Luna released</title>
      <description>Eclipse Luna has been released</description>
      <link>http://eclipse.org/luna/</link>
      <pubDate>Wed, 25 June 2014 09:00:00 -0500</pubDate>
    </item>
  </channel>
</rss>
```

Unfortunately, since this is XML, it will require parsing. There are several ways of doing this, but using a `DocumentBuilder` instance will allow the elements to be iterated through and pull out the `title` and `link` elements, along with `pubDate`.

Create an `RSSFeedParser` class (with a couple of helper methods) to parse a date from the **RFC822** format and a mechanism to parse a text value from an `Element`, as shown in the following code snippet:

```
package com.packtpub.e4.advanced.feeds.internal;
public class RSSFeedParser implements IFeedParser {
  public List<FeedItem> parseFeed(Feed feed) {
    …
  }
  private Date parseDate(String date) {
    try {
      return new SimpleDateFormat("EEE, dd MMM yyyy HH:mm:ss zzz")
       .parse(date);
    } catch (Exception e) {
      return null;
    }
  }
  private String getTextValueOf(Node item, String element) {
    try {
      return ((Element) item).getElementsByTagName(element).
        item(0).getTextContent();
    } catch (Exception e) {
      return null;
    }
  }
}
```

These helper methods can be used to parse the elements out of the feed by parsing the URL of the `Feed` with a `DocumentBuilder` instance and then using `getElementsByName` to find the `item` elements. The `parseFeed` method will be similar to the following code:

```
public List<FeedItem> parseFeed(Feed feed) {
  try {
    List<FeedItem> feedItems = new ArrayList<FeedItem>();
    DocumentBuilder builder = DocumentBuilderFactory.newInstance()
     .newDocumentBuilder();
    Document doc = builder.parse(
      new URL(feed.getUrl()).openStream());
    NodeList items = doc.getElementsByTagName("item");
    for (int i = 0; i < items.getLength(); i++) {
```

```
        Node item = items.item(i);
        Builder feedItem = new FeedItem.Builder(feed);
        feedItem.setTitle(getTextValueOf(item,"title"));
        feedItem.setUrl(getTextValueOf(item,"link"));
        feedItem.setDate(parseDate(getTextValueOf(item,"pubDate")));
        feedItems.add(feedItem.build());
      }
      return feedItems;
    } catch (Exception e) {
      return null;
    }
  }
```

This looks for elements called `item`, finds child text elements with `title` and `link`, and sets them into the feed.

To add this to the Eclipse instance, add `RSSFeedParser` to the `plugin.xml` file in the `feedParser` extension point:

```
<extension point="com.packtpub.e4.advanced.feeds.feedParser">
  <feedParser class=
   "com.packtpub.e4.advanced.feeds.internal.RSSFeedParser"/>
</extension>
```

If the `MockFeedParser` instance is still present, the ordering in the `plugin.xml` file will be important. By default, the order returned in the array is the same as they are in the file. `FeedParserFactory` returns the first parser that successfully parses the feed; therefore, if the `MockFeedParser` is first, then the real content of the feed will not be returned.

> The feed parser is non-optimal; the feed will be parsed and potentially reacquired multiple times. It would be desirable to have the contents of the source document cached, but this is an optimization left for you.

Run the Eclipse application and use the add feed wizard to add a feed for the Packt Publishing RSS feed, `http://www.packtpub.com/rss.xml`.

Adding support for Atom

Not all feeds use RSS as a feed type, partly because RSS was incompletely specified and had several slightly different incompatible feed formats. **Atom** was designed to resolve the issues with RSS but, in practice, there are approximately an equal number of feeds specified in RSS and Atom.

An Atom feed looks like:

```
<feed xmlns="http://www.w3.org/2005/Atom">
  <title>AlBlue's Blog</title>
  <entry>
    <title>Eclipse 4 Book Published</title>
    <updated>2013-07-01T12:00:00+01:00</updated>
    <link href="
http://alblue.bandlem.com/2013/07/eclipse-book-published.html"/>
  </entry>
</feed>
```

Parsing it will not be significantly different from before; the structure can be used to pull out the `entry` and the contained `title`, `link`, and `updated` references. However, there are a couple of points that are worth noting in this example:

- The Java Date APIs do not understand colons in time zones, so `+01:00` must be converted to `+0100` to be parsed
- The reference for the link is stored inside an `href` attribute instead of as a text node

An `AtomFeedParser` class can be created as follows:

```
public class AtomFeedParser implements IFeedParser {
  public List<FeedItem> parseFeed(Feed feed) {
    try {
      List<FeedItem> feedItems = new ArrayList<FeedItem>();
      DocumentBuilder builder = DocumentBuilderFactory
       .newInstance().newDocumentBuilder();
      Document doc = builder.parse(
       new URL(feed.getUrl()).openStream());
      NodeList items = doc.getElementsByTagName("entry");
      for (int i = 0; i < items.getLength(); i++) {
        Node item = items.item(i);
        Builder feedItem = new FeedItem.Builder(feed);
        feedItem.setTitle(getTextValueOf(item, "title"));
        feedItem.setUrl(getTextValueOfAttribute(
          item, "link", "href"));
        feedItem.setDate(parseDate(getTextValueOf(
         item,"updated")));
        feedItems.add(feedItem.build());
      }
      return feedItems;
```

```
      } catch (Exception e) {
        return null;
      }
    }
    ...
  }
```

The `parseDate` method is similar to the following code:

```
private Date parseDate(String date) {
  try {
    if (date.length() > 22 && date.charAt(22) == ':') {
      date = date.substring(0, 22) + date.substring(23);
    }
    return new SimpleDateFormat("yyyy-MM-dd'T'HH:mm:ssZ")
     .parse(date);
  } catch (Exception e) {
    return null;
  }
}
```

To parse an attribute value out from XML, an additional helper method can be created as follows:

```
private String getTextValueOfAttribute(Node item, String element,
 String attribute) {
  try {
    return ((Element) item).getElementsByTagName(element).item(0)
     .getAttributes().getNamedItem(attribute).getNodeValue();
  } catch (Exception e) {
    return null;
  }
}
```

Adding the class into the extension points will allow the element to be parsed if the feed is not an RSS feed as follows:

```
<extension point="com.packtpub.e4.advanced.feeds.feedParser">
  <feedParser class=
   "com.packtpub.e4.advanced.feeds.internal.RSSFeedParser"/>
  <feedParser class=
   "com.packtpub.e4.advanced.feeds.internal.AtomFeedParser"/>
</extension>
```

Now when the feed is downloaded, it will attempt to parse it as RSS first and then fall back to Atom afterwards.

Making the parser namespace aware

The Atom specification uses **XML namespaces**. To parse the feed properly, the document builder must be specified as **namespace aware** and the elements lookup needs to use the equivalent `getElementsByTagNameNS`.

In the `AtomFeedParser` class, define a `static` constant to hold the Atom namespace:

```
private static final String ATOM = "http://www.w3.org/2005/Atom";
```

Then, replace the calls to `getElementsByTagName` with the namespace aware equivalent `getElementsByTagNameNS`, as shown in the following code:

```
// NodeList items = doc.getElementsByTagName("entry");
NodeList items = doc.getElementsByTagNameNS(ATOM, "entry");
...
// return ((Element) item)
//   .getElementsByTagName(element).item(0)
return ((Element) item)
  .getElementsByTagNameNS(ATOM,element).item(0)
```

Finally, to ensure that the document builder is using namespace aware parsing, the `DocumentBuilderFactory` instance needs to be appropriately configured before `DocumentBuilder` is instantiated. The code is as follows:

```
// DocumentBuilder builder = DocumentBuilderFactory.newInstance()
//   .newDocumentBuilder();
DocumentBuilderFactory factory =
 DocumentBuilderFactory.newInstance();
factory.setNamespaceAware(true);
DocumentBuilder builder = factory.newDocumentBuilder();
```

When the Atom feed is parsed, it will be correctly represented if there are multiple namespaces or a default namespace is not specified.

Priority and ordering

The order of the `IConfigurationElement` instances returned by the registry should not be relied upon for consistency. Relying on a specific order will prevent others from easily being able to contribute additional implementations from other plug-ins. If an ordering is desired, additional metadata should be added to the extension to allow the ordering to be calculated after retrieval.

In this case, MockFeedParser should have the lowest priority and RSSFeedParser should have a higher priority than AtomFeedParser. To implement this, an extra attribute priority will be added to the extension point so that the results can be processed after loading.

Although any ordering can be used (for example, high/medium/low, or top/bottom), it is easier to deal with numerical priorities and perform an integer sort. Using both positive and negative numbers allows a full range of priorities and also allows some extensions to register themselves as less desirable than the default, which can remain at zero.

Modify the extension point schema feedParser.esxd and add a new attribute under the **feedParser** element called priority. Since the XML schema for extension points does not permit numeric values, use **string** as the type and the value can be parsed afterwards. This is shown in the following screenshot:

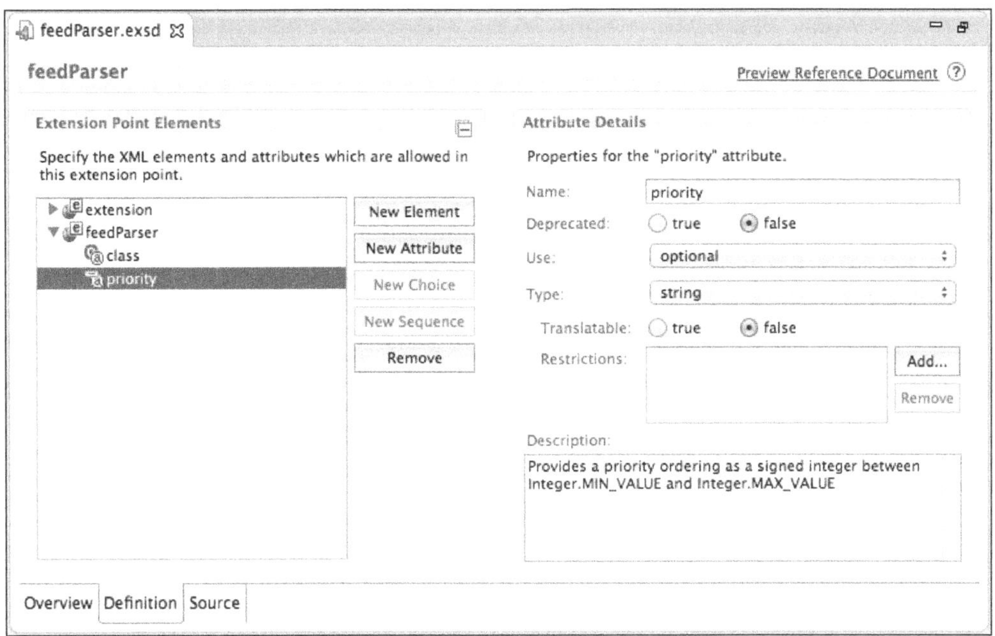

Now, in the plugin.xml file where the feeds are defined, add a priority of -1 to MockFeedParser and a priority of 1 to RSSFeedParser:

```
<extension point="com.packtpub.e4.advanced.feeds.feedParser">
  <feedParser priority="1"
   class="com.packtpub.e4.advanced.feeds.internal.RSSFeedParser"/>
  <feedParser
```

```
    class="com.packtpub.e4.advanced.feeds.internal.AtomFeedParser"/>
    <feedParser priority="-1"
    class="com.packtpub.e4.advanced.feeds.internal.MockFeedParser"/>
</extension>
```

Since the `IFeedParser` interface doesn't have a priority attribute that can be set, the `IConfigurationElement` instances must be sorted after retrieval, but before iteration. To do this, the `Arrays` class can be used by calling `sort` with an appropriate `Comparator`.

Create a class called `FeedParserConfigurationComparator` in the `internal` package, and then make it implement `Comparator` with a target type of `IConfigurationElement`. Write a helper method to parse an integer from a string, treating a missing value (`null`) or integers that cannot be parsed as a zero value.

The class will be similar to the following code:

```
public class FeedParserConfigurationComparator implements
 Comparator<IConfigurationElement> {
  private static final String PRIORITY = "priority";
  public int compare(IConfigurationElement o1,
   IConfigurationElement o2) {
    String a1 = o1.getAttribute(PRIORITY);
    String a2 = o2.getAttribute(PRIORITY);
    return parseInt(a2) - parseInt(a1);
  }
  private int parseInt(String string) {
    try {
      return Integer.parseInt(string);
    } catch (Exception e) {
      return 0;
    }
  }
}
```

This will sort the extensions based on the numerical value of the `priority` attribute. To invoke it, call a `sort` method after the configuration elements are accessed in `FeedParserFactory`:

```
IConfigurationElement[] elements =
 extensionPoint.getConfigurationElements();
Arrays.sort(elements, new FeedParserConfigurationComparator());
```

Now when the extensions are processed, they will be done in priority order.

Using a singleton for comparators?

It's possible to use the singleton pattern for the comparator, since it uses no instance variables. By making the constructor private and instantiating a `public static final` constant, it can be referred to with `FeedParserConfigurationComparator.INSTANCE`. This is useful if the comparator is being used in a lot of places, since the same instance will be reused. However, if it is used infrequently, creating and disposing the comparator will be fairly fast and will not permanently stay in memory when not in use. The tradeoff between memory and CPU utilization will depend on the expected use cases.

Executable extensions and data

When an extension point is created, it is called with a zero-argument constructor. The result is that most extensions in Eclipse are pre-configured with whatever data they need with no further customization.

It is possible to pass through additional configuration data in the `plugin.xml` file and have that parsed at start-up. To do this, the `IExecutableExtension` interface provides a `setInitializationData` method that passes in information defined statically within the `plugin.xml` file.

By adding the `IExecutableExtension` interface to the concrete feed parser instance, it's possible to have additional data from the `plugin.xml` file passed into the class itself. This may allow the same implementation to perform in different ways based on values contained within the `plugin.xml` file; for example, a limit could be placed on the parser to indicate how many feed entries would be shown in the list.

Add the `IExecutableExtension` interface to the `AtomFeedParser` class, and then add following code:

```
private int max = Integer.MAX_VALUE;
public void setInitializationData(IConfigurationElement config,
 String propertyName, Object data) throws CoreException {
  if (data instanceof String) {
    try {
      max = Integer.parseInt((String) data);
    } catch (Exception e) {
      // Ignore
    }
  }
}
```

The max field can be used to limit the number of elements returned from the feed:

```
for (int i = 0; i < items.getLength() && i < max; i++)
```

The data can be passed in a couple of different ways. The easiest way (if it's a single value or can be represented as a string) is to pass it after the class name of the attribute with a colon. Modify the plugin.xml as shown:

```
<feedParser class="com.packtpub.e4.advanced.feeds.internal.
AtomFeedParser:2"/>
```

Note the :2 at the end of the class name. Upon initialization of the feed parser, the value will be passed in as the data object.

> The value of propertyName in this case will be class, which is taken from the createExecutableExtension method call previously and refers to the XML attribute class in this entry.

Now when the application is run, Atom feeds such as http://alblue.bandlem.com/atom.xml will only return a maximum of two values. The same change can be applied to RSSFeedParser.

> There are several ways of pulling configuration information out from an extension. The simplest way is to parse the string appropriately after the class name, and this suffices for most cases.
>
> More complex cases can simply parse the IConfigurationElement interface (shown in the next example).
>
> There is also an ancient plug-in configuration process that can be invoked if null is passed as an attribute name and where elements and parameters use a specific hardcoded pattern. Parameters are parsed from name/value pairs and passed into the data as a Hashtable:

```
<feedParser>
  <parser class="class.name">
    <parameter name="maxCount" value="1">
  </parser>
</feedParser>
```

> This is for compatibility with older versions of Eclipse and should not be used.

Executable extension factories

Sometimes, it's not possible to add an interface to the class that requires instantiation. This is either because it doesn't make sense for the component itself to implement `IExecutableExtension`, or because it's a closed source component, such as a database driver that cannot be modified.

Note that the `DBFactory` example is not used or needed by the `Feed` example; it's used to demonstrate the need to introduce factories where the user has no ability to change the class being instantiated. It is provided here just as an example.

This issue can be resolved by using an **executable extension factory**. This permits a factory to be used to instantiate the extension. For example, if a database connection was defined in an extension point, it might be similar to the following:

```
<database user="example" pass="pass" url="jdbc:h2:/tmp/test"/>
```

The desired result of this would be to provide an instantiated JDBC `Connection` object of the right type. Clearly, the driver itself cannot be modified to implement the `IExecutableExtension` interface; but it is possible to provide it as an extension with a factory:

```
public class DBFactory implements IExecutableExtension,
 IExecutableExtensionFactory {
  private String url;
  private String user;
  private String pass;
  public void setInitializationData(IConfigurationElement config,
   String propertyName, Object data) throws CoreException {
    url = config.getAttribute("url");
    user = config.getAttribute("user");
    pass = config.getAttribute("pass");
  }
  public Object create() throws CoreException {
    try {
      return DriverManager.getConnection(url, user, pass);
    } catch (SQLException e) {
       throw new CoreException(new Status(IStatus.ERROR,
         "com.packtpub.e4.advanced.feeds",
         "Failed to get driver connection for " + url, e));
    }
  }
}
```

The preceding example shows another way of getting the configuration data—by direct parsing of the `IConfigurationElement` class. Of course, placing user IDs and passwords hardcoded into an extension point is not good practice; the example here is used because the `Connection` interface will be familiar to many readers.

Note that since the `DriverManager` class does a lookup based on the URL to acquire the database connection, it will be necessary to have those driver classes available on the bundle's classpath—either as a direct import or as a bundle dependency.

It's fairly common for an `IExecutableExtensionFactory` instance to also inherit `IExecutableExtension`, as that is the only way of receiving data if it is required. If the factory does not need such data (for example, it is instantiating an in-memory structure, or using external file configuration), it might be possible to have an `IExecutableExtensionFactory` interface that does not implement `IExecutableExtension`.

Using the extension registry outside of OSGi

Although the extension registry can work outside of OSGi, it's not easy to do so. This is partly is due to the set of libraries that are required and partly because there is additional setup required in order to provide the registry with the right state.

There are a number of dependencies that need to be provided for the extension registry to work, including the **Equinox Supplemental** bundle. The supplemental bundle provides commonly used features such as `NLS` and `Debug`, which are liberally spread around the Equinox codebase and are required for running outside of Equinox. In addition (in Kepler and below), the `Debug` class transitively depends on the OSGi `ServiceTracker`, which means that even when running outside of OSGi, this package is required.

The minimum setup for a Java application (running outside of OSGi) to use the extension registry is as follows:

- `org.eclipse.equinox.registry`
- `org.eclipse.equinox.common` (provides `CoreException`)
- `org.eclipse.equinox.supplement` (provides `NLS` and `Debug`)
- `org.osgi.core` (provides `ServiceTracker`)

Note that if running in a non-Equinox OSGi container, `org.osgi.core` will not be needed. If running in Equinox, then the supplemental bundle is not needed, as this provides a copy of the public classes and interfaces used.

In Eclipse Luna and above (`org.eclipse.equinox.supplement` version 3.5.100 or higher), the dependency on `org.osgi.core` has been removed so this particular dependency is no longer necessary.

> The supplemental bundle can be downloaded from the Equinox downloads page at `http://download.eclipse.org/equinox/`; navigate to the latest release builds and go to the **Add-on Bundles** section. For example, the download URL for Kepler SR2 is `http://download.eclipse.org/equinox/drops/R-KeplerSR2-201402211700/download.php?dropFile=org.eclipse.equinox.supplement_1.5.0.v20130812-2109.jar`.

To configure the registry to run outside of OSGi, it is necessary to set up a registry instance. There is an `IRegistryProvider` interface that can be used to define what registry instance should be returned when `RegistryFactory.getRegistry` is called. By default, this will return `null` until a registry has been set; in an OSGi runtime, this is done by the registry bundle itself starting.

To create a `Registry` instance directly, there is a `RegistryFactory.create` method that takes a `RegistryStrategy` instance along with a couple of tokens. The tokens can be used in secure environments to prevent callers from modifying or adding to the registry. All three elements can be left as `null`.

The net effect is that adding this to the start-up of a Java application, which needs the registry, will work:

```
public class NonOsgi {
  private final main(String[] args) throws Exception {
    RegistryFactory.setDefaultRegistryProvider(
     new IRegistryProvider() {
      private final IExtensionRegistry registry =
       RegistryFactory.createRegistry(null, null, null);
      public IExtensionRegistry getRegistry() {
        return registry;
      }
    });
    … // register or look up contributions
  }
}
```

Once the registry has been set, it can be acquired from the `RegistryFactory` interface:

```
IExtensionRegistry reg = RegistryFactory.getRegistry();
```

However, unlike OSGi (where the registry automatically scans for bundles as they are inserted and registers the extension elements), in a standalone Java application this needs to be done manually.

To load a single `plugin.xml` file into the registry, it is necessary to first create a contributor (which in OSGi is the bundle, but in a Java application can be a different mechanism) and then add a contribution. The contribution itself is an `InputStream` that represents the `plugin.xml` file, called `feeds.xml` here:

```
IContributor contributor = ContributorFactorySimple
  .createContributor("com.packtpub.e4.advanced.feeds");
reg.addContribution(Main.class.getResourceAsStream("/feeds.xml"),
  contributor, false, "/feeds.xml", null, null);
```

This loads the file `feeds.xml` from the classpath and uses that to register the feeds plug-in mentioned previously. This XML file may be built in-memory or loaded from other input sources, but has the same effect and content as the `plugin.xml` of the original bundle.

> Unfortunately, it isn't possible to use `plugin.xml` as the filename, as the `org.eclipse.equinox.registry` bundle also has a file called `plugin.xml`, and the standard Java `getResourceAsStream` will load the first one that it sees. As a result, depending on whether your class or the registry JAR is first on the path, you might see a different result. See the *Loading all extensions from the classpath* section to find out how to handle this.

The extension can then be acquired as usual or via the `FeedParserFactory` method defined previously.

Using the extension registry cache

In typical Eclipse usage, the extension registry remains the same between Eclipse restarts, and adding (or removing) plug-ins updates the registry appropriately. To save time at start-up, the **extension registry cache** is used to store its contents at shutdown, and if available, loads it at start-up.

Contributions can be **persistent** or **non-persistent**. A persistent registration is kept such that a restart of the application will have the same value; a non-persistent registration is for this JVM only and will be lost on restart. Eclipse uses this mechanism at start-up to ensure a faster start-up time and to avoid having to reparse the `plugin.xml` files each time.

To take advantage of the cache, a `RegistryStrategy` instance must be provided with one or more cache directories to store the content. If at least one directory is writable, the registry can save new extensions; if the list of directories is empty or all of the directories are read-only, then the registry will not persist content between restarts.

Modify the `IRegistryProvider` interface in the `NonOsgi` class to return a directory, and then pass that into `RegistryStrategy` along with an array of `false` values:

```
new IRegistryProvider() {
  private final IExtensionRegistry registry = RegistryFactory
   .createRegistry(getRegistryStrategy(), null, null);
  private RegistryStrategy getRegistryStrategy() {
    File cache = new File(
     System.getProperty("java.io.tmpdir"),"cache");
    return new RegistryStrategy(
     new File[] { cache }, new boolean[] { false } );
}
```

The second parameter to `RegistryStrategy` is an array of `boolean` values (one per entry in the `File` array) that indicates whether the cache is read-only or not. If this parameter is `null`, then the cache directories are all considered read-only.

Finally, note that if using the registry in caching mode, it is necessary to stop the registry after use. This causes the data entries to be persisted to disk:

```
reg.stop(null);
```

To enable the contribution to be added persistently, the `boolean persist` parameter should be specified as `true`:

```
reg.addContribution(Main.class.getResourceAsStream("/feeds.xml"),
 contributor, /* false */ true, "/feeds.xml", null, null);
```

Now, if the contribution is added and the line is commented out, then re-running the application will load the entry from the cache.

If the cache needs to be rebuilt, then the `clearRegistryCache` method of `ExtensionRegistry` will need to be called at start-up. This is equivalent to passing the `-clean` parameter to Eclipse at start-up. Since this is not an interface method, the call will need to be cast to the explicit `ExtensionRegistry` class. Alternatively, the cache directory can be deleted prior to starting the registry, and it will be rebuilt automatically.

Loading all extensions from the classpath

The `getResourceAsStream` method returns the first element found in the classpath. For applications that can span many JAR files, it's desirable to be able to find all the files with that name, not just the first one. Fortunately, `ClassLoader` has a means to scan all of the individual elements with the `getResources` method, which returns an enumeration of URLs from which streams can be individually obtained.

The solution is to call `getResources` with an argument of `plugin.xml` and then iterate through each of those JARs to instantiate the required contributions. By default, the contribution name is the name of the bundle, so it is necessary to parse out the `Bundle-SymbolicName` header from the manifest. There are standard OSGi classes to do this, but the `Manifest` class from the standard JDK libraries can be used.

The `Bundle-SymbolicName` header can have additional metadata after the bundle name, separated by a semicolon (which delimits OSGi directives). The most common one is `;singleton=true`, but others can also exist such as `;mandatory` and `;fragment-attachment`.

Instead of adding a single `feeds.xml` file into the registry, all JARs can have their bundles scanned by changing the following code in `NonOsgi`:

```
// IContributor contributor = ContributorFactorySimple
// .createContributor("com.packtpub.e4.advanced.feeds");
// reg.addContribution(Main.class.getResourceAsStream(
//  "/feeds.xml"), contributor, false, "/feeds.xml", null, null);
Enumeration<URL> resources = getClass().getClassLoader().
 getResources("plugin.xml");
while (resources.hasMoreElements()) {
  URL url = (URL) resources.nextElement();
  String plugin_xml = url.toString();
  String manifest_mf = plugin_xml.replace(
    "plugin.xml","META-INF/MANIFEST.MF");
  Manifest manifest = new Manifest(
    new URL(manifest_mf).openStream());
  String bsn = manifest.getMainAttributes().
   getValue("Bundle-SymbolicName");
  int semi = bsn.indexOf(';');
  if (semi != -1) {
    bsn = bsn.substring(0, semi);
  }
  IContributor contributor =
```

```
        ContributorFactorySimple.createContributor(bsn);
      reg.addContribution(url.openStream(), contributor, persist,
        plugin_xml, null, null);
    }
```

After running this code, all JARs on the classpath will have extensions from their `plugin.xml` files registered.

Unfortunately, there's a minor problem with any projects that are open in the Eclipse workbench. An open project in PDE doesn't put the `plugin.xml` or `MANIFEST.MF` files available on the project's classpath, which means that the classpath loading mechanism doesn't work. This is generally a problem with PDE and means that (for example) `bundle.getEntry` and `class.getResourceAsStream` in a PDE project differ from how they will run when exported and installed into a runtime as a JAR.

Fortunately, there is a way of fixing this: adding the `plugin.xml` and `META-INF/**` files as explicit sources in JDT, which copies them to the output directory. As a result, the `getResource` methods work in both runtime and outside of runtime.

Right-click on the project and go to the **Java Build Path**. In the **Source** tab, add a folder by clicking on **Add Folder** and selecting the root of the project. Click on **Edit** and then add `plugin.xml` and `META-INF/**` as entries to be included. This is shown in the following screenshots:

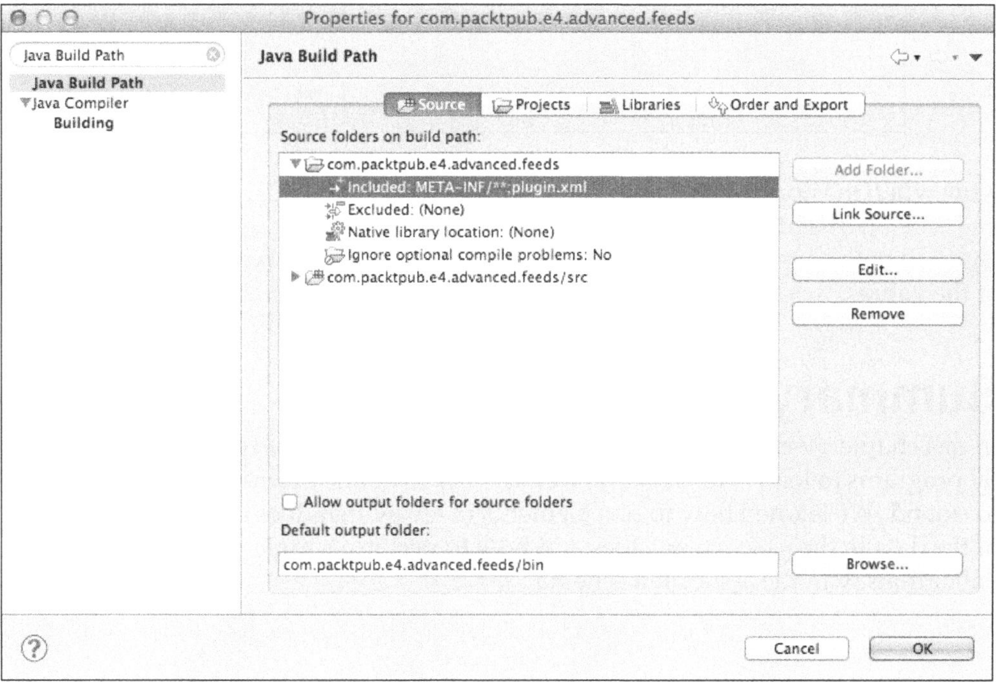

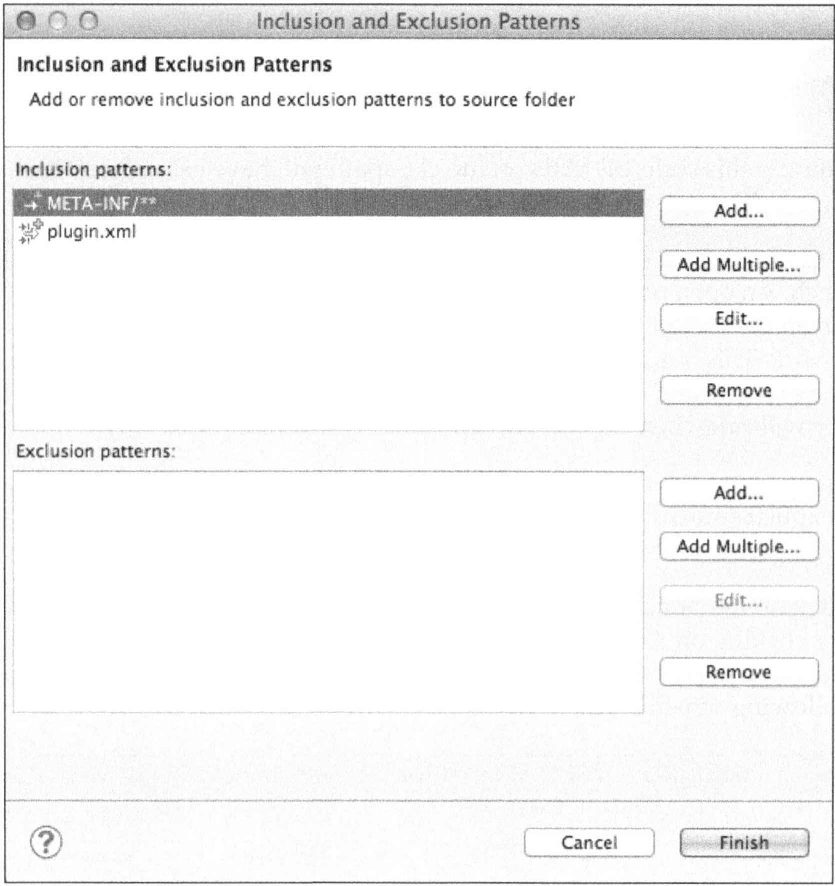

Now when the application is run, `plugin.xml` from the `org.eclipse.equinox.registry` JAR and `plugin.xml` from the `com.packtpub.e4.advanced.feeds` JAR will both be registered and the default feed parsers will be able to return all of the values.

Summary

In this chapter, we looked at the Eclipse extension registry and how it can be used by programs to load extensions, as well as how to define extension points for others to extend. We learned how to sort elements in a way that does not rely on the order of the data in the `plugin.xml` files and how to perform simple definitions and validations with the associated schema.

The extension registry can also be used to customize different instances of extensions, and we looked at both of the ways in which this is done in Eclipse—with executable extensions and with extension factories (for classes whose inheritance hierarchy cannot be modified).

Finally, we looked at how the registry can be used outside of an OSGi runtime, which permits application code to be well behaved both inside and outside of OSGi.

In the next chapter, we will look at how similar extensions can be achieved with OSGi services.

3

Using OSGi Services to Dynamically Wire Applications

This chapter will present **OSGi services** as a means to communicate with and connect applications. Unlike the Eclipse extension point mechanism, OSGi services can have multiple versions available at runtime and can work in other OSGi environments, such as Felix or other commercial OSGi runtimes.

Overview of services

In an Eclipse or OSGi runtime, each individual bundle is its own separate module, which has explicit dependencies on library code via `Import-Package`, `Require-Bundle`, or `Require-Capability`. These express static relationships and provide a way of configuring the bundle's classpath.

However, this presents a problem. If services are independent, how can they use contributions provided by other bundles? In Eclipse's case, the extension registry covered in *Chapter 2, Creating Custom Extension Points*, provides a means for code to look up providers. In a standalone OSGi environment, OSGi services provide a similar mechanism.

A **service** is an instance of a class that implements a **service interface**. When a service is created, it is **registered** with the services framework under one (or more) interfaces, along with a set of properties. Consumers can then **get** the service by asking the framework for implementers of that specific interface.

> Services can also be registered under an abstract class, but this is not recommended. Providing a service interface exposed as an abstract class can lead to unnecessary coupling of client to implementation.

The following diagram gives an overview of services:

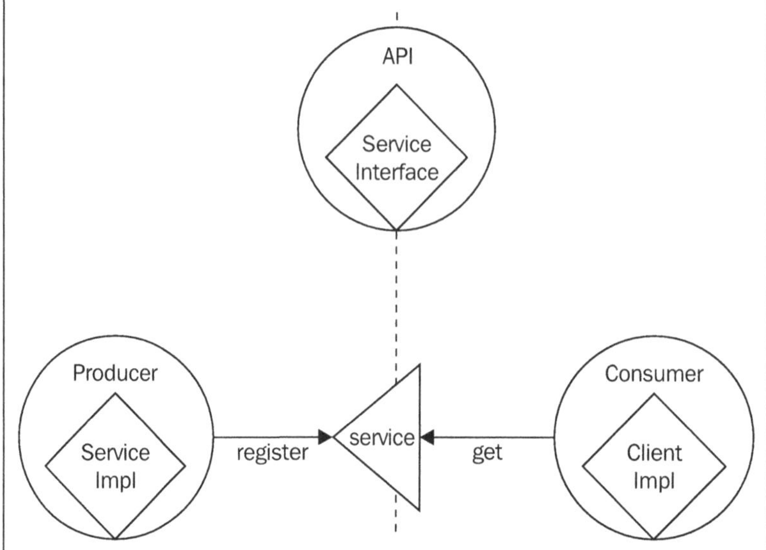

This separation allows the consumer and producer to depend on a common API bundle, but otherwise be completely decoupled from one another. This allows both the consumer and producer to be mocked out or exchange with different implementations in the future.

Registering a service programmatically

To register a service, an instance of the implementation class needs to be created and registered with the framework. Interactions with the framework are performed with an instance of `BundleContext`—typically provided in the `BundleActivator.start` method and stored for later use. The `*FeedParser` classes from the previous chapter will be extended to support registration as a service instead of the Equinox extension registry.

Creating an activator

A bundle's **activator** is a class that is instantiated and coupled to the lifetime of the bundle. When a bundle is started, if a manifest entry `Bundle-Activator` exists, then the corresponding class is instantiated. As long as it implements the `BundleActivator` interface, the `start` method will be called. This method is passed as an instance of `BundleContext`, which is the bundle's connection to the hosting OSGi framework.

Create a class in the `com.packtpub.e4.advanced.feeds` project called `com.packtpub.e4.advanced.feeds.internal.FeedsActivator`, which implements the `org.osgi.framework.BundleActivator` interface.

The quick fix may suggest adding `org.osgi.framework` as an imported package. Accept this, and modify the `META-INF/MANIFEST.MF` file as follows:

```
Import-Package: org.osgi.framework
Bundle-Activator:
 com.packtpub.e4.advanced.feeds.internal.FeedsActivator
```

The framework will automatically invoke the `start` method of the `FeedsActivator` when the bundle is started, and correspondingly, the `stop` method when the bundle is stopped. Test this by inserting a pair of `println` calls:

```
public class FeedsActivator implements BundleActivator {
  public void start(BundleContext context) throws Exception {
    System.out.println("Bundle started");
  }
  public void stop(BundleContext context) throws Exception {
    System.out.println("Bundle stopped");
  }
}
```

Now run the project as an OSGi framework with the `feeds` bundle, the Equinox console, and the Gogo shell. The required dependencies can be added by clicking on **Add Required Bundles**, although the **Include optional dependencies** checkbox does not need to be selected. Ensure that the other workspace and target bundles are deselected with the **Deselect all** button, as shown in the following screenshot:

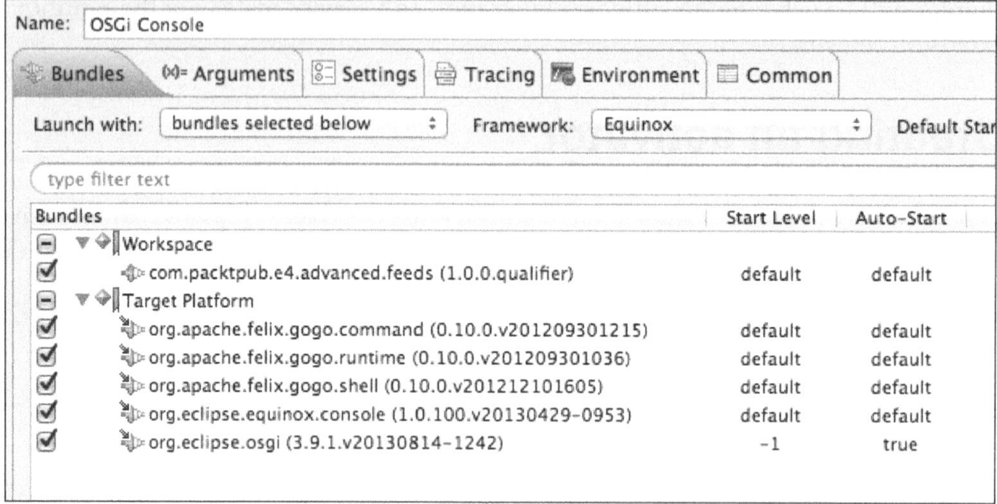

The required bundles are as follows:

- `com.packtpub.e4.advanced.feeds`
- `org.apache.felix.gogo.command`
- `org.apache.felix.gogo.runtime`
- `org.apache.felix.gogo.shell`
- `org.eclipse.equinox.console`
- `org.eclipse.osgi`

On the console, when the bundle is started (which happens automatically if the **Default Auto-Start** is set to `true`), the **Bundle started** message should be seen.

If the bundle does not start, `ss` in the console will print a list of bundles and `start 2` will start the bundle with the ID `2`. Afterwards, `stop 2` can be used to stop bundle `2`. Bundles can be stopped/started dynamically in an OSGi framework.

Registering the service

Once the FeedsActivator instance is created, a BundleContext instance will be available for interaction with the framework. This can be persisted for subsequent use in an instance field and can also be used directly to register a service.

The BundleContext class provides a registerService method, which takes an interface, an instance, and an optional Dictionary instance of key/value pairs. This can be used to register instances of the feed parser at runtime. Modify the start method as follows:

```
public void start(BundleContext context) throws Exception {
  context.registerService(IFeedParser.class,
   new RSSFeedParser(), null);
  context.registerService(IFeedParser.class,
   new AtomFeedParser(), null);
  context.registerService(IFeedParser.class,
   new MockFeedParser(), null);
}
```

Now start the framework again. In the console that is launched, look for the bundle corresponding to the feeds bundle:

```
osgi> bundles | grep feeds
com.packtpub.e4.advanced.feeds_1.0.0.qualifier [4]
  {com.packtpub.e4.advanced.feeds.IFeedParser}={service.id=56}
  {com.packtpub.e4.advanced.feeds.IFeedParser}={service.id=57}
  {com.packtpub.e4.advanced.feeds.IFeedParser}={service.id=58}
```

This shows that bundle 4 has started three services, using the interface com.packtpub.e4.advanced.feeds.IFeedParser, and with service IDs 56, 57, and 58.

It is also possible to query the runtime framework for services of a known interface type directly using the services command and an LDAP style filter:

```
osgi> services (objectClass=com.packtpub.e4.advanced.feeds.IFeedParser)
{com.packtpub.e4.advanced.feeds.IFeedParser}={service.id=56}
  "Registered by bundle:"
    com.packtpub.e4.advanced.feeds_1.0.0.qualifier [4]
  "No bundles using service."
{com.packtpub.e4.advanced.feeds.IFeedParser}={service.id=57}
  "Registered by bundle:"
```

```
    com.packtpub.e4.advanced.feeds_1.0.0.qualifier [4]
  "No bundles using service."

{com.packtpub.e4.advanced.feeds.IFeedParser}={service.id=58}
  "Registered by bundle:"
    com.packtpub.e4.advanced.feeds_1.0.0.qualifier [4]
  "No bundles using service."
```

The results displayed represent the three services instantiated. They can be introspected using the `service` command passing the `service.id`:

```
osgi> service 56
com.packtpub.e4.advanced.feeds.internal.RSSFeedParser@52ba638e
osgi> service 57
com.packtpub.e4.advanced.feeds.internal.AtomFeedParser@3e64c3a
osgi> service 58
com.packtpub.e4.advanced.feeds.internal.MockFeedParser@49d5e6da
```

Priority of services

Services have an implicit order, based on the order in which they were instantiated. Each time a service is registered, a global `service.id` is incremented.

It is possible to define an explicit **service ranking** with an integer property. This is used to ensure relative priority between services, regardless of the order in which they are registered. For services with equal `service.ranking` values, the `service.id` values are compared.

OSGi R6 adds an additional property, `service.bundleid`, which is used to denote the ID of the bundle that provides the service. This is not used to order services, and is for informational purposes only. Eclipse Luna uses OSGi R6.

To pass a priority into the service registration, create a helper method called `priority`, which takes an `int` value and stores it in a `Hashtable` with the key `service.ranking`. This can be used to pass a priority to the service registration methods. The following code illustrates this:

```
private Dictionary<String,Object> priority(int priority) {
  Hashtable<String, Object> dict = new Hashtable<String,Object>();
  dict.put("service.ranking", new Integer(priority));
  return dict;
}
```

```
public void start(BundleContext context) throws Exception {
  context.registerService(IFeedParser.class,
    new RSSFeedParser(), priority(1));
  context.registerService(IFeedParser.class,
    new MockFeedParser(), priority(-1));
  context.registerService(IFeedParser.class,
    new AtomFeedParser(), priority(2));
}
```

Now when the framework starts, the services are displayed in order of priority:

```
osgi> services | (objectClass=com.packtpub.e4.advanced.feeds.IFeedParser)
{com.packtpub.e4.advanced.feeds.IFeedParser}={service.ranking=2, service.
id=58}
"Registered by bundle:" com.packtpub.e4.advanced.feeds_1.0.0.qualifier [4]
"No bundles using service."
{com.packtpub.e4.advanced.feeds.IFeedParser}={service.ranking=1, service.
id=56}
"Registered by bundle:"
com.packtpub.e4.advanced.feeds_1.0.0.qualifier [4]
"No bundles using service."
{com.packtpub.e4.advanced.feeds.IFeedParser}={service.ranking=-1,
service.id=57}
"Registered by bundle:" com.packtpub.e4.advanced.feeds_1.0.0.qualifier [4]
  "No bundles using service."
```

`Dictionary` was the original Java `Map` interface, and `Hashtable` the original `HashMap` implementation. They fell out of favor in Java 1.2 when `Map` and `HashMap` were introduced (mainly because they weren't synchronized by default) but OSGi was developed to run on early releases of Java (JSR 8 proposed adding OSGi as a standard for the Java platform). Not only that, early low-powered Java mobile devices didn't support the full Java platform, instead exposing the original Java 1.1 data structures. Because of this history, many APIs in OSGi refer to only Java 1.1 data structures so that low-powered devices can still run OSGi systems.

Using the services

The `BundleContext` instance can be used to acquire services as well as register them. `FeedParserFactory`, which originally used the extension registry, can be upgraded to refer to services instead.

To obtain an instance of `BundleContext`, store it in the `FeedsActivator.start` method as a `static` variable. That way, classes elsewhere in the bundle will be able to acquire the context. An accessor method provides an easy way to do this:

```
public class FeedsActivator implements BundleActivator {
  private static BundleContext bundleContext;
  public static BundleContext getContext() {
    return bundleContext;
  }
  public void start(BundleContext context) throws Exception {
    // register methods as before
    bundleContext = context;
  }
  public void stop(BundleContext context) throws Exception {
    bundleContext = null;
  }
}
```

Now the `FeedParserFactory` class can be updated to acquire the services. OSGi services are represented via a `ServiceReference` instance (which is a sharable object representing a handle to the service) and can be used to acquire a service instance:

```
public class FeedParserFactory {
  public List<IFeedParser> getFeedParsers() {
    List<IFeedParser> parsers = new ArrayList<IFeedParser>();
    BundleContext context = FeedsActivator.getContext();
    try {
      Collection<ServiceReference<IFeedParser>> references =
        context.getServiceReferences(IFeedParser.class, null);
      for (ServiceReference<IFeedParser> reference : references) {
        parsers.add(context.getService(reference));
        context.ungetService(reference);
      }
    } catch (InvalidSyntaxException e) {
      // ignore
    }
    return parsers;
  }
}
```

In this case, the service references are obtained from the bundle context with a call to `context.getServiceReferences(IFeedParser.class,null)`. The service references can be used to access the service's properties, and to acquire the service.

The service instance is acquired with the `context.getService(ServiceReference)` call. The contract is that the caller "borrows" the service, and when finished, should return it with an `ungetService(ServiceReference)` call. Technically, the service is only supposed to be used between the `getService` and `ungetService` calls as its lifetime may be invalid afterwards; instead of returning an array of service references, the common pattern is to pass in a unit of work that accepts the service and then call `ungetService` afterwards. However, to fit in with the existing API, the service is acquired, added to the list, and then released immediately afterwards.

Lazy activation of bundles

Now run the project as an Eclipse application, with the `feeds` and `feeds.ui` bundles installed. When a new feed is created by navigating to **File** | **New** | **Other** | **Feeds** | **Feed**, and a feed such as `http://alblue.bandlem.com/atom.xml` is entered, the feeds will be shown in the navigator view. When drilling down, a `NullPointerException` may be seen in the logs, as shown in the following:

```
!MESSAGE An exception occurred invoking extension:
com.packtpub.e4.advanced.feeds.ui.feedNavigatorContent
 for object com.packtpub.e4.advanced.feeds.Feed@770def59
!STACK 0
java.lang.NullPointerException
  at com.packtpub.e4.advanced.feeds.FeedParserFactory.
   getFeedParsers(FeedParserFactory.java:31)
  at com.packtpub.e4.advanced.feeds.ui.FeedContentProvider.
   getChildren(FeedContentProvider.java:80)
  at org.eclipse.ui.internal.navigator.extensions.
   SafeDelegateTreeContentProvider.
    getChildren(SafeDelegateTreeContentProvider.java:96)
```

Tracing through the code indicates that the `bundleContext` is `null`, which implies that the `feeds` bundle has not yet been started. This can be seen in the console of the running Eclipse application by executing the following code:

```
osgi> ss | grep feeds
866 ACTIVE   com.packtpub.e4.advanced.feeds.ui_1.0.0.qualifier
992 RESOLVED com.packtpub.e4.advanced.feeds_1.0.0.qualifier
```

While the `feeds.ui` bundle is active, the `feeds` bundle is not. Therefore, the services haven't been instantiated, and `bundleContext` has not been cached.

By default, bundles are not started when they are accessed for the first time. If the bundle needs its activator to be called prior to using any of the classes in the package, it needs to be marked as having an **activation policy** of **lazy**. This is done by adding the following entry to the `MANIFEST.MF` file:

```
Bundle-ActivationPolicy: lazy
```

The manifest editor can be used to add this configuration line by selecting **Activate this plug-in when one of its classes is loaded**, as shown in the following screenshot:

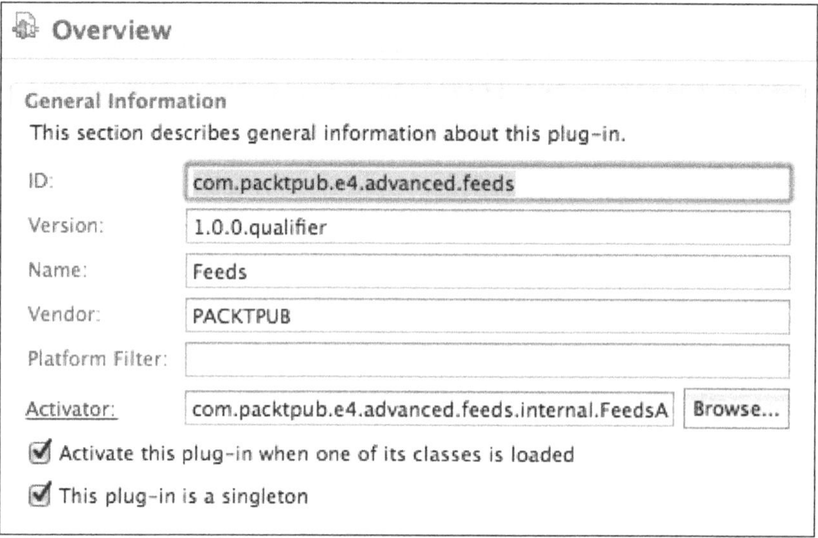

Now, when the application is run, the feeds will resolve appropriately.

Comparison of services and extension points

Both mechanisms (using the extension registry and using the services) allow for a list of feed parsers to be contributed and used by the application. What are the differences between them, and are there any advantages to one or the other?

Both the registry and services approaches can be used outside of an Eclipse runtime. They work the same way when used in other OSGi implementations (such as Felix) and can be used interchangeably. The registry approach can also be used outside of OSGi, although that is far less common.

The registry encodes its information in the `plugin.xml` file by default, which means that it is typically edited as part of a bundle's install (it is possible to create registry entries from alternative implementations if desired, but this rarely happens). The registry has a notification system, which can listen to contributions being added and removed.

The services approach uses the OSGi framework to store and maintain a list of services. These services don't have an explicit configuration file and, in fact, can be contributed by code (such as the `registerService` calls previously covered) or by declarative representations (which are covered in the next section).

The separation of how the service is created versus how the service is registered is a key difference between the service and the registry approach. Like the registry, the OSGi services system can generate notifications when services come and go.

One key difference in an OSGi runtime is that bundles depending on the Eclipse registry must be declared as **singletons**; that is, they have to use the `;singleton:=true` directive on `Bundle-SymbolicName`. This means that there can only be one version of a bundle that exposes registry entries in a runtime, as opposed to multiple versions in the case of general services.

While the registry does provide mechanisms to be able to instantiate extensions from factories, these typically involve simple configurations and/or properties that are hard-coded in the `plugin.xml` files themselves. They would not be appropriate to store sensitive details such as passwords. On the other hand, a service can be instantiated from whatever external configuration information is necessary and then registered, such as a JDBC connection for a database.

Finally, extensions in the registry are declarative by default and are activated on demand. This allows Eclipse to start quickly because it does not need to build the full set of class loader objects or run code, and then bring up services on demand. Although the approach previously didn't use declarative services, it is possible to do this as covered in the next section.

Registering a service declaratively

Registering services imperatively in the `start` method of an `Activator` class is one way of installing services in an OSGi framework. However, it requires that the bundle be started, which in turn requires that either the bundle is started automatically or has classes (such as API classes) accessed by default. Both approaches will mean that additional code will have to be run to bring the system into the desired state.

An alternative is to use one of the declarative service approaches, which represents the service definition in an external file. These are processed using an **extender pattern**, which looks out for bundles with a given file or files and then instantiates the service from this definition. It combines the declarative nature of the extension registry with the flexibility of OSGi services.

There are two providers of declarative service support. Both achieve a similar result but use slightly different configuration files and approaches. They are **Declarative Services** and **Blueprint**.

Declarative Services

Declarative Services (**DS**) was the original declarative implementation to instantiate services in a declarative fashion during OSGi runtime. Both Equinox and Felix have DS modules, and it is a required part of the Eclipse 4 runtime, so it can be trivially expected to be present. In the OSGi specification, it is referred to as the **Services Component Runtime** (**SCR**), which is why the associated package names use `org.osgi.service.component`.

The DS bundle needs to be started before it can process bundles; as a result, it is typically started early on in the start-up process. It listens to bundles being installed and then looks for a specific header in the `META-INF/MANIFEST.MF` file:

```
Service-Component: OSGI-INF/*.xml
```

If the DS bundle finds this header, it looks for files contained in the bundle itself, matching the file pattern specified. This is a comma-separated list, and can use a single wildcard `*` character (which will match filenames but not directories).

The **service document** is then loaded and parsed, and used to instantiate and register services with the OSGi runtime environment. The XML document uses namespaces to represent the component, using `http://www.osgi.org/xmlns/scr/v1.2.0`. Different versions of SCR use different endings; v1.0.0 is defined as the first version, with v1.1.0 the second. The current version (as of the writing of this book) is v1.2.0, and the next version (which is in development at the time of writing this book) will use the suffix v1.3.0.

Each service document defines a single service, which has an implementation class as well as an identifier. The service can be registered under one or more interfaces as well as optional properties.

This can be used to replace the custom code in the `FeedActivator` class created previously:

```
public class FeedsActivator implements BundleActivator {
  public void start(BundleContext context) throws Exception {
    // context.registerService(IFeedParser.class,
    //  new RSSFeedParser(), priority(1));
    // context.registerService(IFeedParser.class,
    //  new MockFeedParser(), priority(-1));
    // context.registerService(IFeedParser.class,
    //  new AtomFeedParser(), priority(2));
    bundleContext = context;
  }
  ...
}
```

If the application is run now, the feeds won't be parsed. To register these as OSGi services, create a file called `OSGI-INF/atomfeedparser.xml`:

```
<?xml version="1.0" encoding="UTF-8"?>
<scr:component xmlns:scr="http://www.osgi.org/xmlns/scr/v1.1.0"
 name="AtomFeedParser">
 <implementation
  class="com.packtpub.e4.advanced.feeds.internal.AtomFeedParser"/>
  <service>
   <provide
    interface="com.packtpub.e4.advanced.feeds.IFeedParser"/>
  </service>
  <property name="service.ranking" type="Integer" value="2"/>
</scr:component>
```

Don't forget to tell Eclipse to consider this part of the build by adding `OSGI-INF/` to the `build.properties` file in the `bin.includes` property.

As long as a Declarative Services provider is installed in the application and started, the service will be created on demand.

In future (Eclipse Mars and above), client bundles will be able to express a dependency on a Declarative Services provider by adding:

```
Require-Capability:
 osgi.extender;osgi.extender="osgi.component"
```

This is being planned to be added to version 1.3.0 of the Declarative Services specification, which is scheduled to be released in March 2015; visit `http://www.osgi.org/Specifications/` for more details.

Properties and Declarative Services

Declarative Services can also be used to register properties with a service when it is registered. These properties can be sourced either from the services XML file, or an external properties file.

To add the `service.ranking` property to the registered service, add the following code to the services document:

```
<?xml version="1.0" encoding="UTF-8"?>
<scr:component xmlns:scr="http://www.osgi.org/xmlns/scr/v1.1.0"
 name="AtomFeedParser">
  …
  <property name="service.ranking" type="Integer" value="2"/>
</scr:component>
```

Now, when the application is restarted, the `services` console command will show that the `service.ranking` property is associated with the feed service:

```
osgi> services | grep IFeed
{com.packtpub.e4.advanced.feeds.IFeedParser}=
 {service.ranking=2,
  component.name=AtomFeedParser,
  component.id=0,
  service.id=37}
```

If the property isn't listed, add a `-clean` argument to the Eclipse runtime console; sometimes the files are cached and **Plug-in Development Environment** (**PDE**) doesn't always notice when files are changed.

The property types can be one of the following:

- `String` (default)
- `Long`
- `Double`
- `Float`
- `Integer`
- `Byte`
- `Character`
- `Boolean`
- `Short`

Additionally, arrays of elements can be specified by placing them in the body of the element instead of as an attribute:

```
<?xml version="1.0" encoding="UTF-8"?>
<scr:component xmlns:scr="http://www.osgi.org/xmlns/scr/v1.1.0"
 name="AtomFeedParser">
  ...
  <property name="compass.point" type="String">
    NORTH
    EAST
    SOUTH
    WEST
  </property>
</scr:component>
```

Service references in Declarative Services

Along with hardcoded values, it is also possible to set up references to services in DS. A service has the `bind` and `unbind` methods, which are called when a service becomes available or becomes inactive.

These can be mandatory or optional; if the dependency is mandatory, then the service is not instantiated until its dependencies are available. If they are optional, the service can come up and be assigned later. They can also be single- or multi-valued. These are encoded in the relationship **cardinality**:

- `0..1`: This service is optional with either zero or one instance needed
- `1..1`: This service is mandatory with exactly one instance needed (default)
- `0..n`: This service is optional and may have zero or more instances
- `1..n`: This service is mandatory and may have one or more instances

This can be used to inject a `LogService` instance into the component. Modify the `AtomFeedParser` class to accept an instance of `LogService` by adding the `setLog` and `unsetLog` methods:

```
private LogService log;
public void setLog(LogService log) {
  this.log = log;
}
public void unsetLog(LogService log) {
  this.log = null;
}
```

The following code can be used to report on the success of feed parsing, or to log errors if they occur:

```
public List<FeedItem> parseFeed(Feed feed) {
  try {
    List<FeedItem> feedItems = new ArrayList<FeedItem>();
    // parse feed items
    if(log != null) {
      log.log(LogService.LOG_INFO, feedItems.size() +
       " atom feed items parsed from " + feed.getUrl());
    }
    return feedItems;
  } catch (Exception e) {
    if (log != null) {
      log.log(LogService.LOG_WARNING, "Problem parsing feed "+e);
    }
    return null;
  }
}
```

To configure DS to provide a log service, the following code must be added to the `atomfeedparser.xml` file:

```
<scr:component name="AtomFeedParser"
 xmlns:scr="http://www.osgi.org/xmlns/scr/v1.1.0">
 …
 <reference interface="org.osgi.service.log.LogService"
  cardinality="0..1" name="log"
  bind="setLog" unbind="unsetLog"/>
</scr:component>
```

This tells DS that the log service is optional (so it will bring the feed parser service up before a `LogService` is available) and `setLog(log)` will be called when it is available. DS also provides an `unbind` method that can be used to remove the service if it becomes inactive. The instance is provided for both the `setLog` and `unsetLog` methods, which may look strange, but when setting multiple elements, the methods are typically called `addXxxListener` and `removeXxxListener`, where having a value is more appropriate.

Multiple components and debugging Declarative Services

Although the example so far has only contained a single component, it is possible to have multiple components defined in a single XML file. An XML parent can be defined with multiple `scr` namespaced children; in fact, all elements outside the `scr` namespace are ignored, so it is possible to embed an XHTML document with an `scr` namespaced element inside, and still have it picked up by Declarative Services:

```
<xhtml>
  <h1>Example HTML file with SCR elements</h1>
  <h2>Component One</h2>
  <scr:component name="One" xmlns:scr="http://...">
    …
  </scr:component>
  <h2>Component Two</h2>
  <scr:component name="Two" xmlns:scr="http://...">
    …
  </scr:component>
</xhtml>
```

Note that many developers will use a one-to-one mapping between service components and the corresponding XML files; it is rare to see a single XML file with multiple service components. It is recommended to only put one component per XML file for ease of maintenance.

When using DS inside Equinox, using `-Dequinox.ds.print=true` can give additional diagnostic information on the state of the Declarative Services, including highlighting which services that are waiting. For Felix, specifying `-Dds.showtrace=true` can increase logging, and so can `-Dds.loglevel=4`.

Dynamic service annotations

Although XML allows flexibility, it has fallen out of fashion in the Java community in favor of Java annotations. Version 1.2 of the OSGi DS specification provides annotations that can be used to mark the code such that a build time processor can create the service component XML files automatically.

Note that the standard OSGi annotations are not read at runtime by the service but only build-time tools such as `maven-scr-plugin`. As a result, they should be optionally imported, since they aren't needed at runtime or with the `compile` scope if using a Maven-based build.

To use the annotations, add the following as an `Import-Package` for the bundle in the `MANIFEST.MF` file:

```
Import-Package:
 org.osgi.service.component.annotations;
 version="1.2.0";
 resolution:=optional
```

The `@Component` annotation can now be added to the individual classes that should be represented as services. Add the following to `RSSFeedParser`:

```
@Component(name="RSSFeedParser",
 service={IFeedParser.class},
 property={"service.ranking:Integer=1"})
public class RSSFeedParser implements
 IFeedParser, IExecutableExtension {
  ...
}
```

There are also Felix annotations (`org.apache.felix.scr.annotations`) that predate the standard OSGi ones. Both the Felix annotations and the OSGi core annotations are available in Maven Central.

Processing annotations at Maven build time

If using Maven Tycho to build bundles, it is possible to add a Maven plug-in to generate service XML files from the components. (See the book's GitHub repository for an example if unfamiliar with Maven Tycho.)

Maven Tycho is covered in more detail in chapter 10 of *Eclipse 4 Plug-in Development by Example Beginner's Guide, Packt Publishing,* as well as on the Tycho home page at `http://www.eclipse.org/tycho/`.

To configure the maven-scr-plugin for a build, first add the following dependency to the pom.xml file:

```
<dependencies>
  <dependency>
    <groupId>org.apache.felix</groupId>
    <artifactId>org.apache.felix.scr.ds-annotations</artifactId>
    <version>1.2.0</version>
    <scope>compile</scope>
  </dependency>
</dependencies>
```

This dependency provides both the org.osgi.service.component.annotations classes as well as the processing engine necessary to generate the components. Note that even if other dependencies are given (say, osgi.enterprise or equinox.ds), this isn't sufficient on its own to generate the service.xml files.

Next, the plug-in needs to be added to the pom.xml file:

```
<build>
  <plugins>
    <plugin>
      <groupId>org.apache.felix</groupId>
      <artifactId>maven-scr-plugin</artifactId>
      <version>1.15.0</version>
      <configuration>...</configuration>
      <executions>...</executions>
    </plugin>
  </plugins>
  <sourceDirectory>src</sourceDirectory>
</build>
```

The sourceDirectory needs to be specified to match the value of the source attribute of the build.properties file (which is used by eclipse-plugin instead of sourceDirectory); otherwise, the maven-scr-plugin cannot find the source files.

The plug-in needs to be configured specifically for eclipse-plugin projects. Firstly, the supported projects default to jar and bundle for maven-scr-plugin, so it needs to be given additional configuration to permit processing eclipse-plugin projects.

Secondly, the service files are written to `target/scr-plugin-generated/` by default. Although this will work, it makes for more difficult debugging in Eclipse. Instead, `maven-scr-plugin` can be configured to write it to the project root, which will place the service files under `OSGI-INF`. This permits the code to be tested and exported in Eclipse using the standard build tools:

```
<configuration>
  <supportedProjectTypes>
    <supportedProjectType>eclipse-plugin</supportedProjectType>
  </supportedProjectTypes>
  <outputDirectory>${basedir}</outputDirectory>
</configuration>
```

Finally, to hook it in with the standard build process, add the following configuration to the build:

```
<executions>
  <execution>
    <id>generate-scr</id>
    <goals>
      <goal>scr</goal>
    </goals>
  </execution>
</executions>
```

When the package is built, the service descriptor XML file will be automatically regenerated based on the annotations. The filename is derived from the service name.

Blueprint

Although Declarative Services has been present in OSGi since the 4.0 release, a new specification called **Blueprint** was made available in the 4.2 release. This provides the same kind of capabilities as Declarative Services, in that dependencies between services can be defined externally to the source code. However, the format of the corresponding XML file is slightly different and there is some difference in behavior.

The Blueprint service can be installed through a couple of implementations: **Gemini** or **Aries**.

Installing Gemini Blueprint

The Blueprint service is provided through a number of bundles as follows:

- `gemini-blueprint-core-1.0.2.RELEASE.jar`
- `gemini-blueprint-extender-1.0.2.RELEASE.jar`
- `gemini-blueprint-io-1.0.2.RELEASE.jar`

However, these bundles also need the following Spring dependencies. Since Spring doesn't contain OSGi metadata (since version 3), the bundles must be acquired through the now defunct **SpringSource EBR** at `http://ebr.springsource.com`:

- `com.springsource.org.aopalliance-1.0.0.jar`
- `org.springframework.aop-3.2.5.RELEASE.jar`
- `org.springframework.beans-3.2.5.RELEASE.jar`
- `org.springframework.context-3.2.5.RELEASE.jar`
- `org.springframework.core-3.2.5.RELEASE.jar`
- `org.springframework.expression-3.2.5.RELEASE.jar`

The Gemini Blueprint implementation suffers from being built on Spring thereby dragging in the Spring dependencies as well. This is because the Gemini implementation can handle both the native OSGi Blueprint service as well as Spring bundle contexts.

For existing Spring-based applications that have migrated to OSGi, Gemini Blueprint may provide an easy transition path. For greenfield or non-Spring applications, using Aries may allow a reduced set of dependencies.

The `gemini-blueprint-extender` bundle must be started in order to automatically register Blueprint services.

Installing Aries Blueprint

The Aries Blueprint service only needs three bundles: the Blueprint bundle and the Aries proxy, which in turn needs the Aries util bundle:

- `org.apache.aries.blueprint-1.1.0.jar`
- `org.apache.aries.proxy-1.0.1.jar`
- `org.apache.aries.util-1.0.1.jar`

In addition, the Aries code requires an implementation of SLF4J, which can be acquired from the following:

- `slf4j-api-1.7.5.jar`
- `slf4j-simple-1.7.5.jar`

Once installed, and the `org.apache.aries.blueprint` and `org.apache.aries.proxy` bundles are started, other bundles in the framework will have their Blueprint services automatically registered.

Using the Blueprint service

Blueprint files are stored under `OSGI-INF/blueprint/` by default, and end in a `.xml` extension. These follow a Spring-inspired format to represent the services and beans.

To add a Blueprint file for the `MockFeedParser`, create a file `mockfeedparser.xml` in the `OSGI-INF/blueprint/` directory. The contents should be as follows:

```
<blueprint xmlns="http://www.osgi.org/xmlns/blueprint/v1.0.0">
  <service interface="com.packtpub.e4.advanced.feeds.IFeedParser"
   activation="eager">
    <service-properties>
      <entry key="other.property">
        <value type="java.lang.Integer">314</value>
      </entry>
    </service-properties>
    <bean
 class="com.packtpub.e4.advanced.feeds.internal.MockFeedParser"/>
  </service>
</blueprint>
```

Now create a run configuration for an Eclipse application or an OSGi framework, and ensure that either the Gemini bundles or Aries bundles are installed and started.

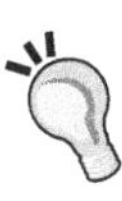

> By default, Eclipse will set the DS bundle to start automatically when creating a new configuration, but it does not do this for Blueprint bundles. If the Blueprint bundle is not started, then Blueprint services will also not be started.

The GitHub project for this book contains a copy of the required libraries for the bundles, which can be seen at `https://github.com/alblue/com.packtpub.e4.advanced/`.

Passing properties in Blueprint

To pass properties to the service when it is registered, the Blueprint XML can have a `service-properties` element added. Like the DS specification, this allows entries to be added in key/value pairs.

Modify the `mockfeedparser.xml` file to add a `service-properties` element:

```
<service interface="com.packtpub.e4.advanced.feeds.IFeedParser"
 activation="eager">
  <service-properties>
    <entry key="other.property">
      <value type="java.lang.Integer">314</value>
    </entry>
  </service-properties>
  …
</service>
```

For single value types, the element can be specified as a single `value`. If an array of elements is required, it must be wrapped in an `<array>` element:

```
<service-properties>
  <entry key="other.property">
    <array>
      <value type="java.lang.Integer">314</value>
      <value type="java.lang.Integer">271</value>
    </array>
  </entry>
</service-properties>
```

It is possible to define non-standard objects as property types by specifying a different class name. At runtime, introspection is used to find an appropriate single argument constructor and the value in the XML file is passed in.

> Note that service properties are generally meant to be portable between different runtimes, and in some cases, exported over a network. It is recommended that the values be serializable and, where possible, use a `String` representation instead of a parsed object representation for portability.

Although it might seem possible to use this to register `service.ranking`, the following does not work:

```
<service-properties>
  <entry key="service.ranking">      <!-- does not work -->
    <value type="java.lang.Integer">-1</value>
  </entry>
</service-properties>
```

This happens because the Blueprint specification defines an alternate key for the service ranking, which is used to override the value given. If Blueprint services need to specify a ranking, then the following code must be used instead:

```
<blueprint xmlns="http://www.osgi.org/xmlns/blueprint/v1.0.0">
  <service interface="com.packtpub.e4.advanced.feeds.IFeedParser"
   activation="eager" ranking="-1">
    …
  </service>
</blueprint>
```

Finally, although a single interface is the most common approach, it is possible to register multiple interfaces against a single service. The implementation class must implement these interfaces; otherwise, an error is logged by the Blueprint extender:

```
<service ranking="-1" activation="eager">
  <interfaces>
    <value>com.packtpub.e4.advanced.feeds.IFeedParser</value>
    <value>java.lang.Cloneable</value>
  </interfaces>
  …
</service>
```

Bean references and properties

Blueprint provides an easy means to name the created beans and relate them to other beans. Each bean may have an ID associated with it, which can then be used by a `ref` in another bean or by name.

Properties can be set on a bean by using the <property> element inside the bean's constructor. These are used to invoke JavaBean style setters on the instantiated object itself. For example, if the MockFeedParser had a method setNumberOfItems(int) to configure the number of returned values, the value could be set in the Blueprint XML file as follows:

```
<bean
 class="com.packtpub.e4.advanced.feeds.internal.MockFeedParser">
  <property name="numberOfItems" value="5"/>
</bean>
```

The property syntax also supports dotted property names; so if the MockFeedParser had a config property, and that config object had a value property, then the name could be specified as config.value.

References to other properties can be specified in the beans. A reference can be defined either through an ID defined in the same bundle, or from an OSGi service reference elsewhere. To set a LogService on MockFeedParser, the following code can be used:

```
private LogService log;
public void setLog(LogService log) {
  this.log = log;
}
```

This can be used when setting the number of items in the previous feed:

```
public void setNumberOfItems(int numberOfItems) {
  this.numberOfItems = numberOfItems;
  if (log != null) {
    log.log(LogService.LOG_INFO, "Setting number of items to "
      + numberOfItems);
  }
}
```

Finally, to get Blueprint to provide LogService to the bean, it needs to be acquired as a reference, as shown:

```
<blueprint xmlns="http://www.osgi.org/xmlns/blueprint/v1.0.0">
  <reference id="logService"
   interface="org.osgi.service.log.LogService" />
  <service ranking="-1" activation="eager">
  …
    <bean
```

```
    class="com.packtpub.e4.advanced.feeds.internal.MockFeedParser">
        <property name="log" ref="logService"/>
        <property name="numberOfItems" value="5"/>
      </bean>
    </service>
  </blueprint>
```

Comparison of Blueprint and DS

Both Blueprint and Declarative Services allow one or more services to be registered declaratively and instantiated on demand when requested. They are advantageous because they can defer the creation of the service until it is first needed, which in turn means that the bundle does not have to start until as late as possible.

In runtimes with large numbers of bundles, this reduced start-up time can result in faster overall start-up of the application. This is used in many of the enterprise Java services to provide functionality that may not all be needed at first.

There are a couple of significant differences that are worth knowing when comparing the two services.

Firstly, DS will create services and unbind them dynamically, so throughout the lifetime of a bundle's use, the services may come and go (in other words, they may be `null`). Code must be defensive when consuming services in case they are no longer present.

Blueprint, on the other hand, creates proxy objects that remain the same for the lifetime of the object. If a `LogService` instance is requested, a dynamic `LogService` proxy class is created and injected into the class. This instance will stay with the class for its entire life, even if log services come and go over time.

For Java code that isn't adapted to using OSGi services, particularly their dynamism, the ability to have a non-null placeholder object that can be passed to other objects provides an easy way to migrate from a non-OSGi solution to a full OSGi-based system. On the other hand, the proxy object is set to block until a service becomes available, so clients attempting to log a message may inadvertently block until either a real `LogService` instance is found or a timeout error is thrown.

There are many more configuration properties available for Blueprint services, including complex expressions and the ability to wire and connect up objects through injection. This additional flexibility can introduce additional problems when developing and testing a Blueprint solution; since the XML file can be complex, it's possible for the file to not be valid. Unfortunately, if a bundle's XML file is invalid, then no services will be registered; however, proxy classes can still be registered in client bundles that will silently hang when called.

Finally, the Blueprint extender will scan every bundle installed, looking for files in `OSGI-INF/blueprint/*.xml`. As a result, frameworks that use Blueprint may notice a slightly delayed start-up time.

> If migrating a Spring-based application to an OSGi runtime, then Blueprint may provide an easy way forward. If you are creating a dynamic OSGi application without prior Spring involvement, use Declarative Services instead.

Dynamic services

The OSGi specification defines the following four different layers:

- **Security Layer**: All actions are checked against a security permissions model
- **Module Layer**: Modules are specified as bundles that have dependencies
- **Life Cycle Layer**: Bundles that come and go
- **Service Layer**: Dynamic services that come and go

The services layer allows bundles to communicate by defining an API that can cross bundle layers. However, the services layer also allows the services to come and go dynamically, instead of being fixed at runtime.

This mechanism allows services to be exported over a network, and since the network can come and go (as can the remote endpoint), the OSGi services layer can replicate that same functionality.

Responding to services that dynamically come and go may add a slight difficulty to the client code, but it will be more robust in case of failure. The next sections will present different ways to achieve dynamism in services.

Resolving services each time

The easiest way of working with dynamic services is to list the services each time they are needed. The feed parser example so far uses this technique of allowing different parsers to be contributed; each time a feed is parsed, a list of feed parser services are acquired. If a feed parser goes, or one is added, the next time a feed is parsed the new service will be part of the list.

This technique can work if the list of services is infrequently needed. However, each time a lookup is performed, there is a cost to the acquisition which may not be desirable.

Using a ServiceTracker

The OSGi framework provides a `ServiceTracker` class that can be used to simplify the acquisition of one or more services in a standard way. Provided in the `org.osgi.util.tracker` package, the `ServiceTracker` class has a constructor that takes a class and a `BundleContext` object, along with an optional filter specification.

> The `ServiceTracker` class has an `open` method that must be called prior to use; otherwise, it will not return any services.

Add the package to the feed plug-in's manifest as an import:

```
Import-Package: org.osgi.util.tracker
```

Modify the `FeedParserFactory` class so that a `ServiceTracker` instance is acquired in the constructor and `open` is called. This simplifies the `getFeedParser` method to simply delegate to the service tracker:

```
public class FeedParserFactory {
  private final ServiceTracker<IFeedParser, IFeedParser> st;
  private FeedParserFactory() {
    st = new ServiceTracker<IFeedParser, IFeedParser>(
      FeedsActivator.getContext(), IFeedParser.class, null);
    st.open(); // Remember to call this!
  }
  ...
  public List<IFeedParser> getFeedParsers() {
    return Arrays.asList(st.getServices(new IFeedParser[]{}));
  }
}
```

`ServiceTracker` also has a `close` method that should be called when services are no longer required to be tracked. For this reason, sometimes the `ServiceTracker` instance is set up and managed in the appropriate `Activator`, since the `open` and `close` methods can be tied to the bundle's life cycle. Alternatively, the `close` method can be associated with the factory's `finalize` method:

```
protected void finalize() throws Throwable {
  st.close();
  super.finalize();
}
```

Generally, tying the service tracker's life cycle to another life cycle is more appropriate, as otherwise this can leak implementation.

Sorting services

Unfortunately, `ServiceTracker` differs from the previous implementation in that the services returned are in an arbitrary order, not in the correct service ordering. Instead of acquiring an array of services as in the initial implementation, it will be necessary to get a list of the `ServiceReference` objects and perform the sort manually.

Switch the implementation of `getFeedParsers` to use `st.getServiceReferences` instead. This can be sorted using `Arrays`, using a comparator that is built using the standard `ServiceReference` comparable interface.

Note that the default sort order will end up being lowest-to-highest, which is the reverse of what's desired. So, the order of the arguments has to be swapped.

The resulting code thus becomes:

```
public List<IFeedParser> getFeedParsers() {
  ServiceReference<IFeedParser>[] srs = st.getServiceReferences();
  Arrays.sort(srs, new Comparator<ServiceReference<?>>() {
    public int compare(ServiceReference<?> o1,
                       ServiceReference<?> o2) {
      return o2.compareTo(o1);
    }
  });
  List<IFeedParser> list = new ArrayList<IFeedParser>(srs.length);
  for (ServiceReference<IFeedParser> sr : srs) {
    list.add(st.getService(sr));
  }
  return list;
}
```

Now, when the services are acquired, they are in the correct order.

Filtering services

The service tracker, as it is currently implemented, returns all compatible services that implement the interface (if `true` is passed to the `open` call, both compatible and incompatible services are returned; although this should generally not be used).

It is also possible to use a filter to restrict the list of services that are returned. Filters in OSGi are specified using the LDAP filter syntax that uses a prefix notation and parenthesis to group elements. The following shows how to read it:

LDAP filter	Meaning
`(&(A)(B))`	A and B
`(|(A)(B))`	A or B
`(!(A))`	Not A
`(A=B)`	A equals B
`(A=*B*)`	A contains B

The `services` command in the Equinox console allows a filter to be specified. Each service is published into the registry, and the filter `objectClass=` allows services matching a particular interface to be found, as was done earlier in this chapter:

```
osgi> services (objectClass=*.IFeedParser)
{com.packtpub.e4.advanced.feeds.IFeedParser}={service.ranking=2,
 component.name=AtomFeedParser, component.id=0, service.id=40}
{com.packtpub.e4.advanced.feeds.IFeedParser}={service.ranking=1,
 component.name=RSSFeedParser, component.id=1, service.id=41}
{com.packtpub.e4.advanced.feeds.IFeedParser}={service.ranking=-1,
 other.property=[314,222], service.id=43}
```

It's possible to filter other properties as well. For example, DS registers a `component.id` property with a service, so this can be used to create a filter for just DS registered components:

```
osgi> services "(&(objectClass=*.IFeedParser)(component.id=*))"
{com.packtpub.e4.advanced.feeds.IFeedParser}={service.ranking=2,
component.name=AtomFeedParser, component.id=0, service.id=40}
{com.packtpub.e4.advanced.feeds.IFeedParser}={service.ranking=1,
component.name=RSSFeedParser, component.id=1, service.id=41}
```

This looks for services ending in `IFeedParser` and that have a value for the `component.id` property. Filters can be included in `ServiceTracker` to ensure that only desired services are picked up. For example, to include only the `MockFeedParser` (actually, any service that isn't registered by DS), the following can be included in `ServiceTracker`:

```
Filter filter = context.createFilter(
 "(&(objectClass=*.IFeedParser)(!(component.id=*)))");
st = new ServiceTracker<IFeedParser, IFeedParser>(
 context, filter, null);
st.open();
```

> The value of the service filter can be overridden by a property to enable debugging, for example. Note that the `createFilter` method throws a checked syntax exception if it is invalid, which must be handled in the code.

Obtaining a BundleContext without using an activator

Since `ServiceTracker` needs the `BundleContext` instance to register a listener, it is conventional to set up a `BundleActivator` instance for the sole purpose of acquiring an instance of `BundleContext`.

Because this incurs a performance penalty, using a different mechanism to acquire the context will speed the start-up process. Fortunately, there is a class, `FrameworkUtil`, which can be used to acquire a `Bundle` instance for any given class, and from there, the `BundleContext` instance. This allows the implementation of the `FeedsActivator` to be removed:

```
// BundleContext context = FeedsActivator.getContext();
BundleContext context = FrameworkUtil.
  getBundle(FeedParserFactory.class).getBundleContext();
```

Using this mechanism adds no performance penalty and should be used in favor of a global static instance for `BundleContext`. It also potentially allows the bundle's activator to be removed from the bundle.

> If the bundle is not started, it does not have a `BundleContext` instance and so the returned value here may be `null`. Code should defensively handle this case. The bundle can be started by calling `bundle.stat(Bundle.START_TRANSIENT)`, after which the `BundleContext` will not be `null`.

A note on ServiceReference

The OSGi specification has the ability to find instances of `ServiceReference`. This is a wrapper that represents a single service (a single `service.id`) and can be shared between bundles. The `getService` call performs a resolution of the service instance on demand.

The problem with storing a `ServiceReference` instance is that the service may subsequently disappear; when it does, the `getService` method will return `null`. In other words, it doesn't perform a lookup if that single service goes away or is restarted/replaced.

The only reason to use `ServiceReference` is to either translate directly into the service interface (as was done in the initial implementation of `FeedParserFactory` in the *Using the services* section), or if only specific properties of the service are required instead. The `ServiceReference` instances should not be stored or used indefinitely unless the service is known to be a singleton.

Dependent services

It is fairly common that an OSGi service depends on other OSGi services. As such, it can help if the services are set up and made available when the bundles are available.

The Blueprint approach wires dependencies into bundles that can block until services become available, but the Declarative Services approach can be used to register services on demand when the requirements are satisfied. Both allow dependencies to be encoded in relationships.

For DS, if the cardinality of the relationship is not optional (in other words, the relationship is `1..1` or `1..n`), then the service won't be started until the required dependent services are available. For example, a menu service may not be required until the graphical user interface service is present, and services that wish to contribute to the menu service won't be able to work until the menu service is present.

Delaying the creation of the services until they are needed will result in shorter start-up times of the application, as illustrated in the following diagram:

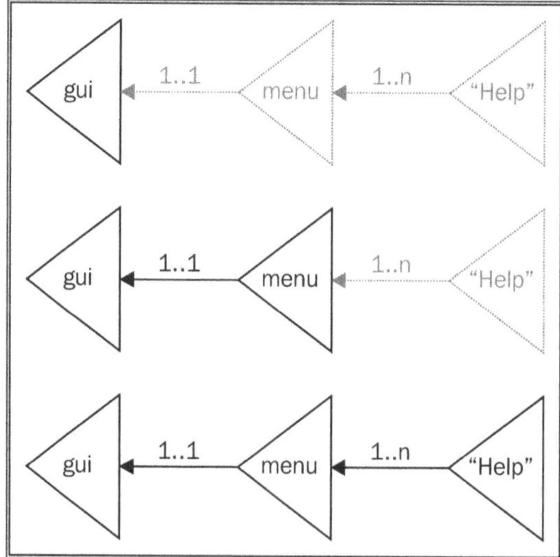

Dynamic Service Configuration

OSGi provides a standard configuration mechanism called **Config Admin**. This allows the location of configuration information to be decoupled from the code that requires the configuration. Configuration is passed through to services via a `Map` or `Hashtable`, and they can then configure themselves appropriately.

As with other parts in OSGi, this can also be dynamically updated. When the configuration source changes, an event can flow through to the service or component in order to allow it to reconfigure itself.

Installing Felix FileInstall

Config Admin itself is an OSGi service, and it may be supplied by different configuration agents. A de facto standard is Apache Felix's **FileInstall**, which can also be used to install bundles into an OSGi runtime.

FileInstall is available from the Apache Felix site at `http://felix.apache.org` as well as Maven Central. Download `org.apache.felix.fileinstall-3.2.8.jar` and import it into Eclipse as a plug-in project by navigating to **File** | **Import** | **Plug-in Development** | **Plug-ins and Fragments** to enable it to run at test runtime.

To use FileInstall, a system property `felix.fileinstall.dir` must be specified. It defaults to `./load` from the current working directory, but for the purposes of testing, this can be specified by adding a VM argument in the launch configuration that appends `-Dfelix.fileinstall.dir=/tmp/config` or some other location. This can be used to test modifications to the configuration later.

Make sure that FileInstall is configured to start when runtime begins, so that it picks up configurations. This can be done by specifying the start level on the OSGi framework launch configuration page.

Installing Config Admin

To configure services, Config Admin needs to be installed into the runtime as well. The two standard implementations of these are Felix Config Admin and Equinox Config Admin. The latter does not come with Eclipse by default, and the Felix version is available from Maven Central and should be preferred. Download `org.apache.felix.configadmin-1.8.0.jar` from Maven Central or from the book's GitHub repository.

Import this as a plug-in project to Eclipse by navigating to **File** | **Import** | **Plug-in Development** | **Plug-ins and Fragments** so that it can be used as a bundle in the OSGi framework.

Configuring Declarative Services

A component created by Declarative Services can have configuration passed in a `Map`. A component can have an `activate` method, which is called after the component's dependencies have become available (along with a corresponding `deactivate` method). There is also a `modified` method that can be used to respond to changes in the configuration without stopping and restarting the component.

To configure `AtomFeedParser` with Config Admin, add a `configure` method that takes a `Map` of values. If it's not `null`, and there is a key `max`, then parse it as `int` and use that as the `max` value, as shown in the following code:

```
private int max = Integer.MAX_VALUE;
public void configure(Map<String, Object> properties) {
  max = Integer.MAX_VALUE;
  if (properties != null) {
    String maxStr = (String) properties.get("max");
    if (maxStr != null) {
      max = Integer.parseInt(maxStr);
    }
  }
}
```

To ensure that the method gets called, modify the service component document to add the `activate="configure"` and `modified="configure"` attributes:

```
<scr:component xmlns:scr="http://www.osgi.org/xmlns/scr/v1.1.0"
  modified="configure" activate="configure"
  name="AtomFeedParser">
```

Finally, create a properties file called `AtomFeedParser.cfg` with the content `max=1`, and place it in the location of `felix.fileinstall.dir`.

Now when the application is run, the configuration should be loaded and should configure `AtomFeedParser`, such that when a feed is added, it shows a maximum of one value. Modify the configuration file and refresh the feeds during the Eclipse runtime, and it should pick up the new value.

If nothing is seen, verify that `felix.fileinstall.dir` is specified correctly using `props | grep felix` from the OSGi console. Also, verify that the Felix `fileinstall` and `configadmin` bundles have started. Finally, verify that the methods in the component are `public void` and are defined correctly in the component config.

Config Admin outside of DS

It is possible to use Config Admin outside of the Declarative Services specification. Services can be configured directly using the `ManagedService` interface of the Config Admin specification.

When a service requires configuration, it is registered under the `ManagedService` interface in the registry with an associated **Persistent ID (PID)**. Config Admin will notice the service being published and use that to feed updated configuration information through the `updated` method. Since the specification has been with OSGi for some time, it uses a `Dictionary` to specify property values instead of a `Map`.

This technique can be used to acquire configuration information for a singleton, such as a `BundleActivator`. If the activator registers itself as a `ManagedService` interface, then it will receive configuration updates through Config Admin. For example, to aid in testing the user interface, the mock feed can be enabled through a debug mode in the `Activator` class in the `feeds.ui` plug-in.

Modify the `META-INF/MANIFEST.MF` file of the `com.packtpub.e4.advanced.feeds.ui` plug-in to include `org.osgi.service.cm` as an imported package, and add the `ManagedService` interface to the `Activator` class. In the `start` method, register an instance of itself as the managed service:

```
public void start(BundleContext context) throws Exception {
  super.start(context);
  plugin = this;
  Dictionary<String, String> properties =
   new Hashtable<String, String>();
  properties.put(Constants.SERVICE_PID,
   "com.packtpub.e4.advanced.feeds.ui");
  context.registerService(ManagedService.class, this, properties);
}
```

In the implementation of the `updated` method, detect whether the configuration is passed in an element `debug` with the value `true`. If so, set a `boolean debug` field to be `true`. Expose this via an accessor method `isDebug`. Having a print method can enable debugging and verify that the configuration changes are being applied for testing purposes:

```
private boolean debug;
public boolean isDebug() {
  return debug;
}
public void updated(Dictionary<String, ?> configuration)
 throws ConfigurationException {
  debug = configuration != null
```

```
    && "true".equals(configuration.get("debug"));
    if (debug) {
      System.out.println("Debugging enabled");
    } else {
      System.out.println("Debugging disabled");
    }
}
```

Finally, to see the mentioned behavior in action, modify the `FeedContentProvider` class to skip class implementation names when the service name implementation does not contain the string "`Mock`" and is in the `debug` mode:

```
public Object[] getChildren(Object parentElement) {
  ...
  if (parentElement instanceof Feed) {
    Feed feed = (Feed)parentElement;
    FeedParserFactory factory = FeedParserFactory.getDefault();
    List<IFeedParser> parsers = factory.getFeedParsers();
    for (IFeedParser parser : parsers) {
      if(Activator.getDefault().isDebug()) {
        if(!parser.getClass().getName().contains("Mock")) {
          continue;
        }
      }
    }
  }
  ...
}
```

Now run the test application, create a new feed, and point it at a valid Atom or RSS feed. When the bookmarks project is refreshed, the real entries will be seen. To enable the `debug` mode, create a configuration properties file at `/tmp/config/com.packtpub.e4.advanced.feeds.ui.cfg` with the content `debug=true`. Provided that DS is working correctly, it should display **Debugging enabled** in the console window, and subsequent refreshing of the feed should show the mock entries being created instead.

Services and ManagedService

It is possible to register services that implement both a service (such as `AtomFeedParser`) and the `ManagedService` interface (to acquire configuration). However, the problem comes when the service is registered without any configuration data. Should the service be valid if there is no configuration data present? Or will the defaults work as expected? If there must be configuration data, how will the service be prevented from being called until the configuration data is available?

The best way is to rely on something like Declarative Services to do the right thing (and with less work), but if for whatever reason it needs to be implemented then this can be done as well.

If the service can run without explicit configuration data, then the service can be registered both as its service interface (such as `IFeedParser`) as well as the `ManagedService` interface. The two interfaces will be registered at the same time, and hence, clients may call the service before the configuration is available.

If the service needs to have configuration data before being made available, then the service can be registered under the `ManagedService` interface only. When the `updated` method is called with configuration data, it can call the `registerService` method to register itself under the service interface. When the `updated` method is called with no data, it can unregister the service.

Since this is a case where the full life cycle of the service is used, it is appropriate to use a `ServiceRegistration` instance to keep a handle on the configured service.

> Note that the `ServiceRegistration` objects are not supposed to be shared between bundles, but only used by the bundle that registered them.

Creating an EmptyFeedParser class

Create a new feed parser, `EmptyFeedParser`, but place it in the UI bundle (since it needs an `Activator` class or some other start-up process to register it as a service, it needs to be hooked onto the UI package for ease of testing). The `EmptyFeedParser` class should implement both `IFeedService` and `ManagedService`:

```
public class EmptyFeedParser implements
 IFeedParser, ManagedService {
  public void updated(Dictionary<String, ?> properties)
   throws ConfigurationException {
  }
  public List<FeedItem> parseFeed(Feed feed) {
    return new ArrayList<FeedItem>(0);
  }
}
```

To register this, add a line in the `start` method of the `Activator` class that registers this as a `ManagedService` interface. It should use the PID `com.packtpub.e4.advanced.feeds.ui.EmptyFeedParser`, to allow for easy configuration testing:

```
public void start(BundleContext context) throws Exception {
  ...
  Dictionary<String, String> properties
   = new Hashtable<String, String>();
  properties.put(Constants.SERVICE_PID,
   EmptyFeedParser.class.getName());
  context.registerService(ManagedService.class,
   new EmptyFeedParser(), properties);
}
```

The final piece is to implement the `updated` method so that it registers the service when a configuration is provided, and remove it when it is no longer needed. If the configuration is not `null`, then a new service can be registered and the resulting registration object stored in an instance variable. If the configuration is `null`, then the registration object should be removed, if it existed. The implementation will look like the following:

```
private ServiceRegistration<IFeedParser> registration;
public void updated(Dictionary<String, ?> properties)
 throws ConfigurationException {
  BundleContext context = FrameworkUtil
   .getBundle(EmptyFeedParser.class)
   .getBundleContext();
  if (properties != null) {
    if (registration == null) {
      System.out.println(
       "Registering EmptyFeedParser for the first time");
      registration = context.registerService(
       IFeedParser.class, this, properties);
    } else {
      System.out.println("Reconfiguring EmptyFeedParser");
      registration.setProperties(properties);
    }
  } else {
    if (registration != null) {
      System.out.println("Deconfiguring EmptyFeedParser");
      registration.unregister();
    }
    registration = null;
  }
}
```

This shows the use of a `ServiceRegistration` object that permits both service reconfiguration (via the `setProperties` method) as well as unregistration via the `unregister` method. This can be used independently of Config Admin.

Configuring the EmptyFeedParser

Running the application followed by creating a configuration properties file at `/tmp/config/com.packtpub.e4.advanced.feeds.ui.EmptyFeedParser.cfg` should result in the output being seen in the console that the service is being created. Similarly, changes to the file will show the updated messages being displayed, and when the file is removed, the service will go away.

Felix has a default timeout of two seconds to scan for changes, which can be configured to a different value via the `felix.fileinstall.poll` property, which takes a number in milliseconds between polls.

First, find out what `bundle.id` is being used for the `feeds.ui` bundle:

```
osgi> ss | grep feeds.ui
27 ACTIVE com.packtpub.e4.advanced.feeds.ui_1.0.0.qualifier
```

Now the bundle identifier is found (27 in this case), it can be used to ensure that it is started and investigate what services are provided:

```
osgi> start 27
osgi> bundle 27 | grep service.pid
{org.osgi.service.cm.ManagedService}={service.id=294,
 service.pid=com.packtpub.e4.advanced.feeds.ui}
{org.osgi.service.cm.ManagedService}={service.id=295,
 service.pid=com.packtpub.e4.advanced.feeds.ui.EmptyFeedParser}
```

The two managed services are the ones created earlier in this chapter; the one that controls debugging and the one that controls the `EmptyFeedParser` class just created.

Now create an empty file in the configuration directory (the value specified by the `felix.fileinstall.dir` property) `/tmp/config/com.packtpub.e4.advanced.feeds.ui.EmptyFeedParser.cfg`. The following can be seen in the console:

```
Registering EmptyFeedParser for the first time
osgi> bundle 27 | grep service.pid
{org.osgi.service.cm.ManagedService}={service.id=294,
```

```
 service.pid=com.packtpub.e4.advanced.feeds.ui}
{org.osgi.service.cm.ManagedService}={service.id=295 ,
 service.pid=com.packtpub.e4.advanced.feeds.ui.EmptyFeedParser}
{com.packtpub.e4.advanced.feeds.IFeedParser}={service.id=296,
 service.pid=com.packtpub.e4.advanced.feeds.ui.EmptyFeedParser,
 felix.fileinstall.filename=file:/tmp/config/
 com.packtpub.e4.advanced.feeds.ui.EmptyFeedParser.cfg}
```

The creation of the external configuration file has resulted in the service being registered automatically. Now add a line, `a=banana`, in the `EmptyFeedParser.cfg` file and see what happens:

```
Reconfiguring EmptyFeedParser
osgi> bundle 27 | grep service.pid
{org.osgi.service.cm.ManagedService}={service.id=294,
 service.pid=com.packtpub.e4.advanced.feeds.ui}
{org.osgi.service.cm.ManagedService}={service.id=295,
 service.pid=com.packtpub.e4.advanced.feeds.ui.EmptyFeedParser}
{com.packtpub.e4.advanced.feeds.IFeedParser}={service.id=296,
 service.pid=com.packtpub.e4.advanced.feeds.ui.EmptyFeedParser,
 a=banana, felix.fileinstall.filename=file:/tmp/config/
 com.packtpub.e4.advanced.feeds.ui.EmptyFeedParser.cfg}
```

In addition to the service being reconfigured (with the reconfiguring debug message shown), the additional service property `a=banana` has been added to the list.

Because the service method `registration.setProperties` was used, the same service stays bound. An alternative strategy is to `unregister` the service and `register` a new one. Doing so will require clients to rebind themselves to the new service, so if this can be avoided, it makes the clients easier to reason about.

Finally, remove the configuration file and see what happens:

```
Deconfiguring EmptyFeedParser
osgi> bundle 27 | grep service.pid
{org.osgi.service.cm.ManagedService}={service.id=294,
 service.pid=com.packtpub.e4.advanced.feeds.ui}
{org.osgi.service.cm.ManagedService}={service.id=295,
 service.pid=com.packtpub.e4.advanced.feeds.ui.EmptyFeedParser}
```

Service factories

A **service factory** can be used to create services on demand, rather than being provided up front. OSGi defines a number of different service factories that have different behaviors.

Ordinarily services published into the registry are shared between all bundles. OSGi R6 adds a **service.scope** property, and uses the `singleton` value to indicate that the same instance is shared between all bundles. Services that are not factories will have this value.

Service factories allow multiple instances to be created, and these are the following three different types:

- `ServiceFactory`: This creates a new instance per bundle (registered with `service.scope=bundle` in OSGi R6)
- `ManagedServiceFactory`: This uses Config Admin to create instances per configuration/PID (registered with `service.scope=bundle` in OSGi R6)
- `PrototypeServiceFactory`: This allows multiple instances per bundle (newly added in OSGi R6 registered with `service.scope=prototype`)

The `ServiceFactory` interface was added to allow a per-client bundle instance to be created, to avoid bundles sharing state. When a client bundle requests a service, if the bundle has already requested the service, then the same instance is returned; if not, a service is instantiated. When the client bundle goes away, so does the associated service instance.

A `ManagedServiceFactory` interface provides a means to instantiate multiple services instead of a single service per component. The `EmptyFeedParser` example is a configured singleton. If the configuration file exists, a service is registered; if not, no service is registered (multiple instances of a service can be created, each with their own configuration using `service.pid-somename.cfg`). Each bundle shares the instances of these services, but other client bundles will instantiate their own. Like `ServiceFactory`, if the service has been requested before, the same bundle will be returned.

The `PrototypeServiceFactory` interface was added in OSGi R6 (available in Eclipse Luna and later) as a means to provide a bundle with multiple instances of the same service. Instead of caching the previously delivered service per bundle, a new one is instantiated each time it is looked up. The client code can use `BundleContext.getServiceObjects(ref).getService()` to acquire a service through the `PrototypeServiceFactory` interface. This allows stateful services to be created.

Creating the EchoServer class

As an example, consider an `EchoServer` class that listens on a specific `ServerSocket` port. This can be run on zero or many ports at the same time. This code will be used by the next section, and simply creates a server running on a port and sets up a single thread to accept client connections and reflect what is typed. The code here is presented without explanation (other than of its purpose), and will be used to create multiple instances of this service in the next section.

When this is instantiated on a port (for example, when `new EchoServer(1234)` is called), it will be possible to `telnet` to the `localhost` on port `1234` and have content reflected as it is typed. To close the stream, use *Ctrl* + *]* and then type `close`. The code is as follows:

```
public class EchoServer implements Runnable {
  private ServerSocket socket;
  private boolean running = true;
  private Thread thread;
  public EchoServer(int port) throws IOException {
    this.socket = new ServerSocket(port);
    this.thread = new Thread(this);
    this.thread.setDaemon(true);
    this.thread.start();
  }
  public void run() {
    try {
      byte[] buffer = new byte[1024];
      while (running) {
        Socket client = null;
        try {
          client = socket.accept();
          InputStream in = client.getInputStream();
          OutputStream out = client.getOutputStream();
          int read;
          while (running && (read = in.read(buffer)) > 0) {
            out.write(buffer, 0, read);
            out.flush();
          }
        } catch (InterruptedIOException e) {
          running = false;
        } catch (Exception e) {
        } finally {
          safeClose(client);
        }
      }
```

```
      } finally {
        safeClose(socket);
      }
    }
    public void safeClose(Closeable closeable) {
      try {
        if (closeable != null) {
          closeable.close();
        }
      } catch (IOException e) {
      }
    }
    public void stop() {
      running = false;
      this.thread.interrupt();
    }
  }
```

Creating an EchoServiceFactory class

Create an `EchoServiceFactory` class that implements `ManagedServiceFactory`, and register it in the `Activator` class as before:

```
public void start(BundleContext context) throws Exception {
  ...
  properties = new Hashtable<String, String>();
  properties.put(Constants.SERVICE_PID,
   EchoServiceFactory.class.getName());
  context.registerService(ManagedServiceFactory.class,
   new EchoServiceFactory(), properties);
}
```

The `EchoServiceFactory` class is responsible for managing the children that it creates, and since they will be using threads, to appropriately stop them afterwards. The `ManagedServiceFactory` interface has three methods; `getName`, which returns a name of the service, and `updated` and `deleted` methods for reacting to configurations coming and going. To track them, create an instance variable in the `EchoServiceFactory` class called `echoServers`, which is a map of `pid` to `EchoServer` instances:

```
public class EchoServiceFactory implements ManagedServiceFactory {
  private Map<String, EchoServer> echoServers =
   new TreeMap<String, EchoServer>();
  public String getName() {
    return "Echo service factory";
```

```
    }
    public void updated(String pid, Dictionary<String, ?> props)
     throws ConfigurationException {
    }
    public void deleted(String pid) {
    }
}
```

The `updated` method will do two things; it will determine whether a `port` is present in the properties, and if so, instantiate a new `EchoServer` on the given port. If not, it will deconfigure the service:

```
public void updated(String pid, Dictionary<String, ?> properties)
 throws ConfigurationException {
  if (properties != null) {
    String portString = properties.get("port").toString();
    try {
      int port = Integer.parseInt(portString);
      System.out.println("Creating echo server on port " + port);
      echoServers.put(pid, new EchoServer(port));
    } catch (Exception e) {
      throw new ConfigurationException("port",
       "Cannot create a server on port " + portString, e);
    }
  } else if (echoServers.containsKey(pid)) {
    deleted(pid);
  }
}
```

If an error occurs while creating the service (because the port number isn't specified, isn't a valid integer, or is already in use), an exception will be propagated back to the runtime engine, which will be appropriately logged.

The `deleted` method removes it if present, and stops it:

```
public void deleted(String pid) {
  System.out.println("Removing echo server with pid " + pid);
  EchoServer removed = echoServers.remove(pid);
  if (removed != null) {
    removed.stop();
  }
}
```

Configuring EchoService

Now that the service is implemented, how is it configured? Unlike singleton configurations, the `ManagedServiceFactory` expects the value of `pid` to be a prefix of the name, followed by a dash (-), and then a custom suffix.

Ensure that the `feeds.ui` bundle is started, and that `EchoServiceFactory` is registered and waiting for configurations to appear:

```
osgi> ss | grep feeds.ui
27 ACTIVE com.packtpub.e4.advanced.feeds.ui_1.0.0.qualifier
osgi> start 27
osgi> bundle 27 | grep service.pid
{org.osgi.service.cm.ManagedService}={service.id=236,
 service.pid=com.packtpub.e4.advanced.feeds.ui}
{org.osgi.service.cm.ManagedService}={service.id=237,
 service.pid=com.packtpub.e4.advanced.feeds.ui.EmptyFeedParser}
{org.osgi.service.cm.ManagedServiceFactory}={service.id=238,
service.pid=com.packtpub.e4.advanced.feeds.ui.EchoServiceFactory}
```

Now create a configuration file in the Felix install directory `/tmp/config/com.packtpub.e4.advanced.feeds.ui.EchoServiceFactory.cfg` with the content `port=1234`. Nothing happens.

Now rename the file to something with a - extension at the end, such as `-1234`, for example, `/tmp/config/com.packtpub.e4.advanced.feeds.ui.EchoServiceFactory-1234.cfg`. The suffix can be anything, but conventionally naming it for the type of instance being created (in this case, a service listening on port `1234`) makes it easier to keep track of the services. When this happens, a service will be created:

```
Creating new echo server on port 1234
```

Telnetting to this port can see the output being returned:

```
$ telnet localhost 1234
Connected to localhost.
Escape character is '^]'.
hello
hello
```

```
world
world
^]
telnet> close
Connection closed by foreign host.
```

Creating a new service PID will start a new service; create a new file called `/tmp/config/com.packtpub.e4.advanced.feeds.ui.EchoServiceFactory-4242.cfg` with the content `port=4242`. A new service should be created:

```
Creating new echo server on port 4242
```

Test this by running `telnet localhost 4242`. Does this echo back content?

Finally, remove the service configuration for port `1234`. This can be done by either deleting the configuration file, or simply renaming it with a different extension:

```
Removing echo server
```

Verify that the service has stopped:

```
$ telnet localhost 1234
Trying 127.0.0.1...
telnet: unable to connect to remote host
```

`FileInstall` only looks at `*.cfg` files, so renaming it to `*.cfg.disabled` has the same effect as deleting it, while making it easy to restore it subsequently.

Summary

This chapter looked at OSGi services as an alternative means to provide dependent services in an Eclipse or OSGi application. By registering services either imperatively at bundle start-up in an activator, or by using one of the declarative services representations, an operational system can evolve by connecting services together during a single runtime. Different approaches for configuration were shown with either embedded values in the service component document, or derived from external properties or configuration with Config Admin.

The next chapter will look in more detail at how the console shell works and how commands can be contributed to an OSGi runtime.

4
Using the Gogo Shell and Commands

Although not defined as an OSGi specification, all (non-embedded) OSGi frameworks have had a console to provide a means to interact with the framework. Some, such as Equinox, had a console built into the core JAR; others, such as Felix, provided console services through separate bundles.

In this chapter, we'll look at the Gogo shell, which is used by Felix and Equinox, and learn how to write commands in Gogo script as well as Java.

Consoles in Equinox

Until the end of Eclipse 3.7, Equinox supported a built-in console that was available by running the `org.eclipse.osgi` JAR file with a `-console` argument:

```
$ java -jar org.eclipse.osgi_3.7*.jar -console
Framework is launched.
osgi>
```

With the release of Eclipse 4.2 (Juno) and onwards, this console is no longer available by default:

```
$ java -jar org.eclipse.osgi_3.8*.jar -console
```

This is because the implementation provider for the console defers to the Gogo shell, which was developed by the Apache Felix project.

Eclipse 4.2 and 4.3 provided an `osgi.console.enable.builtin` flag to enable the older console, but this was removed in Eclipse 4.4 (Luna).

With Equinox 3.8 (Eclipse Juno 4.2 and above), it is necessary to install additional bundles at start-up to provide a console. This is covered in the *Running Equinox from the command line* section later in this chapter.

Host OSGi Console

The easiest way to experiment with the console is to use Eclipse's **Console View**. This is typically used for seeing the output of running Java programs, but in fact the console view can show many other types of consoles as well. In the top-right corner of the view, there is a dropdown that can show alternative consoles.

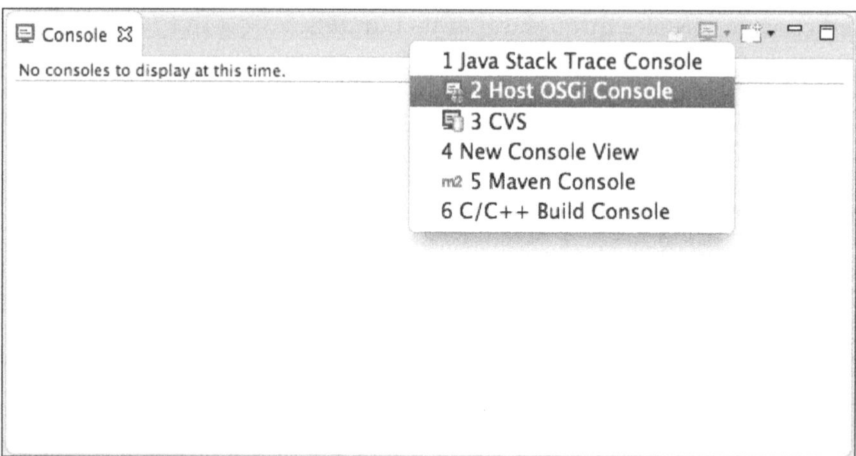

Choosing the **Host OSGi Console** action creates a new Gogo shell. It warns that the console is connected to the running Eclipse instance; typing `exit` will call `System.exit` and terminate Eclipse and the JVM:

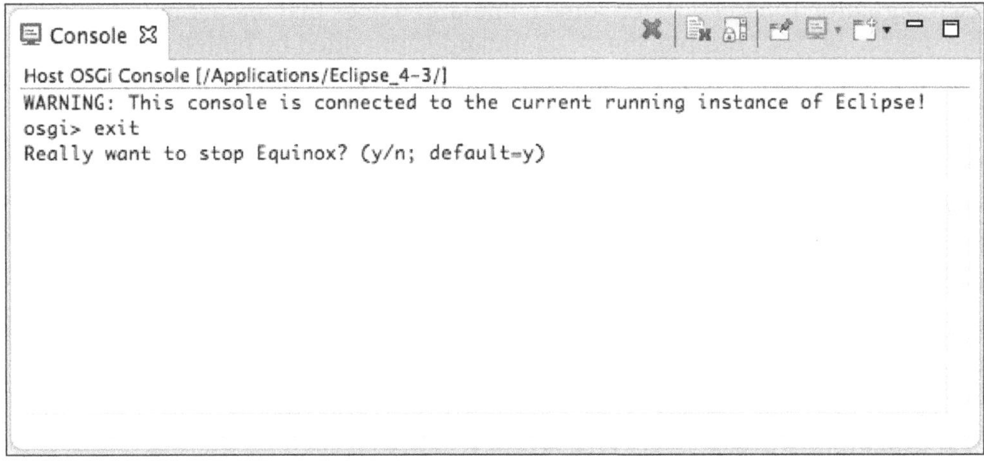

The console has a built-in help system that can be used to find out what commands are available and what their individual functions are. The `help` command will provide a list of all the available commands, and running `help command` will give more information:

```
osgi> help getprop
getprop - displays the system properties with the given name, or all of them
   scope: equinox
   parameters:
      String[]   name of system property to display
osgi> getprop os.name
os.name=Mac OS X
```

Running commands

Each command has a **scope** and a **name**. Optionally, it may require a number of parameters. Many commands take no arguments, but the help text should say what is required. Some commands have limited help, but they will display additional information when run with no arguments.

Commands may be prefixed with their scope to avoid ambiguity. These two commands are therefore equivalent:

```
osgi> echo Hello World
Hello World
osgi> gogo:echo Hello World
Hello World
```

Disambiguation is necessary for some command names that are defined in more than one scope. For example, the `ls` command is provided by both the `equinox` scope (to list the Declarative Services components) and by the `felix` scope (to list the contents of the current directory):

```
osgi> felix:ls
/Applications/Eclipse.app/Contents/MacOS/eclipse
/Applications/Eclipse.app/Contents/MacOS/eclipse.ini
osgi> equinox:ls
All Components:
ID State      Component Name
1  Registered org.eclipse.e4.core.services.preferences
2  Registered org.eclipse.e4.core.services.events
...
```

By default, the shell prints out a value after each statement. To disable this, run `.Gogo.format=false` (with the correct capitalization):

```
osgi> 'Hello World'
Hello World
osgi> .Gogo.format=false
osgi> 'Hello World'
osgi> .Gogo.format=true
true
osgi> 'Hello World'
Hello World
```

With formatting disabled, the `echo` or `format` commands can be used to display results. Along with printing the output, `format` will also return the value. This may result in two values being displayed if autoformatting is turned on:

```
osgi> echo 'hello'
hello
osgi> format 'hello'
hello
hello
osgi>
```

Variables and pipes

The shell has a way to set and get variables, which can be useful when interacting with bundle identifiers or names. Variables can be assigned with the equals sign (`=`) and can be evaluated with a dollar symbol (`$`), similar to Unix shell scripts. Identifiers start with an extended alphabet followed by alphanumeric characters (including underscores):

```
osgi> name = Alex
Alex
osgi> echo Hello $name
Hello Alex
osgi> id = 0
0
osgi> headers $id
Bundle headers:
 Built-By = e4Build
 Bundle-Description = OSGi System Bundle
 Bundle-SymbolicName = org.eclipse.osgi; singleton:=true
...
```

The special variable `$_` is used to store the result of the last command. Other variables are also predefined; `exception` is used to store the result of the last exception and `e` is a function that will print out the last exception's stack trace. The `set` command will print out all the currently defined variables:

```
osgi> 'hello'
hello
osgi> echo $_
hello
osgi> set
null            0               null
String          SCOPE           equinox:*
null            _               null
Closure         e               $exception printStackTrace
HeapCharBuffer  prompt          osgi>
osgi> misteak
gogo: CommandNotFoundException: Command not found: misteak
```

```
osgi> $exception
Command                 misteak
Cause                   null
Message                 Command not found: misteak
osgi> e
  org.apache.felix.gogo.runtime.CommandNotFoundException:
   Command not found: misteak
  at org.apache.felix.gogo.runtime.Closure.executeCmd
  at org.apache.felix.gogo.runtime.Closure.executeStatement
```

Along with being able to assign variables from literal values on the command line, it is also possible to capture the output of a command and assign that to a variable. While the command `cat` copies output from a source to the console, `tac` works in the opposite direction:

```
osgi> contents = (felix:ls | tac)
/Applications/Eclipse.app/Contents/MacOS/eclipse /Applications/Eclipse.
app/Contents/MacOS/eclipse.ini
osgi> echo $contents
/Applications/Eclipse.app/Contents/MacOS/eclipse /Applications/Eclipse.
app/Contents/MacOS/eclipse.ini
```

It is possible to pipe the content through other commands; the most useful one is `grep`, which can be used to search for specific patterns:

```
osgi> lb -s | grep osgi
   0|Active  |0|org.eclipse.osgi (3.9.1.v20140110-1610)
 185|Resolved|4|org.eclipse.osgi.services (3.3.100.v20130513-1956)
 186|Resolved|4|org.eclipse.osgi.util (3.2.300.v20130513-1956)
1103|Resolved|4|osgi.enterprise (4.2.0.v201108120515)
```

The `grep` command doesn't support a full set of POSIX arguments, but it does provide some options. The built-in help documentation does not show it, but if run without arguments, it provides more useful output:

```
osgi> help grep
grep
   scope: gogo
   parameters:
      CommandSession
      String[]
osgi> grep
```

```
grep: no pattern supplied.
Usage: grep [OPTIONS] PATTERN [FILES]
  -? --help                show help
  -i --ignore-case         ignore case distinctions
  -n --line-number         prefix each line with line number
  -q --quiet, --silent     suppress all normal output
  -v --invert-match        select non-matching lines
gogo: IllegalArgumentException: grep: no pattern supplied.
```

Functions and scripts

Besides providing an interactive **Read Evaluate Print Loop** (**REPL**), the console also permits the creation of **functions** and **scripts**. This allows common functions to be defined in a persistent file and then be reused between sessions.

A function is defined in curly braces, and it can use the special variables `$args` or `$argv` to refer to arguments, just like the Unix shell's `$*` or Windows' `%*`. It is possible to refer to the first nine arguments with `$1` to `$9`, or `$it` as an alias for the first argument; `$it` is commonly used in `each` with an anonymous function, covered in the *Processing a list with each* section later in this chapter.

```
osgi> pwd
gogo: CommandNotFoundException: Command not found: pwd
osgi> pwd = {getprop user.dir}
getprop user.dir
osgi> pwd
user.dir=/Applications/Eclipse.app/Contents/MacOS
osgi> greeting = {echo Hello $args}
echo Hello $args
osgi> greeting World
Hello World
```

Functions can be saved in an external file and then loaded into a Gogo shell session. Create a file called `fns` in the temp directory (`/tmp` on Unix/OS X and `c:\TEMP` on Windows) as follows:

```
# Lines beginning with # are comments

# Blank lines are also permitted
#      v  curly braces  v
pwd = {getprop user.dir}
greeting = {echo Hello $args}
```

From the Gogo shell, run the following:

```
osgi> source /tmp/fns # source c:\TEMP\fns on Windows
Loaded file successfully
osgi> pwd
user.dir=/Applications/Eclipse.app/Contents/MacOS
osgi> greeting Alex
Hello Alex
```

Literals and objects

Strings that are passed in are interpreted as string literals. Strings surrounded with double quotes allow replacement of variables with `$`, whereas those with single quotes do not perform replacement:

```
osgi> name=Alex
Alex
osgi> 'Hello $name'
Hello $name
osgi> "Hello $name"
Hello Alex
```

Numbers are available as both floating point and integers. By default, they are represented as `Double` and `Long` instances respectively. They can be used to pass into methods that expect smaller types (such as `float` and `int`) and are cast down automatically. Suffix flags of `f` and `d` are used to denote floating point values, but both are converted to `Double`:

```
osgi> lightspeed = 299792458
299792458
osgi> ncc = 1701d
1701.0
```

It is possible for lists and maps to be entered in literal form in the console. They are separated by spaces rather than commas, and the syntax for maps is almost the same, with the addition of keys:

```
osgi> numbers = [ 1 2 3 ]
1
2
3
osgi> words = [ one=1 two=2 three=3 ]
```

```
one                     1
two                     2
three                   3
osgi> echo $one
null
```

Note that using the syntax `one=1` does not perform an assignment, as shown in the example. It defines a key for the map. If the key contains special characters or spaces, it must be specified in quotes.

There are explicit literals for boolean values `true` and `false`.

The console allows objects to be instantiated with the `new` command. The fully qualified name of the class is passed in along with any arguments:

```
osgi> new java.util.ArrayList
osgi> random = new java.util.Random
java.util.Random@768c5708
```

Calling and chaining methods

The values displayed on the console are actually Java objects, so `true` is a literal that maps to `Boolean.TRUE` and `false` maps to `Boolean.FALSE`. Similarly, integral values are represented under the covers as `Long` instances and strings are all instances of `String`.

The Gogo shell can invoke arbitrary methods on instance methods using the dot (`.`) operator. It's possible to chain more than one method call by using one dot operator after another:

```
osgi> "hello" . length
5
osgi> "hello" . getClass . getName
java.lang.String
```

Since the Gogo shell is dynamic and the methods are looked up dynamically, the methods can be specified in a case-insensitive manner:

```
osgi> "hello" . getclass . getname
java.lang.String
```

Although methods can be called in a case-insensitive manner, variable names are case sensitive. Note that the dot (`.`) operator can be left out for the first method call, as everything else will be interpreted as arguments:

```
osgi> $numbers . get 0
1
osgi> $words get one
1
```

Parentheses can be used to evaluate nested expressions, as in other languages:

```
osgi> ("hello" getClass) getName
java.lang.String
osgi> (("hello" getClass) getPackage) getName
java.lang
```

Control flow

The Gogo shell supports basic control flow, including `if` and `each`:

```
osgi> if {true} {echo Yes}
Yes
osgi> if {false} {echo Yes}
osgi> if {false} {echo Yes} {echo No}
No
```

Multiple commands can be put inside the braces, separated by semicolons:

```
osgi> if {true} {echo Yes; echo Still yes}
Yes
Still yes
```

There are also other functions such as `not`, which can be used to negate the result of a boolean expression:

```
osgi> if {not {true}} {echo Yes} {echo No}
No
```

Although there aren't built-in functions for logical operators such as `and` and `or`, it's possible to create functions to do this fairly simply:

```
osgi> and = { if {$1} {if {$2} {true} {false}} {false}}
osgi> or  = { if {$1} {true} {if {$2} {true} {false}}}
osgi> or true false
true
osgi> and true false
false
```

Finally, the `each` command allows iteration over an array of elements:

```
osgi> directions = [ "Up" "Down" ]
osgi> each $directions { echo $it }
Up
Down
osgi> each $directions { echo "->$it<-" }
->Up<-
->Down<-
```

The `each` command actually provides a **map** function (which takes an array of values), invokes a function on each element, and returns an array of results. This allows operations to be nested:

```
osgi> (each [ "" 1 true ] { ($it getClass) getName }) get 0
java.lang.String
```

Running Equinox from the command line

To launch Equinox as a standalone OSGi application with a Gogo shell, the minimal dependencies are as follows:

- `org.apache.felix.gogo.shell` (provides the I/O processing and parser)
- `org.apache.felix.gogo.runtime` (provides the language runtime)
- `org.eclipse.osgi` (the Equinox kernel)

The `org.apache.felix.gogo.command` bundle provides a number of the built-in functions such as `ls` and `start`, as well as those that interact with repositories. It is useful but not necessary to run a basic shell.

To run Equinox as a launch in Eclipse, go to the **Run** menu and then choose **Run Configurations...** after which a dialog will appear. Choose **OSGi Framework** and set it up with the mentioned bundles (a quick way is to add the `org.apache.felix.gogo.shell` bundle, then deselect the **Include optional dependencies** option and click on **Add Required Bundles**). The resulting launch configuration now looks like the following screenshot:

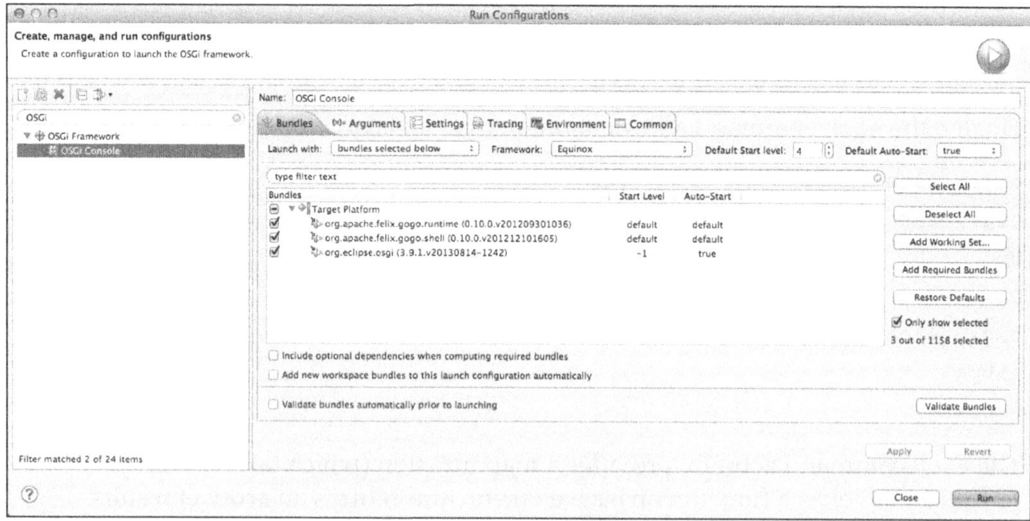

Click on **Run** and a console will be launched.

An exception may be thrown at start-up if the `org.eclipse.equinox.console` bundle is not found:

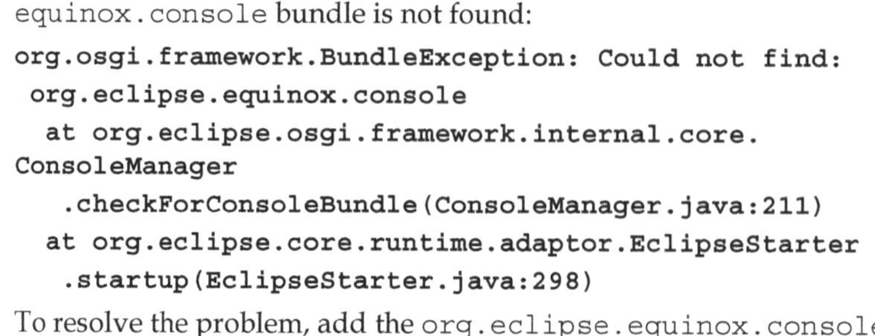

```
org.osgi.framework.BundleException: Could not find:
 org.eclipse.equinox.console
  at org.eclipse.osgi.framework.internal.core.
ConsoleManager
   .checkForConsoleBundle(ConsoleManager.java:211)
  at org.eclipse.core.runtime.adaptor.EclipseStarter
   .startup(EclipseStarter.java:298)
```

To resolve the problem, add the `org.eclipse.equinox.console` bundle to the runtime.

To run from a command line instead of an Eclipse launch configuration, the bundles need to be specified as either relative files or URLs. Equinox supports the `osgi.bundles` system property, which provides a comma-separated list of the JARs that the framework should attempt to bring up at boot. Note that `@start` is required to bring the console up when the `org.eclipse.equinox.console` bundle isn't present:

```
$ java -Dosgi.bundles=
 org.apache.felix.gogo.runtime_0.10.0.v201209301036.jar@start,
 org.apache.felix.gogo.shell_0.10.0.v201212101605.jar@start
 -jar org.eclipse.osgi_3.9.1.v20140110-1610.jar -console
osgi> bundles
0|Active|0|org.eclipse.osgi (3.9.1.v20140110-1610)
1|Active|4|org.apache.felix.gogo.shell (0.10.0.v201212101605)
2|Active|4|org.apache.felix.gogo.runtime (0.10.0.v201209301036)
```

Relative paths may be used by starting with `./` or `file:./` and absolute paths may be used with `/` or `file:///`.

The `-jar` argument runs the `org.eclipse.osgi` JAR using `Main-Class` from the manifest (which is `org.eclipse.core.runtime.adaptor.EclipseStarter` in Equinox).

Finally, the `-console` argument is passed to the running Eclipse instance inside `String[] args`, which indicates that Equinox should start up the console.

> The version numbers may differ; these were taken from Kepler SR2. Eclipse Luna (4.4.0) uses `org.eclipse.osgi_3.10.0.v20140606-1445.jar` as the entry point.

The Equinox commands (those in `scope equinox:`) are provided by the `org.eclipse.osgi.console` bundle. Adding this removes the exception highlighted previously and supplies some of the commands such as `ss` (short status) and `b` (bundle).

Understanding osgi.bundles and config.ini

The Equinox runtime can be configured in a couple of different ways. One way is to specify system properties on the command line with the `-Dosgi.*` parameters. (Despite being prefixed with `osgi`, they aren't standardized by an OSGi specification; they're all specific to Equinox.)

To prevent large command-line arguments, properties may instead be specified in a file called `config.ini`, which is stored in the configuration area of Eclipse. The **configuration area** is a directory that stores Equinox runtime information, and it is typically referred to as the `configuration` directory, since that is the default value. Running Equinox with `-config` can specify a different directory to be used.

One advantage of the `config.ini` file is that it can be updated by installers. P2 has a means to amend the contents of this file, which is used when updating between releases of Eclipse and in which the filenames (which have embedded version numbers) can be modified. Equinox reads the `config.ini` file and sets lines as system properties for the application.

When a stock Eclipse application runs, either the Equinox framework (if launched via the `-jar` option) or the `eclipse.exe` executable boots the JVM with the framework on the classpath, and then Equinox reads the `osgi.bundles` property (potentially set from the `config.ini` file) to bring it into a started state.

In the case of Eclipse, the `org.eclipse.equinox.simpleconfigurator` bundle is started, which reads a file named `bundles.info`, containing a list of bundles that need to be installed. Each line represents a single bundle, which is comma-separated and contains the following parts:

- The bundle name
- The bundle version number
- The location of the bundle (either as a relative path or as a fully qualified URL)
- The start level of the plug-in
- Whether the bundle should be started

For example, the Gogo shell is installed with the following (as a single line):

```
org.apache.felix.gogo.shell,
0.10.0.v201212101605,
plugins/org.apache.felix.gogo.shell_0.10.0.v201212101605.jar,
4,
false
```

When bundles are installed via P2, the `bundles.info` file is updated to reflect the new state of the system. Upon restart, the new set of bundles are used. The file is written by the utilities in `org.eclipse.equinox.simpleconfigurator.manipulator`, and it is sorted alphabetically by the bundle identifier and then in reverse version order. When changes are made, the entries are updated and the sorting ensures minimal changes to the content.

Sorting the bundles in reverse version order means that the highest version is considered first.

Connecting remotely

The Gogo shell has a telnet daemon that can be used to listen for network connections. This can be started interactively from the console with `telnetd`, or it can be run from the command line with the `-console` argument and an associated port:

```
$ java -Dosgi.bundles=… -jar org.eclipse.osgi_*.jar -console
osgi> telnetd --port=1234 start

$ java -Dosgi.bundles=… -jar org.eclipse.osgi_*.jar -console 1234
```

Note that the console-with-port from the command line requires the `org.eclipse.equinox.console` bundle to be installed in addition to the Gogo shell. Alternatively, the system property `-Dosgi.console=1234` can be specified at the command line or via the `config.ini` file.

Once the daemon is running, the Equinox process can be connected to via `telnet`:

```
$ telnet localhost 1234
Trying ::1...
telnet: connect to address ::1: Connection refused
Trying 127.0.0.1...
Connected to localhost.
Escape character is '^]'.
osgi> bundles
org.eclipse.osgi_3.9.1.v20140110-1610 [0] Id=0, Status=ACTIVE
...
```

Securing the connection

While telnet is good for debugging, it is not a secure way of connecting to a networked machine. SSH provides a way of connecting securely to remote machines.

Equinox can start an SSH daemon, but it requires more bundles to be added as well as an appropriate means to verify users and passwords. Unlike the command-line console or the telnet daemon, the SSH service requires that the Equinox console implementation be available. The full set of bundles is as follows:

- `org.apache.felix.gogo.shell` (provides the I/O processing and parser)
- `org.apache.felix.gogo.runtime` (provides the language runtime)
- `org.eclipse.osgi` (the Equinox kernel)
- `org.eclipse.equinox.console` (the Equinox console service)
- `org.eclipse.equinox.console.jaas.fragment` (adds JAAS support to the SSHD server)
- `org.eclipse.equinox.console.ssh` (the SSHD server support)
- `org.apache.sshd.core` (the SSHD server libraries)
- `org.apache.mina.core` (needed by the SSH server libraries)
- `slf4j-api` (the logging framework used by the libraries)

These bundles are available from the Equinox downloads page at `http://download.eclipse.org/equinox/` and the Orbit downloads page at `http://download.eclipse.org/tools/orbit/downloads/`. The GitHub repository, `https://github.com/alblue/com.packtpub.e4.advanced`, associated with this book has a set of the required bundles along with a demonstration runtime in the `com.packtpub.e4.advanced.console.ssh` directory.

To start an SSHD server in Equinox, it is easier to use a `config.ini` file instead of passing in many arguments via the command line. (However, either approach will still work, so use whichever is more convenient.)

Creating a JAAS configuration

JAAS is used to provide user ID/password authentication. To do this, a **JAAS configuration file** needs to be created with an `equinox_console` entry. As with other Java programs, this login module is set with the `java.security.auth.login` system property.

Create a file called `jaas.config` in the `configuration` directory with the following content:

```
equinox_console {
  org.eclipse.equinox.console.jaas.SecureStorageLoginModule
    REQUIRED;
};
```

The `java.security.auth.login` property can be set in the `config.ini` file that lists the bundles required:

```
osgi.console.ssh=1234
osgi.console.ssh.useDefaultSecureStorage=true
org.eclipse.equinox.console.jaas.file=configuration/store
ssh.server.keystore=configuration/hostkey.ser
java.security.auth.login.config=configuration/jaas.config
osgi.bundles=\
 ./org.apache.felix.gogo.runtime_0.10.0.v201209301036.jar@start,\
 ./org.apache.felix.gogo.shell_0.10.0.v201212101605.jar@start,\
 ./org.apache.mina.core_2.0.2.v201108120515.jar,\
 ./org.apache.sshd.core_0.7.0.v201303101611.jar,\
 ./org.eclipse.equinox.console.ssh_1.0.0...jar@start,\
 ./org.eclipse.equinox.console.jaas.fragment_1.0.0...jar,\
 ./org.slf4j.api_1.7.2.v20121108-1250,\
 ./org.eclipse.equinox.console_1.0.100.v20130429-0953.jar
```

Understanding the configuration options

The `osgi.console.ssh` port `1234` is used to start up the SSH server. If this configuration line is missed out, the SSH server won't be started.

The `osgi.console.ssh.useDefaultSecureStorage` property is required if the `SecureStorageLoginModule` is used. It is possible to use alternative `LoginModules` here, but this is not covered in this book. See the tutorials on JAAS on the Java home page for more information.

The `org.eclipse.equinox.console.jaas.file` property specifies where the `SecureStorageLoginModule` writes the user/password values. If not specified, it uses `configuration/store` as default.

> The secure storage login module uses a fairly simple means to store hashed passwords. It first generates an MD5 hash of the password, concatenates the password with this hash, and then stores the resulting SHA1 hash. So, `password` becomes `password5f4dcc3b5aa765d61d8327deb882cf99` and then ends up as `0d85584b3529eaac630d1b7ddde2418308d56317`.

The `ssh.server.keystore` file contains a serialized Java object (`java.security.KeyPair`) of the host's SSH key, which is automatically generated and persisted on first run. It defaults to `hostkey.ser`.

Finally, `java.security.auth.login.config` is the standard JAAS property that refers to a configuration file that defines the JAAS modules. The final property, `osgi.bundles`, lists the bundles that are required and the ones that should be started.

Launching the SSH daemon

Now a console can be accessed via SSH:

```
$ ssh -p 1234 equinox@localhost
The authenticity of host '[localhost]:1234 ([::1]:1234)' can't be established.
DSA key fingerprint is 0c:40:ff:ba:0a:c8:bc:3d:a9:72:9f:05:5f:c6:96:35.
Are you sure you want to continue connecting (yes/no)? Yes
Warning: Permanently added '[localhost]:1234' (DSA) to the list of known hosts.
equinox@localhost's password:
Currently the default user is the only one; since it will be deleted after first login, create a new user:
username: alex
password:
Confirm password:
roles:
osgi> ss
"Framework is launched."
id State       Bundle
0  ACTIVE      org.eclipse.osgi_3.9.1.v20140110-1610
1  ACTIVE      org.apache.felix.gogo.runtime_0.10.0.v201209301036
2  ACTIVE      org.apache.felix.gogo.shell_0.10.0.v201212101605
3  RESOLVED    org.apache.mina.core_2.0.2.v201108120515
4  RESOLVED    org.apache.sshd.core_0.7.0.v201303101611
  Fragments=6
5  ACTIVE      org.eclipse.equinox.console.ssh_1.0.0...
6  RESOLVED    org.eclipse.equinox.console.jaas.fragment_1.0.0...
  Master=4
7  RESOLVED    org.slf4j.api_1.7.2.v20121108-1250
8  ACTIVE      org.eclipse.equinox.console_1.0.100.v20130429-0953
```

Note that the jaas.fragment bundle has been wired to the org.apache.sshd.core bundle, which allows the sshd.core bundle to connect to the SecureStorageLoginModule. In fact, an investigation of the jaas.fragment bundle shows that it is almost empty; the only thing it has is a manifest file with the following content:

```
DynamicImport-Package: org.eclipse.equinox.console.jaas
Fragment-Host: org.apache.sshd.core;bundle-version="0.5.0"
```

The preceding snippet says that the fragment's host is the sshd.core bundle, and it should add a DynamicImport-Package of the org.eclipse.equinox.console.jaas package. As a result, although the org.apache.sshd.core bundle doesn't know anything about the Equinox secure storage module, when the fragment is injected, it permits the bundle to be wired up to the Equinox bundle:

```
osgi> bundle 4 | grep equinox
org.eclipse.equinox.console.jaas; version="0.0.0"
 <org.eclipse.equinox.console.ssh_1.0.0.v20130515-2026 [5]>
org.eclipse.equinox.console.jaas.fragment_1.0.0.v20130327-1442 [6]
```

Fragments are covered in more detail in *Chapter 5, Native Code and Fragment Bundles.*

Extending the shell

There are two different ways of extending the shell. One of them is to use the osgi:addcommand function that comes with Gogo. This allows one or more static methods from a class to be defined as functions in the console. Another way is to write custom Java classes and register them as OSGi services.

Adding commands from existing methods

In Java, the Integer class has a static method called toHexString, which converts an integer into its hexadecimal representation. Although this can be invoked via method calls, it is easier if it can be added as a command natively to the console.

The osgi:addcommand command takes a prefix (scope), a class object, and optionally a method to import. Without the last parameter, all public static methods will be added as commands.

When Gogo starts, it runs the gosh_profile script that uses this technique to add the methods of the System class under the system scope.

Getting a class from an existing instance

There are two ways to acquire a class in Gogo. One is to use the `getClass` method on an instance to acquire a `class` object, and the second way is to load the class dynamically using `loadClass`:

```
osgi> loadClass = (0 getClass)
osgi> addcommand number $loadClass toHexString
osgi> number:toHexString 255
ff
osgi> toHexString 255
ff
```

Loading a class via a ClassLoader

For classes that aren't immediately available, it is necessary to load them via a `ClassLoader`. For standard Java packages, the system `ClassLoader` instance should be used; for bundle-specific classes, the bundle's own `ClassLoader` instance should be used.

A bundle's `ClassLoader` instance can be acquired from the bundle, and should be available from the bundle context. Bundle zero (`0`) is the system bundle and can be used to load the standard Java packages:

```
osgi> arraysClass = (context:bundle 0) loadClass java.util.Arrays
osgi> addcommand arrays $arraysClass
```

This is necessary because many of the OSGi libraries return arrays, and the Gogo commands don't deal well with array types. Having loaded the `Arrays` class and registered it with the `arrays` prefix, it is now possible to convert an array of bundles into a list of bundles:

```
osgi> context:bundles
 0|Active|0|org.eclipse.osgi (3.9.1.v20140110-1610)
 1|Active|1|org.eclipse.equinox.simpleconfigurator (1.0.400)
 2|Active|4|com.ibm.icu (50.1.1.v201304230130)
...
osgi> (context:bundles) size
gogo: NumberFormatException: For input string: "size"
osgi> (arrays:asList (context:bundles)) size
820
```

Writing commands in Java

Although commands can be written in Gogo script or imported from static methods, it's more common to use POJO classes to implement commands. Because the Gogo shell works with reflection, there aren't any specific interfaces or features that need to be added for the commands to work. Instead, there are just implementations of commands that will be registered by the shell upon start-up.

How does the shell know what the commands are if there are no interfaces? It uses a couple of **service properties** (covered in the previous chapter) to annotate services as being usable by the shell framework. A service must be registered with the following two properties to be recognized as commands:

- `osgi.command.scope`: This is the name of the prefix of the command (such as `equinox` or `gogo`)
- `osgi.command.function`: This is an array of commands by name, which correspond to methods of the same name in the implementation class

A service can be registered in any supported way into the runtime, for example, using Declarative Services, Blueprint, bundle activation, or other ways of calling `context.registerService`. This example will use Declarative Services, since it is bundled by default in Eclipse.

Creating the project

Create a new plug-in project called `com.packtpub.e4.advanced.console` and create a class `com.packtpub.e4.advanced.console.MathsCommand`. Inside that class, create the methods `add`, `subtract`, `divide`, and `multiply` that operate on `Number` instances, casting to a `Double` if either argument is a floating point value and `Long` otherwise. The code is as follows:

```
public class MathsCommand {
  public Number add(Number n1, Number n2) {
    if (n1 instanceof Double ||
        n1 instanceof Float  ||
        n2 instanceof Double ||
        n2 instanceof Float) {
      return new Double(n1.doubleValue() + n2.doubleValue());
    } else {
      return new Long(n1.longValue() + n2.longValue());
    }
  }
  ...
}
```

Having created methods that allow mathematical operations, the next step is to have them registered with the framework at start-up. This can be done by registering an instance of `MathsCommand` as an OSGi service. Typically, services are registered as implementations of a common interface, but since the class does not implement an explicit interface, `java.lang.Object` can be used instead.

Using `java.lang.Object` means that clients don't inadvertently pick up or cache the bundle's implementation class, which might prevent reloading.

Using Declarative Services to register the command

To create declarative service, create a folder called `OSGI-INF` and place a file called `maths.xml` in it which has the following content:

```
<?xml version="1.0" encoding="UTF-8"?>
<scr:component xmlns:scr="http://www.osgi.org/xmlns/scr/v1.1.0"
 immediate="true" name="MathsCommand">
  <implementation
   class="com.packtpub.e4.advanced.console.MathsCommand"/>
  <property name="osgi.command.scope" type="String"
   value="maths"/>
  <property name="osgi.command.function" type="String">
    add
    subtract
    divide
    multiply
  </property>
  <service>
    <provide interface="java.lang.Object"/>
  </service>
</scr:component>
```

The `implementation class` attribute specifies the class name that will be instantiated by Declarative Services upon component start-up. By marking it as `immediate="true"`, the component will be instantiated as soon as the OSGi runtime installs and starts the Declarative Services implementation.

The properties specified allow the console to recognize the services as console functions. In this case, the command `maths:add` will be defined in the shell, which will correspond to the implementation in `MathsCommand.add`. Multiple commands can be added against a single implementation; in this case, an array of four strings is used (the type `String` is used to denote a string type, and the value-per-line means that it is an array rather than a single value).

Now, add the `OSGI-INF` folder to the `MANIFEST.MF` file so that component XML files are picked up by the framework:

```
Service-Component: OSGI-INF/*.xml
```

Verify that the folder is also added to the `build.properties` file so that it's correctly exported by Eclipse when a plug-in is generated (or built by Tycho):

```
output.. = bin/
bin.includes = META-INF/,\
               OSGI-INF/,\
               .
source.. = src/
```

Test the command

Now run an Eclipse instance with the plug-in enabled and create a **Host OSGi Console** from the **Console** view. Inside the console, run the following `maths` commands:

```
osgi> maths:add 1 2
3
osgi> maths:subtract 3 4
-1
osgi> maths:multiply 3 4
12
osgi> maths:divide 3 4
0
osgi> maths:divide 3.0 4
0.75
```

Note that `maths:divide` returns an integer if both arguments are supplied as integral values; the implementation for the `divide` method can be adjusted as necessary or a floating point literal can be used (for example, `3.0` or `3f`).

If this doesn't work, run `type | grep maths` and it should show `maths:4`. If it doesn't, find the bundle by running `bundles | grep com.packtpub.e4.advanced.console`, make a note of the number at the end (such as `123`), then run `start 123` to start the bundle. Repeat the `type | grep maths` step to see if it shows the output.

If it still doesn't show up, check that the `OSGI-INF` directory, referred to in the bundle by running `headers 123 | grep Service-Component`, displays a result such as `Service-Component: OSGI-INF/*.xml`.

If this is shown, check the contents of the XML file by looking at it through the console using the command `((context:bundle 123) getEntry 'OSGI-INF/maths.xml') content`.

Processing objects with console commands

Although the previous example used numbers, the console commands can take any object type and interact with them or generate output to the output stream. As an example, look at the following output generated by `context:bundles`:

```
osgi> context:bundles
 0|Active|0|org.eclipse.osgi (3.9.1.v20140110-1610)
 1|Active|1|org.eclipse.equinox.simpleconfigurator (1.0.400)
 2|Active|4|com.ibm.icu (50.1.1.v201304230130)
...
```

This can be recreated by invoking the `getBundles` method of `BundleContext`, but doing this requires a different way of using Declarative Services; in this case, providing a **component activation method**.

Create a class called `BundlesCommand` and create an `activate` method that takes a `BundleContext` instance as an argument. This will require importing the `org.osgi.framework` package in the manifest:

```
import org.osgi.framework.BundleContext;
public class BundlesCommand {
  private BundleContext context;
  public void activate(BundleContext context) {
    this.context = context;
  }
}
```

The `activate` method is called when the component is started and handed a `BundleContext`. If an exception is thrown in this method, the component is not started. There is a corresponding `deactivate` method that is called (if it exists) when the component is stopped.

Adding the print bundles command

Now a command can be added to print out the list of bundles. It can print out the status of the bundle and its symbolic name to `System.out`; invocation of the command will ensure that the stream is routed to the correct console:

```
public void print() {
  Bundle[] bundles = context.getBundles();
  for (int i = 0; i < bundles.length; i++) {
    Bundle bundle = bundles[i];
    System.out.println(bundle.getBundleId() + " "
      + bundle.getSymbolicName());
  }
}
```

Now add a new component called `bundles.xml` to the `OSGI-INF` directory for `BundlesCommand`:

```
<?xml version="1.0" encoding="UTF-8"?>
<scr:component xmlns:scr="http://www.osgi.org/xmlns/scr/v1.1.0"
 immediate="true" name="BundlesCommand">
  <implementation
   class="com.packtpub.e4.advanced.console.BundlesCommand"/>
  <property name="osgi.command.scope" type="String"
   value="bundles"/>
  <property name="osgi.command.function"
  type="String">print</property>
  <service>
    <provide interface="java.lang.Object"/>
  </service>
</scr:component>
```

Now restart Eclipse and run the `bundles:print` command:

```
osgi> bundles:print
0 org.eclipse.osgi
1 org.eclipse.equinox.simpleconfigurator
...
842 com.packtpub.e4.advanced.feeds.ui
847 com.packtpub.e4.advanced.feeds
851 com.packtpub.e4.advanced.console
```

Note the `immediate="true"` attribute in the component definition, which ensures that the component is started automatically.

Returning a list of bundles

To work with the actual bundle instances, a new command is needed. This will return the array of `Bundle` as a `List` (which saves converting the array to a `List` as done earlier). Add a new method called `list` and add it to the component `bundles.xml` file:

```
public List<Bundle> list() {
  return Arrays.asList(context.getBundles());
}

<property name="osgi.command.function" type="String">
   print
   list
</property>
```

Restart the Eclipse instance and verify that the `bundles:list` command works as expected. If not, find the bundle's ID and uninstall it, and then restart it:

```
osgi> bundles:list
0|Active|0|org.eclipse.osgi (3.9.1.v20140110-1610)
1|Active|1|org.eclipse.equinox.simpleconfigurator (1.0.400)
```

Since the result of `bundles:list` is a `List`, it is possible to get elements from the list with `get`. The elements are indexed from `0`, so won't necessarily correspond with their bundle IDs (use `context:bundle` to look them up by ID):

```
osgi> ((bundles:list) get 0) getSymbolicName
org.eclipse.osgi
```

Processing a list with each

Lists can be processed with `each`, which iterates through values. The `each` function takes a function (lambda) and passes its argument in via `$it` or `$args`, so it can be used to display every bundle that starts with a specific prefix:

```
osgi> each (bundles:list) {
  if {($it getSymbolicName) startsWith "com.packtpub"}
     {echo ($it getSymbolicName) } }
com.packtpub.e4.advanced.feeds.ui
com.packtpub.e4.advanced.feeds
com.packtpub.e4.advanced.console
```

Note that the result of this operation will be to print out the bundles; however, many bundles exist, and also a selection of `null` values (one per bundle). That's because the `each` function returns an element for each of the entries processed. To disable printing, refer to the *Running commands* section that shows how to set `.Gogo.format=false`.

The ability to return a value with `each` provides a powerful way of doing a map operation. For example, to convert the `List<Bundle>` objects to a `List` of `String` names, use the following command:

```
osgi> each (bundles:list) { $it getSymbolicName }
org.eclipse.osgi
org.eclipse.equinox.simpleconfigurator
...
```

With Java 8, it will be possible to filter lists more efficiently, and this will result in improvements to the Gogo shell's ability to perform list processing. The next section will show how to implement a `filter` function in Java.

Calling functions from commands

To permit functions to be callable from other Java commands, it is necessary to provide an implementation of `Function`, which is a Gogo-specific class. To use this, add the following import to the console bundle's manifest:

```
Import-Package:
 org.apache.felix.service.command;status=provisional
 ;resolution:=optional
```

Because the API is marked as provisional (and the OSGi directive `mandatory:=status` is used at the point of export), it is necessary to add the `status=provisional` attribute to the package import.

Since not all commands need to use this package, marking `resolution` as `optional` means that the bundle will still resolve if this package is not available; the net effect is that the methods using the `Function` type will not be able to run correctly.

Create a class called `ListCommand` in the `com.packtpub.e4.advanced.console` package, and create a method called `filter` that allows a `Function` and a `List` of objects to be passed in. It will also need to take in a `CommandSession` argument as well. Since the nested function may throw an exception, propagate this to the caller by defining it on the method signature:

```
package com.packtpub.e4.advanced.console;
import org.apache.felix.service.command.CommandSession;
import org.apache.felix.service.command.Function;
public class ListCommand {
  public List<Object> filter(CommandSession session, Function f,
   List<Object> list) throws Exception {
    …
  }
}
```

Inside the `filter` function, implement the method such that it iterates through all elements of the list, and where the function applied to each element is `true`, add the element to the returned list:

```
List<Object> result = new ArrayList<Object>();
for (Object object : list) {
  List<Object> args = new ArrayList<Object>(1);
  args.add(object);
  if (Boolean.TRUE.equals(f.execute(session, args))) {
    result.add(object);
  }
}
return result;
```

To register the service, create a Declarative Services component XML file called `list.xml`:

```
<?xml version="1.0" encoding="UTF-8"?>
<scr:component xmlns:scr="http://www.osgi.org/xmlns/scr/v1.1.0"
 immediate="true" name="ListCommand">
  <implementation
   class="com.packtpub.e4.advanced.console.ListCommand"/>
  <property name="osgi.command.scope" type="String" value="list"/>
  <property name="osgi.command.function" type="String">
    filter
  </property>
  <service>
    <provide interface="java.lang.Object"/>
```

```
  </service>
</scr:component>
```

This can be tested by using a function that always returns `true` or `false`:

```
osgi> list:filter {true} [ 1 2 3 ]
1
2
3
osgi> list:filter {false} [ 1 2 3 ]
osgi>
```

To provide a more useful filter, it is necessary to have some functions capable of performing comparisons. Since the shell script doesn't have any concept of equality (or inequality), it is necessary to define these as a set of functions. This can be done with a `CompareCommand` class and an associated component XML file called `compare.xml`:

```
public class CompareCommand {
  public boolean eq(Object a, Object b) {
    return a.equals(b);
  }
  public boolean gt(Comparable<Object> a, Comparable<Object> b) {
    return a.compareTo(b) > 0;
  }
  public boolean lt(Comparable<Object> a, Comparable<Object> b) {
    return a.compareTo(b) < 0;
  }
  public int compare(Comparable<Object> a, Comparable<Object> b) {
    return a.compareTo(b);
  }
}
```

```
<?xml version="1.0" encoding="UTF-8"?>
<scr:component xmlns:scr="http://www.osgi.org/xmlns/scr/v1.1.0"
 immediate="true" name="CompareCommand">
  <implementation
   class="com.packtpub.e4.advanced.console.CompareCommand"/>
    <property name="osgi.command.scope" type="String"
     value="compare"/>
    <property name="osgi.command.function" type="String">
     eq
     compare
     gt
     lt
   </property>
   <service>
     <provide interface="java.lang.Object"/>
   </service>
</scr:component>
```

A combination of the `list:filter` and `compare:gt` commands allows lists to be processed:

```
osgi> list:filter {gt $it 2} [ 1 2 3 4 ]
3
4
```

Finally, this allows the list of bundles to be filtered when they are in a particular state. It is possible to implement this as follows:

```
osgi> ACTIVE = 32
32
osgi> filter {eq $ACTIVE ($it getState)} (bundles:list)
osgi>
```

Unfortunately, the preceding code does not work. The reason is subtle, but worth understanding; the implementation of `compare:eq` that was implemented earlier looks like the following:

```
public boolean eq(Object a, Object b) {
  return a.equals(b);
}
```

However, `32` in the console is always represented as a `Long` (for integral values). The return value of the `Bundle.getState` method is an `int`, which is promoted to an `Integer`; unfortunately, the implementation of the `Long` class only permits `Long` values to be compared to other `Long` values, not to any other `Number` type.

```
osgi> ($ACTIVE getClass) getName
java.lang.Long
osgi> (new java.lang.Integer '1') equals (new java.lang.Long '1')
false
```

So, a change needs to be made to the `compare:eq` method such that if the two argument types are `Number` instances, their numeric values are compared instead. The method can be reimplemented as follows:

```
public boolean eq(Object a, Object b) {
  if (a instanceof Number && b instanceof Number) {
    if (a instanceof Double || a instanceof Float
     || b instanceof Double || b instanceof Float) {
      return ((Number)a).doubleValue()==((Number)b).doubleValue();
```

```
        } else {
          return ((Number)a).longValue()==((Number)b).longValue();
        }
      } else {
        return a.equals(b);
      }
    }
```

Now the filter will work as expected:

```
osgi> filter {eq $ACTIVE ($it getState)} (bundles:list)
  0|Active|0|org.eclipse.osgi (3.9.1.v20140110-1610)
  1|Active|1|org.eclipse.equinox.simpleconfigurator (1.0.400)
 ...
858|Active|4|com.packtpub.e4.advanced.console (1.0.0.qualifier)
```

Technically, comparing `double` values requires ensuring that the difference between two values is smaller than an epsilon value, because doubles may not be exactly equal but round off to approximately the same figure. Utilities such as **Apache Commons Math** has `Precision.equals(d1,d2,ulps)` and **JUnit** has `assertEquals(d1,d2,epsilon)` for this reason.

Looping and iteration

Although the `each` function provides a way of iterating over arrays, sometimes it is desirable to perform a fixed number of loops. Although there is a `while` and `until` command built into the shell, neither is particularly useful unless there is some way of keeping a loop counter. Fortunately, with the `maths:subtract` and the `compare:gt` functionality, it's possible to write a `while` function that loops:

```
osgi> n = 5
osgi> while { gt $n 0 } { echo $n; n = (subtract $n 1); }
5
4
3
2
1
```

The `until` loop works in the same way, except that termination occurs when the argument changes from `false` to `true`:

```
osgi> n = 5
5
osgi> until { lt $n 1 }  { echo $n; n = (subtract $n 1); }
5
4
3
2
1
```

Summary

In this chapter, we looked at the Gogo shell and how it can be extended in Equinox. Many of the examples here will work against a Felix implementation as well, although the SSHD example is specific to Equinox. The first part covered basic Gogo syntax, including variables, literals, functions, and how to run the console either locally or via remote access.

The second part of the chapter covered how to extend the console. The simplest kind of extension is with built-in shell functions, which can be iteratively developed or sourced from an external file. However, for more complex commands, shell extensions can be provided in the form of Java objects, which when integrated with Declarative Services or Blueprint, do not need to have any OSGi dependency at all.

The next chapter will look at how native code is used in Java and how native libraries can be loaded into bundles.

5 Native Code and Fragment Bundles

OSGi has support for loading native code in an application, which may be used to provide access to platform-specific functionality or for performance reasons. This chapter will present an overview of the Java Native Interface, and then cover how native code can be bundled in with plug-ins. It will also cover how **fragment bundles** can provide extensions to bundles in an OSGi runtime, such as native code libraries and Java patches.

Native code and Eclipse

The **Java Native Interface** (**JNI**) is a standard way in which any Java program can interact with native code. The process for working with native code can be summarized as follows:

1. Write a Java class with a **native** method.
2. Compile the Java class as normal.
3. Run **javah** with the class name, which generates a header stub.
4. Write the native C function and export it with the given function signature.
5. Compile the code into a dynamically linked library.
6. Load the library into the runtime with `System.loadLibrary`.
7. Execute the native method as normal.

The name of the library is dependent on the operating system; some call the library `name.dll`, some call it `libname.so`, and others `libname.dylib`. However, Java just uses the real portion of the library name; so, all three platforms use the same Java code, `System.loadLibrary("name")`, to load the library.

Creating a simple native library

For the purpose of this chapter, a native library will be created to perform a simple `Maths` operation class that adds two numbers. Although this could be easily implemented in Java, it is used to demonstrate the principles of how native code works.

Create a new plug-in project called `com.packtpub.e4.advanced.c` and, inside that, a class called `Maths` with a package named for the project. In it, create a `native` method called `add`, which takes two `int` arguments and returns an `int`. To ensure the native library is loaded, add a `static` initializer block that calls `System.loadLibrary`:

```
package com.packtpub.e4.advanced.c;
public class Maths {
  static {
    System.loadLibrary("maths");
  }
}
```

Now compile this class and then run `javah` from the command line, specifying the fully qualified class name:

```
$ javah -d native -classpath bin com.packtpub.e4.advanced.c.Maths
$ ls native/
com_packtpub_e4_advanced_c_Maths.h
```

Now implement a C function that has the same signature as defined in the header:

```
#include "com_packtpub_e4_advanced_c_Maths.h"
JNIEXPORT jint JNICALL Java_com_packtpub_e4_advanced_c_Maths_add
 (JNIEnv *env, jclass c, jint a, jint b) {
  return a + b;
}
```

The function signature is generated by `javah`, and uses macros such as `JNIEXPORT` and `JNICALL`, which are platform-specific `#define` statements in case any additional compiler or platform flags are required to register these as exported symbols. The name of the function is calculated from the fully qualified name of the class and method name, using underscores instead of dots. Each JNI function also has a pointer to `JNIEnv`, which is a handle to the JVM, as well as `jclass` (for static methods) or `jobject` (for instance methods).

The final step is to compile it into a platform-specific dynamic link library. The process differs from one operating system to another. This will typically include a path to the location of the JNI header files and output flags that say what the resulting file should be called.

Mac OS X

The Mac OS X developer tools are located either in /Developer or under /Applications/Xcode.app/Contents/Developer. The JNI header is located under the JavaVM.framework/Headers directory, so an include path -I needs to be specified to locate the files. Adjust the path as necessary when building this code, or use xcrun --show-sdk-path to find out where the SDK folder is located:

```
$ xcrun --show-sdk-path --sdk macosx10.9
/Applications/Xcode.app/Contents/Developer/Platforms
/MacOSX.platform/Developer/SDKs/MacOSX10.9.sdk
```

The -dynamiclib option is used to generate a dynamic linked library, which will allow it to be loaded into the Java runtime.

The output filename is declared with -o and, in order to load it into a Java runtime, must be of the form lib<name>.dylib.

The -arch i386 -arch x86_64 compiler flags generate a universal binary, which is a combination of both 32-bit and 64-bit code in the same library. OS X is the only major operating system to support multi-architecture builds by default.

The following command can therefore be used to build the library:

```
$ clang
  com_packtpub_e4_advanced_c_Maths.c
  -dynamiclib
  -o libmaths.dylib
  -I /Applications/Xcode.app/Contents/Developer/Platforms
     /MacOSX.platform/Developer/SDKs/MacOSX10.9.sdk
     /System/Library/Frameworks/JavaVM.framework/Headers
  -arch i386
  -arch x86_64
```

This results in a file named libmaths.dylib.

On OS X, the **dylib** extension is used for dynamic libraries, and conventionally, they have a **lib** prefix.

Linux

Linux distributions currently use GCC, although it may not be installed by default. Consult the operating system's package manager to determine where and how to install it if it is missing. (On Ubuntu and Debian, this will be `apt-get install gcc`, and on Red Hat and derivatives, `yum install gcc`.)

To build a library with `gcc`, the `-I` flag tells the compiler where to find the include files, and `-shared` tells it to create a library. The `-o` flag tells the compiler what to call the output:

```
$ gcc
  com_packtpub_e4_advanced_c_Maths.c
  -shared
  -o libmaths.so
  -I /usr/include/java
```

This results in a file named `libmaths.so`.

On Linux, the **so** extension is used for shared object libraries, and conventionally, they have a **lib** prefix.

Note that depending on the operating system, the installation of the JDK (and therefore its include files) may be located elsewhere. For example, on Debian, this will be located under `/usr/lib/jvm`.

To find the correct location, run `find /usr -name jni.h` and see which directory is reported:

```
$ find /usr -name jni.h
/usr/lib/jvm/java-7-openjdk-i386/include/jni.h
```

Windows

Windows doesn't come with a compiler by default, although there is a Visual Studio Express version that is available at no charge.

The Windows Studio Express download ships with a C compiler and linker called `cl`. Options can be specified with / or - and are interchangeable depending on preference. The `-LD` option tells the compiler to generate a dynamic link library, and the `-Fe` option gives the output name (in this case, `maths.dll`). As with other compilers, `-I` indicates where the include files are placed for the JDK that has been installed:

```
cl
  com_packtpub_e4_advanced_c_Maths.c
  -LD
  -Femaths.dll
  -IC:\Java\include
```

This results in a file called `maths.dll`. Note that the lowercase `e` is part of the `-Fe` option, and not part of the dynamic link library itself.

On Windows, the **dll** extension is used for dynamic link libraries, and there is no prefix.

Loading the native library

Once the binary has been compiled, a simple test for the `Maths` class can exercise the functionality:

```
package com.packtpub.e4.advanced.c;
public class MathsTest {
  public static void main(String[] args) {
    System.out.println(Maths.add(1,2));
  }
}
```

When run, this should print out `3`.

If the native library cannot be found, the following exception will be displayed:

```
Exception in thread "main" java.lang.UnsatisfiedLinkError:
 no maths in java.library.path
  at java.lang.ClassLoader.loadLibrary(ClassLoader.java:1886)
  at java.lang.Runtime.loadLibrary0(Runtime.java:849)
  at java.lang.System.loadLibrary(System.java:1088)
  at com.packtpub.e4.advanced.c.Maths.<clinit>(Maths.java:13)
  at com.packtpub.e4.advanced.c.MathsTest.main(MathsTest.java:14)
```

The `<clinit>` method (which stands for class initializer) in the stack trace is the special name given to the `static` initializer—in this case, the `static` block in the `Maths` class. This is also generated if any `static` variables are assigned non-default values.

The instance constructor is called `<init>`, and is generated whenever instance variables are assigned or if a constructor is provided.

The exception is triggered when the `Maths` class is first used, which is called from `MathsTest`. Note that the `static` initializer of a class is executed prior to any methods being invoked on that class.

If the `System` class is unable to find the library relative to the class, it will consult the list of directories specified in the `java.library.path` system property. If the native library is found, then it will be returned; otherwise, an error is thrown.

To fix the previous error, modify the Java runtime to add a directory (relative or absolute) and invoke it with the system property set accordingly:

```
$ java -classpath . -Djava.library.path=/path/to/dir
  com.packtpub.e4.advanced.c.MathsTest
```

The library must be loaded as a `File` rather than as an embedded resource in a JAR file; in other words, an `InputStream` object cannot be used to load the contents. OSGi runtimes such as Equinox and Felix extract the native libraries on demand to a temporary file so that they can be loaded by the operating system.

Library dependencies

One thing to be aware of is the fact that native libraries go through a slightly different resolution process as compared to libraries loaded by Java. If the JNI library has an external dependency, then this will be loaded automatically by the operating system. However, the operating system won't know about `java.library.path`, and hence may fail to find the required native library dependencies.

For Windows systems, the current directory is always consulted if a library can't be found elsewhere, and this typically results in the library being loadable. It will default to the Windows system directory (such as `c:\Windows\Sytstem32` or similar) if it can't be found in the `PATH` variable.

On Linux and OS X, the value of the `LD_LIBRARY_PATH` variable or the `DYLD_LIBRARY_PATH` variable is consulted. Generally, these are set to include `/usr/lib` and `/lib` by default, so that standard libraries (such as `libc` and `libssl`) can always be loaded.

To see the problem in action, create a new dynamic library called `other`, which defines a single function:

```
// other.h
int otherAdd(int a, int b);
// other.c
#include "other.h"
int otherAdd(int a, int b) { return a+b; }
```

Compile this as a dynamic linked library called `other`. Then, modify the `maths` library to use the `other` library:

```
#include "com_packtpub_e4_advanced_c_Maths.h"
#include "other.h"
JNIEXPORT jint JNICALL Java_com_packtpub_e4_advanced_c_Maths_add
 (JNIEnv *env, jclass c, jint a, jint b) {
  return otherAdd(a,b);
}
```

The `maths` library will need to be passed an argument to link this with the native library as well, such as `-L. -lother` on Unix or by passing the name of the library on the `cl` command line for Windows.

If the `other` library is in the current directory when the Java virtual machine is started, then the `MathsTest` class will work as expected. If it is moved into a different directory, then the test will fail:

```
$ java -Djava.library.path=native
 com.packtpub.e4.advanced.c.MathsTest
Exception in thread "main" java.lang.UnsatisfiedLinkError:
 com.packtpub.e4.advanced/com.packtpub.e4.advanced.c/
  native/libmaths.dylib:
 dlopen(com.packtpub.e4.advanced/com.packtpub.e4.advanced.c/
  native/libmaths.dylib, 1):
Library not loaded: libother.dylib
Referenced from:
 com.packtpub.e4.advanced/com.packtpub.e4.advanced.c/
  native/libmaths.dylib
Reason: image not found
 at java.lang.ClassLoader$NativeLibrary.load(Native Method)
```

The problem is that the value of `java.library.path` is only known by the Java runtime. Java knows where to find the first library, but when that library needs the dependent library and the native operating system needs to resolve it, it will use the operating system's native resolution to find the library.

Java doesn't provide a way to modify environment variables at runtime, and in any case, the operating system's library loader doesn't re-read the environment variables after the start of a process for efficiency reasons.

On Windows, the dependent library may be loaded and cached in memory by calling `System.loadLibrary` separately. The `Maths` class can be changed as follows:

```
static {
  System.loadLibrary("other");
  System.loadLibrary("maths");
}
```

Now when run on Windows, the program works as expected. That's because the Windows platform loads and resolves the symbols in the first library and then loads and resolves the symbols in the second library.

On Unix platforms such as Mac OS X and Linux, this doesn't work, because the library will have an embedded reference to the dependent library. The native loader will complain that the dynamic link library is not satisfied, even if the library has been loaded already. That's because on Unix, the native libraries are loaded lazily (and so not resolved), with the result that when the function is first called, it is resolved on demand.

The solution to this problem is to perform one of the following steps instead:

- In the native code, only rely on system libraries (those in `/usr/lib` or equivalent)
- Statically link any dependent code
- Set the appropriate environment variable to a location containing all the dependencies before launching
- Avoid using JNI libraries to provide operating system hooks
- Use an alternative library such as **jnr** (`https://github.com/jnr`), which includes a POSIX compatibility layer

Native code patterns

When writing native code methods in Java, any time the method signature changes, the method has to be recompiled and relinked. This may be inconvenient for Java developers, especially if multiple platforms need to be rebuilt.

Best practice is to internalize native dependencies by ensuring that all `native` methods are marked as `private`.

Instead of exporting the native function to callers directly, mark it as private and provide Java public methods that wrap the native call:

```
private native static int nativeAdd(int a, int b);
public static int add(int a, int b) {
  return nativeAdd(a,b);
}
```

This permits the native library to be isolated from any Java changes that may occur in future, such as changing the signature type or adding exceptions. In addition, any fixes that are required may be implemented in a Java layer instead of the native layer. For example, in the previous case, if the method needed to be changed to add long values instead, the native layer could still be used in the common case but fall back to a pure Java path in the case the values are larger than the native layer can handle:

```
public static long add(long a, long b) {
  if (a < Integer.MAX_VALUE / 2 && a > Integer.MIN_VALUE / 2
   && b < Integer.MAX_VALUE / 2 && b > Integer.MIN_VALUE / 2) {
    return nativeAdd((int)a, (int)b);
  } else {
    return a+b;
  }
}
```

Note that the arguments are range tested to ensure that the resulting value will be within the int range and that an overflow does not occur. Similar argument testing can be done for other types of arguments before they are passed into the native method. If certain values are known to cause problems, they can be handled in the Java layer appropriately.

Another reason to use a Java frontend is that exceptions are often easier to generate (and messages easier to update) when compiled in Java than in the native layer. JNI provides a means to throw an exception with the (*env)->ThrowNew method, but if there is a requirement to update the information passed into the exception object, it is easier to change this in the Java code once instead of changing it once per platform.

An alternative approach is to provide thin Java bindings over every native method in as close to one-to-one correspondence as possible. SWT provides a means to manipulate the underlying operating system's resources using Java classes; for example, on Mac OS X, the org.eclipse.swt.internal.cocoa package provides objects such as NSView and id that have one-to-one correspondence with their underlying native counterparts. The SWT library is then constructed by manipulating the Java wrappers, in much the same way that AWT abstracts the native libraries in the original GUI toolkit for Java.

Unlike AWT, SWT can be upgraded without requiring a JVM update. The other key reason why AWT is no longer used is that the AWT implementation aimed to provide a least-common-denominator approach, which meant that it always lagged behind OS upgrades. SWT keeps up-to-date with the operating system's new features, adding support for touches, gestures, and new UIs such as GTK3. Wherever possible, the native objects are returned so that the look, feel, and behavior are appropriate for the application; but for operating systems that don't support particular elements, a fallback implementation in Java can often be used.

Native libraries in OSGi bundles

To support loading native code in OSGi bundles, the framework defines a specific header, **Bundle-NativeCode**, which defines the libraries that are available to the bundle via the `System.loadLibrary` call.

The `Bundle-NativeCode` header defines one or more native libraries and a clause which states what operating systems and processor architectures are valid for each library. Calls to `System.loadLibrary` will then look for libraries mentioned in this list and use only those found for the appropriate architecture. In effect, the `Bundle-NativeCode` header replaces the `java.library.path` property.

In the prior example, the `maths` library was used for performing calculations. In an OSGi bundle, this could be packaged with the bundle itself and referred to via a manifest header:

```
Bundle-NativeCode: native/maths.dll
```

When calling `System.loadLibrary("maths")` on Windows, the `native/maths.dll` library will be automatically extracted to a suitable location on the filesystem and passed to the operating system for loading.

Note that the directory of the library in the bundle is neither relevant nor consulted in the loading of the library itself.

If a bundle is being designed to support more than one operating system, then the library needs to be qualified accordingly. To do this, clauses can be appended to each native library to determine which **osname** or operating system they can run on:

```
Bundle-NativeCode:
 native/maths.dll;osname=win32,
 native/libmaths.dylib;osname=macosx,
 native/libmaths.so;osname=linux
```

Now when run on a Windows platform, `System.loadLibrary("maths")` will load the `native/maths.dll` library; for Linux platforms, `native/libmaths.so` will be loaded instead; and for Mac OS X, `native/libmaths.dylib` will be used.

> The OSGi R6 specification translates requirements in the `Bundle-NativeCode` header to a set of generic requirements on the `osgi.native` namespace. An `osname=win32` clause is automatically translated to a `Require-Capability: osgi.native.osname~=win32` clause. This allows resolvers to choose the right dependency automatically. Eclipse Luna has an OSGi R6 compatible version of Equinox.

Although each operating system has its own naming convention (and thus the libraries can all be in the same directory in this instance), this approach doesn't work when providing multiple libraries for the same operating system. Although Mac OS X can create multi-architecture bundles, other operating systems are restricted to a single-processor architecture per library.

If the bundle needs to support both 32-bit and 64-bit operating systems, two versions of the library are required and the **processor** attribute disambiguates between them:

```
Bundle-NativeCode:
 native/x86/maths.dll;osname=win32;processor=x86,
 native/x86_64/maths.dll;osname=win32;processor=x86_64,
 native/libmaths.dylib;osname=macosx,
 native/x86/libmaths.so;osname=linux;processor=x86,
 native/x86_64/libmaths.so;osname=linux;processor=x86_64
```

The correct version of the `maths` library is loaded depending upon whether it is a 32-bit (`x86`) or 64-bit (`x86_64`) processor.

> This is the reason why directories are neither consulted nor necessary in the lookup of the native libraries; this permits the directories themselves to be used to partition the native libraries into different directories without affecting the logical runtime.

Optional resolution of native code

A side effect of the `Bundle-NativeCode` header is that if it is present, then it must have an associated entry that matches the operating system. If it is not, then the bundle will fail to resolve.

As a result, specifying the following will mean that the bundle cannot resolve on platforms other than Mac OS X:

```
Bundle-NativeCode: native/libmaths.dylib;osname=macosx
```

This is desirable in cases where there is a dependency on a framework specific to an operating system (such as a dependency on `Cocoa.framework`), but in other cases, a native library can be useful to accelerate certain actions but will work fine without the native library.

To declare that the native library is optional, place an asterisk (`*`) as another option in the `Bundle-NativeCode` header:

```
Bundle-NativeCode: native/libmaths.dylib;osname=macosx,*
```

This special syntax indicates that the bundle should still resolve normally even if the operating system isn't Mac OS X, but with the expectation that `System.loadLibrary` will only be called when running on a Mac OS X platform; or alternatively, that the code can handle an `UnsatisifedLinkError` when calling the method.

Multiple libraries for the same platform

When providing multiple libraries on a single platform, they all need to be referenced on the same clause. The OSGi resolution iterates through the clauses in order, and stops at the first one matching the current environment. As a result, this will never load the `maths` library:

```
Bundle-NativeCode:
 native/libother.dylib;osname=macosx,
 native/libmaths.dylib;osname=macosx
```

Even though this looks like it should work, calls to `System.loadLibrary("other")` will work as expected, while calls to `System.loadLibrary("maths")` will fail.

To define multiple libraries, concatenate them into the same clause:

```
Bundle-NativeCode:
 native/libother.dylib;native/libmaths.dylib;osname=macosx
```

Now, the resolution of `other` and `maths` will work on the `macosx` platform.

Multiple libraries with the same name

If there are multiple libraries with the same name in the same clause, then only the first one is loaded. For example, if a separate debug version of the maths library was used and placed in a separate directory, then there would be no way to load it:

```
Bundle-NativeCode:
 native/libmaths.dylib;debug/libmaths.dylib;osname=macosx
```

Since folders are ignored and cannot be supplied as part of the `System.loadLibrary` call, any reference to `maths` will always result in the first `native/libmaths.dylib` library.

The right way to resolve this is to either rename the library, for example, `libmaths -debug.dylib`, or use an alternative mechanism, such as the filter or fragment solutions discussed later in this chapter.

Additional filters and constraints

It is possible to attach additional filters and constraints on loading the native libraries in an OSGi bundle. There are a number of standard attributes that can be specified along with a generic filter:

- `osname`: This is the name of the operating system (`win32`, `macosx`, or `linux`)
- `osversion`: This is the version number of the operating system (`8.1`, `10.9`, or `3.2`)
- `processor`: This is the processor type (`x86`, `x86_64`)
- `language`: This is the ISO language code, in case the DLL has textual content
- `selection-filter`: This is an OSGi LDAP filter, which can be applied for other system properties

For a full list of supported values, see the OSGi specification or on the OSGi website at `http://www.osgi.org/Specifications/Reference`.

The `selection-filter` can be used to provide a specific debug variant of an available library by specifying a system property for the Java VM. For example, if two versions of a library were required, one with debugging symbols, then the filter can be set as follows:

```
Bundle-NativeCode:
 native/libmaths.dylib;selection-filter=(!(debug=true))
 debug/libmaths.dylib;selection-filter=(debug=true)
```

Running the VM with a `-Ddebug=true` flag would result in the debug libraries being loaded by `System.loadLibrary`, whereas with any other value (or unset), the normal one would be used.

`selection-filter` can also be used to test for other conditions, for example:

```
Bundle-NativeCode:
 native/libmaths.dylib;selection-filter=(file.encoding=UTF-8)
```

This can be used to selectively load different libraries based on the windowing system installed:

```
Bundle-NativeCode:
 native/libgtk.so;selection-filter=(osgi.ws=gtk),
 native/libcocoa.dylib;selection-filter=(osgi.ws=cocoa),
 native/mfc.dll;selection-filter=(osgi.ws=win32)
```

Reloading native libraries

When a native library is loaded into the JVM, it can only be loaded from a single bundle at a time. If the bundle is restarted or updated, the existing native library is reused for the new version of the bundle. The reason for this is that the JVM ensures that the fully qualified path of the native library is associated with a single `ClassLoader` instance. Subsequent loads of the native library will fail.

If the bundle is uninstalled completely, the native library may be subject to unloading. Note that this only occurs when the `ClassLoader` instance associated with the bundle is garbage collected, which may be some time after the bundle has been stopped.

Note that as discussed earlier in this chapter, the OSGi specification only supports native libraries that have no transitive native dependencies. This restriction is primarily limited to the support in Java for loading such transitive dependencies.

OSGi fragment bundles

An OSGi runtime consists of a set of bundles running in a managed environment. These bundles provide classes and resources, a (sub)set of which can be exported to other bundles. Each bundle has its own class space (provided by its own `ClassLoader` instance) that permits the dependencies and exports to be wired up appropriately.

OSGi also has the ability to manage **fragment bundles** or simply **fragments**. These are like bundles that don't have their own life cycle, but can still contribute classes and package dependencies to a **host bundle** at runtime.

The difference between a fragment bundle and a host bundle is the existence of the **Fragment-Host** header, which specifies the `Bundle-SymbolicName` and, optionally, the `bundle-version` attribute of the bundle to attach to. All other OSGi headers are valid for fragments, except for `Bundle-Activator`. The reason why the activator is not valid is that fragments do not have their own life cycle; they share the life cycle of their parent bundle, and as such cannot be activated.

The `Fragment-Host` header can specify version ranges of bundles to attach to; the syntax is the same for other bundles, for example, `bundle-version="[1.0,2.0)"` to specify a range between 1.0 (inclusive) and 2.0 (exclusive).

Note that on Equinox, the value of `Bundle-ManifestVersion` must be at least 2 to enable fragments to resolve correctly.

Adding native code with fragments

Fragments can be used to contribute native libraries and other resources to a bundle. By embedding the native libraries to the fragment and having it attach to the `Fragment-Host`, the host bundle will be able to look up native resources as usual.

The `Bundle-NativeCode` header is used as before, and filter options can be specified to ensure that only a particular fragment resolves correctly:

```
Bundle-ManifestVersion: 2
Bundle-SymbolicName: com.packtpub.e4.advanced.c.win32.x86
Bundle-Version: 1.0.0
Bundle-NativeCode: win32/x86/maths.dll;processor=x86;osname=win32
Fragment-Host: com.packtpub.e4.advanced.c
```

There are a few points worth noting with the native code and fragment option:

- As with any fragments, they need to be installed prior to the host bundle being resolved, or it will not be bound as expected. This may cause confusion if the native library is required.

- As the platform-specific fragment and the bundle will share the same class space (that is, the same `ClassLoader`), it is necessary to put the native libraries in unique folder names to ensure that they get consulted appropriately. One way of doing this is to use the `processor` and `osname` values as folder names, which help to maintain uniqueness. Otherwise, one fragment may bind tighter to a package name than the desired one, resulting in the desired package not loading. This is especially true when the optional platform binding is used.
- The bundle itself will still be able to resolve, even if the fragment is missing or cannot be resolved at all. This may lead to confusion if the native library is strictly required for the bundle to operate correctly.

In general, if native libraries are required for correct operation, it is recommended that they are stored in the same bundle as the corresponding Java code for all platforms that are supported. The downside of the additional size of the bundle will be outweighed by the convenience of it working as expected when it is installed.

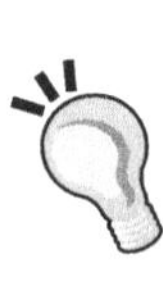

Eclipse provides its native libraries as fragments that are attached to a host bundle. Both the SWT and Equinox launcher have native code that gets loaded from a Java bundle. This allows the specific platform bundle fragment to be loaded, but from an OSGi perspective, the SWT (or Equinox) bundle will resolve without the native code being present. Generally, it is better if an OSGi bundle does not resolve until all the required dependencies are present.

Adding classes to a bundle

A fragment can contribute classes and resources to the classpath for the bundle. If the host bundle does not specify a `Bundle-ClassPath`, then the default is a dot (`.`) which is the content of the bundle itself. A fragment that has one or more classes in the root of the fragment bundle will therefore be available to classes running in the host bundle, and vice versa. As a result, loading classes with `class.forName` allows a class to be loaded from a contributed fragment bundle.

Fragments have their own `Bundle-ClassPath` as well and can be appended to the end of the search path. By itself, this doesn't allow for fragments to replace the bundle content, but it does provide a way to add code to the bundle's search path such as a database driver:

```
Bundle-ManifestVersion: 2
Bundle-SymbolicName: com.packtpub.e4.advanced.db.client
Bundle-Version: 1.0.0
```

```
Bundle-ManifestVersion: 2
Bundle-SymbolicName: com.packtpub.e4.advanced.db.client.h2
Bundle-Version: 1.0.0
Bundle-ClassPath: h2.jar
Fragment-Host: com.packtpub.e4.advanced.db.client
```

When the `com.packtpub.e4.advanced.db.client.h2` fragment is installed and attached to `com.packtpub.e4.advanced.db.client`, it will allow the client bundle to load the h2 drivers.

Patching bundles with fragments

Another common use case for a fragment bundle is to provide a patch to an existing OSGi bundle, but without having to modify or replace the source bundle. The way this is performed is by injecting fragment classes to the front of the host bundle's classpath.

Since the `Bundle-ClassPath` of the fragment is concatenated at the end of the `Bundle-ClassPath` of the host, this in itself is not sufficient to be able to patch a runtime bundle. The search order for a class or resource is to step through the entries in the `Bundle-ClassPath` in order, and stop at the first one found.

The solution is to implement the host bundle in a way that permits later patching, by providing a patch JAR file that is missing in the host bundle but can be contributed by a fragment bundle. Class lookups will ignore the patch JAR if it cannot be found, and consult any fragments that contribute the patch JAR.

To implement this, define the `Bundle-ClassPath` on the host bundle such that a `patch.jar` is placed before the root of the bundle (`.`):

```
Bundle-ManifestVersion: 2
Bundle-SymbolicName: com.packtpub.e4.advanced.host
Bundle-Version: 1.0.0
Bundle-ClassPath: patch.jar,.

Bundle-ManifestVersion: 2
Bundle-SymbolicName: com.packtpub.e4.advanced.host.fragment
Bundle-Version: 1.0.0
Fragment-Host: com.packtpub.e4.advanced.host
Comment: Provides the patch.jar file in the fragment
```

Now when the fragment is installed and bound to the host bundle, classes in the fragment will take priority and can replace those in the host bundle.

Adding imports and exports with fragments

Fragments can also be used to add additional imports and exports to a bundle. By supplying a combination of `Import-Package` and `Export-Package` statements, the original host bundle can be extended or exposed appropriately.

Sometimes a bundle will inadvertently have runtime requirements that are not expressed or exposed in an `Import-Package` statement. Providing a fragment allows a bundle to be corrected without needing to change the source of the original bundle. Another reason to do this is to allow a bundle to see the implementation of a particular driver class (such as a custom `log4j` appender) that it would otherwise not be able to see:

```
Bundle-ManifestVersion: 2
Bundle-SymbolicName: com.packtpub.e4.advanced.log4j
Bundle-Version: 1.0.0
Fragment-Host: org.apache.log4j
Import-Package: com.packtpub.e4.advanced.log4j.custom
```

A similar thing can be done with `Export-Package` as well:

```
Bundle-ManifestVersion: 2
Bundle-SymbolicName: com.packtpub.e4.advanced.log4j.export
Bundle-Version: 1.0.0
Fragment-Host: org.apache.log4j
Export-Package: org.apache.log4j;version="1.2.0"
```

This will attach to an existing bundle and re-export the package, but with a lower version number than present. This may be useful when a package export contains a higher micro version than expected or a tighter constraint is defined in a required bundle.

Note that for both `Import-Package` and `Export-Package`, the required dependencies are ignored if the host bundle already supplies an exact match (since adding them would change nothing). If the packages conflict, then the fragment may fail to resolve. Diagnosing and resolving these errors is a tricky process, and will often involve updating the `uses` directive of the imported/exported packages to ensure a consistent class space. Felix often provides better diagnostic information than Equinox when the `uses` constraint fails.

The **uses directive** specifies what packages are used by classes of the exported package. This allows a resolver to figure out the correct transitive dependencies without the client needing to provide them.

For example, in the Gogo runtime bundle, the `org.apache.felix.gogo.api` package declares that it uses the `org.apache.felix.service.command` package, which means that users of the API package need to be compatible with the `Command` package as well:

```
Export-Package: org.apache.felix.gogo.api;
 uses:="org.apache.felix.service.command"
```

Bnd calculates `uses` constraints automatically, and is used by `maven-bundle-plugin` as well as the Gradle `osgi` plug-in when projects are built with those plug-ins enabled. Maintaining the `uses` constraint manually is not recommended.

Extension bundles

Fragments that bind to the system bundle are known as **extension bundles**. The system bundle has an ID of `0` and uses the symbolic name `system.bundle`, or the specific framework implementation such as `org.apache.felix.framework` or `org.eclipse.osgi` if the fragment is specific to a single framework.

One way of using extension bundles is to provide access to a package that is contained in the JVM but not exported. By default, the OSGi framework will export packages only in the `java.*` package, although both Felix and Equinox default to exporting the `javax.*` packages where available.

Consider a bundle that depends on the internal class `sun.misc.BASE64Decoder`. A bundle that has an `Import-Package: sun.misc` will not resolve in a standard OSGi framework, because no framework will export that package.

Note that depending on the `sun.misc` packages is not recommended as these may be removed in future versions of Java. For Base 64 encoding/decoding, the Apache Commons Codec class can be used, or for Java 6 and above, the `javax.xml.bind.DatatypeConverter` class can be used instead. Java 8 has introduced the `java.util.Base64` class to allow developers to migrate away from `sun.misc`. OpenJDK 8 ships with the `jdeps` tool, which can show when internal class dependencies are present. Running `jdeps -jdkinternals` will show all internal classes that are used on the classpath.

Although the default packages exposed by the OSGi framework can be modified by setting a system property `org.osgi.framework.system.packages.extra`, another way is to create a system bundle extension that exports the package and attaches it to the framework:

```
Bundle-ManifestVersion: 2
Bundle-SymbolicName: com.packtpub.e4.advanced.export.sun.misc
Bundle-Version: 1.0.0
Fragment-Host: system.bundle
Export-Package: sun.misc
```

If this is created as an empty fragment bundle and installed into the framework, it will result in the system bundle exporting the `sun.misc` package, which will allow bundles that need it to bind as normal.

Another use for fragments is to provide standard OSGi services in a bundle outside of the system bundle. Felix uses this to conditionally provide the implementation of the `PermissionAdmin` framework. Such implementations need to use the `extension:=framework` attribute:

```
Bundle-ManifestVersion: 2
Bundle-SymbolicName: org.apache.felix.framework.security
Fragment-Host: system.bundle; extension:=framework
```

OSGi R6 adds the `Extension-BundleActivator` header specifically for framework extensions, so that they may participate in the start-up and shut-down of the framework.

Finally, fragments may be used to add classes to the JVM's **bootclasspath** with extension bundles. This may be necessary if starting a Java agent is required. Note that not all OSGi frameworks support modification of the `bootclasspath`; if they do, the property `org.osgi.supports.bootclasspath.extension` will be `true`. A fragment defined as a `bootclasspath` extension looks like the following:

```
Bundle-ManifestVersion: 2
Bundle-SymbolicName: com.packtpub.e4.advanced.bootclasspath
Fragment-Host: system.bundle;extension:=bootclasspath
```

On Equinox and Felix, this is currently `null`, which means it is not supported:

```
osgi> getProperty org.osgi.supports.bootclasspath.extension
osgi>
```

As a result, attempting to install a bundle with a `bootclasspath` extension results in an error in Felix:

```
org.osgi.framework.BundleException:
 Unsupported Extension Bundle type: bootclasspath java.lang.
UnsupportedOperationException:
 Unsupported Extension Bundle type!
```

The case is similar for Equinox:

```
org.osgi.framework.BundleException:
 Boot classpath extensions are not supported.
```

Modification of the `bootclasspath` extension is not directly supported in OpenJDK for a standalone program (though instrumented JVMs with an agent can obtain an `Instrumentation` class that does have permissions), and as such, modifications of the `bootclasspath` in Equinox and Felix are not directly supported on OpenJDK VMs.

It is however possible to programmatically add classes to the `bootclasspath` by using reflection to invoke the `addURL` method of the `URLClassLoader`, which is used by the system class loader.

Summary

This chapter presented the way in which Java code can call native code. Examples for various operating systems and how they can be loaded from a Java application were shown. This technique was then demonstrated with fragment bundles, along with other kinds of extension mechanisms to export packages and perform additions to the framework itself.

The next chapter will look at the details of service loaders and Thread Context ClassLoaders in an OSGi context.

6
Understanding ClassLoaders

In this chapter, we will look at how OSGi's use of **ClassLoaders** permits bundle separation, and what effect this has on libraries that mistakenly assume there is only one ClassLoader per JVM. We will cover the Java **ServiceLoader** and describe the problems and solutions it has in an OSGi framework. Finally, we will look at how to upgrade such libraries so that they are OSGi compatible.

Overview of ClassLoaders

One of JVM's biggest contributions to runtime loading has been the **ClassLoader** design and infrastructure. This allows a JVM to load the **bytecode** from arbitrary locations or even generate them on demand. It was this infrastructure that enabled **Applets** and **Remote Method Invocation** (**RMI**)—two key technologies that propelled Java toward enterprise use in the late 1990s.

The purpose of a ClassLoader is to take a class name (such as `com.example.Test`) and return an instantiated `Class` object. This typically involves translating the name to some kind of file reference (such as `com/example/Test.class`), loading the content of that file, and passing it to the JVM to define a `Class`. ClassLoaders can also be used to synthesize classes on demand or even weave additional data to the classes at load time.

The most common ClassLoader used in Java is the **URLClassLoader**. This takes an array of URLs that either point to JARs or directory roots, and when a class is requested, it iterates through them in turn attempting to resolve the required class. If a URL looks like an archive file (such as a JAR or ZIP), then the manifest is loaded and the content is inspected; otherwise, it concatenates the base URL with the file reference. This allows a JVM to load classes both from a local filing system (such as the one started from the command line) or from a remote network source (such as `http` used by both Applets and Java WebStart).

Finally, ClassLoaders are also used to load resources. When using methods such as `class.getResource` or `class.getResourceAsStream`, the same set of `ClassLoader` steps occur, allowing code and resources to be loaded from the same place.

ClassLoaders and inheritance

The JVM actually uses multiple ClassLoaders while running Java programs. The **system ClassLoader** is used for most operations, which can be obtained from the `ClassLoader.getSystemClassLoader` method. This is an instance of `URLClassLoader`, with a set of URLs that correspond to the class path specified at launch time from the command line or the `CLASSPATH` environment variable.

A `ClassLoader` typically has a non-null **parent ClassLoader**. This is used to delegate requests that cannot be satisfied internally and for packages in the `java.*` namespace (which must come only from the boot classpath). The standard launcher also has an **extension ClassLoader** that is responsible for loading libraries from the `$JAVA_HOME/jre/lib/ext` directory.

As a result, when looking up a file or resource, the following locations are searched:

- If the class is in the `java.*` namespace, only the boot `ClassLoader` is searched
- The locations or JARs specified in the `-classpath` command-line argument or the `CLASSPATH` environment variable (loaded by the `AppClassLoader`)
- Libraries in `$JAVA_HOME/jre/lib/ext` (loaded by the `ExtClassLoader`)
- Fallback to the boot `ClassLoader`

The combination of these is known as the system ClassLoader, as illustrated in the following diagram:

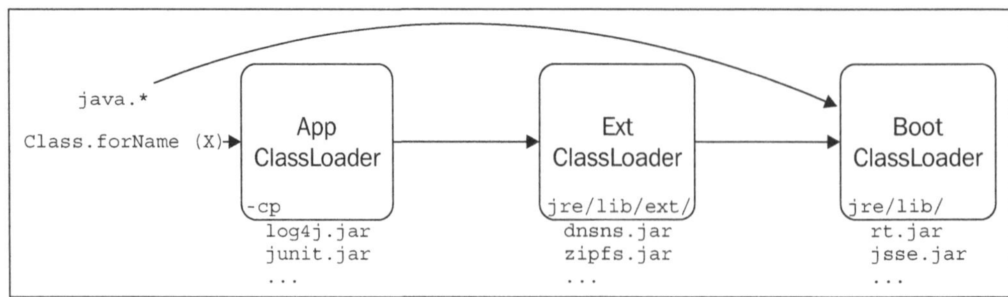

ClassLoaders in web application servers

ClassLoaders are heavily used in web application servers such as Tomcat, GlassFish, and Jetty (as well as their commercial counterparts). Each **Web ARchive (WAR)** installed onto a server has its own `WebappClassLoader`, which loads the webapp's classes and resources as well as delegating to the application servers and ultimately the system `ClassLoader`. As a result, two web applications can have independent resources and classes, and one cannot affect the other. This permits two web applications to use a different version of a common library, such as `log4j`, without any problems, as illustrated in the following diagram:

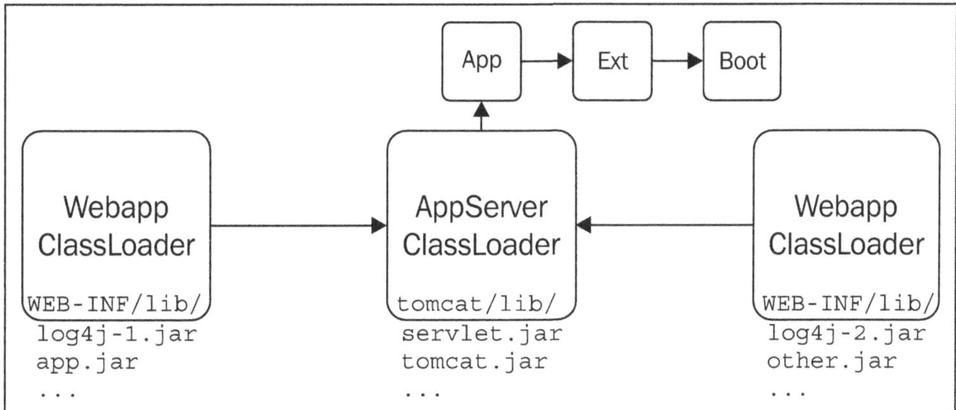

The standard Java platform performs a parent-first search for classes, but in web and enterprise application servers, the child-first search for classes allows independent web applications to load different versions of libraries.

In the context of the web application, both classes and resources are served from the web application's own ClassLoader, and they are distinct from classes loaded by other ClassLoaders.

Although some people incorrectly think that a class name is global within a JVM, the JVM specification (section 5.3) defines uniqueness as the class name *and* the instance of its `ClassLoader`. Without this ability, Java web application servers would not exist, and Java may never have made big inroads to the server side in the late 1990s.

ClassLoaders and garbage collection

One important feature of a `ClassLoader` is that it has a bi-directional relationship with the `Class` instances it has defined. In turn, the `Class` is referenced by every instance of that class, forming a tree of relationships between a set of instances and the `ClassLoader` that loaded them, as shown:

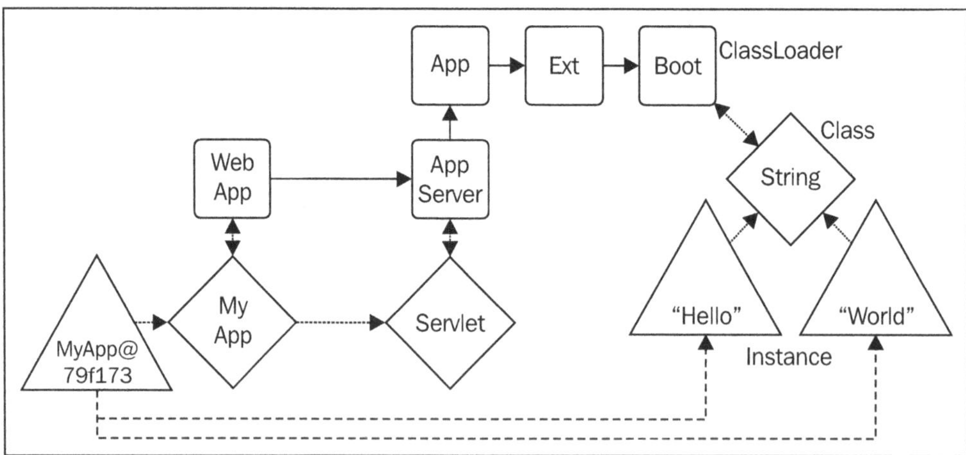

In this case, `MyApp` is a subclass of `Servlet`, whose `toString` method returns `MyApp@79f173`. It refers to two strings, `"Hello"` and `"World"`. Although this diagram may look complicated, it is a common occurrence in every web application server for these kinds of relationships to occur.

The `WebappClassLoader` is owned by the webapp server runtime, which ensures that it and the all classes it defines are pinned in memory so that they are not garbage collected. The `MyApp` servlet is referred to by the runtime as well so it is also not garbage collected.

However, when the webapp server decides that the application must be stopped (either through an administrative command or the WAR being deleted from the filesystem), the corresponding `WebappClassLoader` is released, and this can subsequently be garbage collected. Similarly, the classes it loaded are now no longer referenced and can be garbage collected in their own time.

If the webapp server decides to restart the webapp (for example, a new version has been installed), then a new `WebappClassLoader` instance is created and used to load content. Since the webapp server will route through URLs to the new `MyApp` servlet instance, it effectively means the webapp has been reloaded.

All Java applications that have a reloading ability do so using a per-context `ClassLoader`, then dropping it and instantiating a new one. Hudson/Jenkins, Gerrit, Webapps, OSGi, and other plug-in systems all use this technique.

There are also class redefinition tools, such as JRebel, but these use low-level JVM APIs that permit class redefinition.

OSGi and ClassLoaders

OSGi is a dynamic module system that uses multiple `ClassLoader` instances to provide module-level separation. Just like a webapp server will enforce separation between webapps, an OSGi runtime will enforce separation between bundles.

When a bundle is loaded and activated in an OSGi runtime, a new bundle ClassLoader is created. This is used for all class and resource lookups for classes in that bundle.

Unlike webapps, OSGi bundles are allowed to communicate with each other. As a result, the ClassLoaders form a directed graph to perform lookups between bundles. **Bundle wiring** is handled by the framework to arrange the graph of ClassLoaders, as shown in the following diagram:

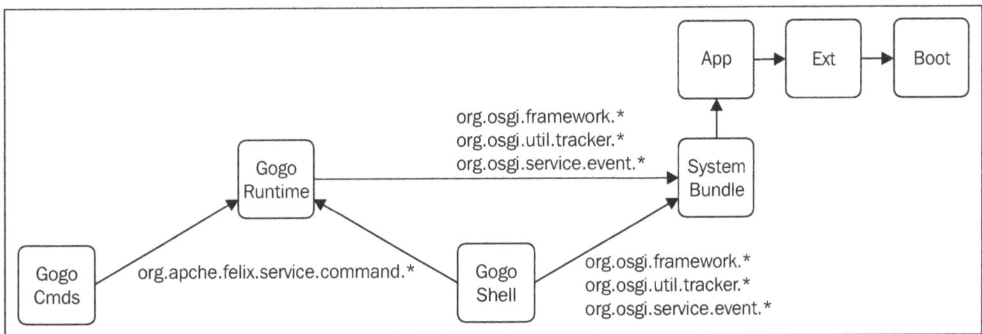

Bundle reloading occurs in the same way as it occurs for other Java applications —the `ClassLoader` is released and the associated instances are garbage collected. The bundle can be reloaded and a new `ClassLoader` is created.

OSGi `ClassLoader` lookups are more powerful than the standard Java lookups. Whereas standard Java lookups only have a single-parent hierarchy, the `ClassLoader` relationships in OSGi form a directed graph. When a request to load a class occurs, that is passed to potentially multiple parent bundles instead of a single parent. Typically, the package name (specified in an `Import-Package`) is used to filter requests, though for a generic `Require-Bundle` dependency all requests may be forwarded.

In the previous diagram, the Gogo Shell consumes classes from the `org.osgi.framework` package of the System Bundle, but `org.apache.felix.service.command` classes come from the Gogo Runtime bundle.

OSGi services and ClassLoaders

Once a `Class` has been loaded by a `ClassLoader`, it is cached for subsequent references. As a result, when looking up classes with `class.forName`, the implementation class is pinned to the requesting bundle's `ClassLoader`, and hence the lifetime of the bundle.

`class.forName` caches the resulting `Class` in the caller's `ClassLoader`. Callers using this tie the resulting `Class`' lifetime to that of the caller's context.

In an OSGi service reference, the API/interface class is pinned to the lifetime of the bundle using that service. However, the implementation class is supplied by the service API and is bound to the lifetime of the supplied service. As a result, the bundle that provides the service can be stopped and reloaded (with a new `ClassLoader` and therefore `Class`) and when the bundle next requests the service, the new implementation will be returned.

This is similar to the webapp servers that use `javax.servlet.http.HttpServlet` as the API/interface, and have the implementation class supplied by the webapp itself. By delegating the implementation class lookup to the webapp's individual `ClassLoader`, the server can cycle through different implementations of the same interface without leaking references.

Note that the instance returned by the OSGi service lookup is tightly coupled to its `Class`, and therefore `ClassLoader` of a bundle. Storing that instance will result in the bundle being pinned in memory, even if the bundle or service is stopped (or otherwise removed from the system). This is why OSGi provides the `ServiceReference` class, which can be stored persistently and then used to return a correct service instance via the `getService` factory method.

Bundles should only cache `ServiceReference` instances to refer to services, and not the actual service instance. The service can be resolved on demand with `getService`, or other techniques can be used instead such as Declarative Services, covered in *Chapter 3, Using OSGi Services to Dynamically Wire Applications*.

ThreadContextClassLoaders

When a class is requested (either implicitly through a class reference or explicitly with `class.forName`), the `ClassLoader` of the calling `Class` is used. This allows an `Applet` or an RMI-based application to refer to other classes that have been acquired from a remote site and ensure that they are downloaded from the same location as well.

However, libraries loaded from one `ClassLoader` cannot necessarily see classes loaded from another `ClassLoader`.

This often occurs with **Object Relational Mapping** (**ORM**) tools such as Hibernate that use configuration files that contain class names. To load the classes, it needs to resolve class names from the application's associated `ClassLoader`.

If the Hibernate library is installed in the same WAR as the webapp, this will be automatic. However, if Hibernate is stored in the webapp server's global classpath or an extension location, then it won't have visibility to the webapp's `ClassLoader`.

To solve this (specifically for the benefit of `RMIClassLoader`), Java 1.2 added a method to the `Thread` class to provide an additional `ClassLoader` that could be used as an extra source of classes called the **ThreadContextClassLoader** (**TCCL**). Each thread has its own unique instance, is accessed with `getContextClassLoader` and set with `setContextClassLoader`. Libraries such as Hibernate use this to resolve additional classes on demand, which they wouldn't otherwise be able to resolve through their own `ClassLoader`.

The context `ClassLoader` is inherited by newly created threads, which allows the context `ClassLoader` to be implicitly available in any executing class. However, it suffers while using `Executors` or other multi-threaded environments because it may not be the case that the initiating `Thread` is the same as the one that needs to subsequently load the class.

Setting the Thread Context `ClassLoader` usually takes the following form:

```
public void runWith(Runnable runnable, ClassLoader other) {
  final Thread current = Thread.currentThread();
  final ClassLoader tccl = current.getContextClassLoader();
  try {
    current.setContextClassLoader(other);
    runnable.run();
  } finally {
    current.setContextClassLoader(tccl);
  }
}
```

Note that this pattern explicitly expects the `runnable` to either be single-threaded, or that any multi-threaded pools will be instantiated during the call (and therefore will inherit the context `ClassLoader`). The Thread Context `ClassLoader` typically works in constrained environments such as webapp and enterprise Java servers since they own the threading and have full control of the life cycle of the applications. They do not work as well in more dynamic environments like OSGi.

Some open source libraries require the use of the Thread Context `ClassLoader` to operate correctly; however, many have been upgraded to take an explicit `ClassLoader` instead of attempting to load everything via the context loader.

Alternatively, mapping tools can be passed explicit `Class` instances, which avoids problems with resolving the `Class` in the first place. For example, `Gson` is used to deserialize a class from a JSON representation and to do so is passed a `Class` instance rather than the name of a class.

Note that Hibernate has been upgraded to support OSGi since version 4.2, and provides an `EntityManagerFactory` as an OSGi service.

Java ServiceLoader

The **ServiceLoader** class in the `java.util` package (added in Java 1.6) provides a means of acquiring an instance of an interface or abstract class. It is used by a variety of different parts in the JDK, where a single implementation is required that cannot be known in advance, such as JDBC drivers.

The `ServiceLoader` class provides a static `load` method that can be used to return a `ServiceLoader`, which in turn provides an `Iterator` over all services available:

```
ServiceLoader<Driver> sl = ServiceLoader.load(Driver.class);
Iterator<Driver> it = sl.iterator();
while (it.hasNext()) {
  Driver driver = (Driver) it.next();
  // do something with driver
}
```

The implementation class for the driver is found by consulting a text file, located under the `META-INF/services/` directory. When looking for implementations for the `java.sql.Driver` class, the service loader will attempt to find files called `META-INF/services/java.sql.Driver`. The contents of these files are fully qualified class names of services that implement the specified interface.

The file may also contain comments, and any whitespace or content after # is ignored; for example:

```
# File is META-INF/services/java.sql.Driver
org.h2.Driver                       # H2 database driver
org.mariadb.jdbc.Driver             # Maria DB driver
org.apache.derby.jdbc.ClientDriver # Apache Derby driver
```

When the `ServiceLoader.load` method is called with a `Driver.class` argument, the three classes will be instantiated and returned in the iterator, in the order that they appear in the file. Any duplicates from this file or from other matching files are filtered from the list.

Problems with ServiceLoader, OSGi, and Eclipse

Although the `ServiceLoader` provides a general mechanism to return instances of classes based on their interface type, there are the three specific problems that prevent its general use with OSGi:

- The implementation class is loaded with `class.forName`, which caches the class in the caller's `ClassLoader`. This prevents the service implementation from being reloaded.
- The `META-INF/services/` folder is not a package, so it cannot be referred to with the normal `Import-Package` OSGi semantics. In addition, the package name (directory) can only be exported by a single bundle, so even if this could be used, it would not be possible to bind to more than one provider.
- The loader for the service is typically taken from the current Thread Context `ClassLoader`, and in OSGi, the calling class is unlikely to have visibility to the implementation package (and in any case, explicitly importing the implementation class defeats the point of having the class unknown until load time).

To solve these problems, the OSGi Enterprise Specification Release 5 provides the **Service Loader Mediator**, implemented by the Apache Aries **SPI-Fly** bundle. This provides the following two key features:

- For consumers, it uses bytecode weaving that can dynamically rewrite `ServiceLoader.load` calls to a more OSGi-appropriate implementation
- For providers, it automatically registers implementations defined in any `META-INF/services` files as OSGi services

In both cases, the consumer and producer need to opt-in explicitly through the use of entries in the MANIFEST.MF to ensure that bundles are weaved (or not) on demand. The weaving bundle org.apache.aries.spifly.dynamic.bundle also needs to be installed and started prior to any consumers starting.

> The org.apache.aries.spifly.dynamic.bundle needs org.apache.aries.util to resolve, and org.objectweb.asm-all to perform the bytecode weaving. It is possible to pre-weave a bundle using org.apache.aries.spifly.static.bundle as documented on the home page at http://aries.apache.org/modules/spi-fly.html.

Creating a service producer

Create a plug-in project called com.packtpub.e4.advanced.loader.producer. This does not need an Activator and will be a standard OSGi bundle that targets **Standard OSGi**.

Create a class in the com.packtpub.e4.advanced.loader.producer package called HelloWorldRunnable that implements Runnable:

```
package com.packtpub.e4.advanced.loader.producer;
public class HelloWorldRunnable implements Runnable {
  public void run() {
    System.out.println("Hello World");
  }
}
```

Create a META-INF/services/java.lang.Runnable file with the following content in order to register it as a service for the ServiceLoader:

```
com.packtpub.e4.advanced.loader.producer.HelloWorldRunnable
```

This is enough for the ServiceLoader to find it with ServiceLoader.load, but in order for it to work in an OSGi runtime, the bundle needs to have additional OSGi metadata. Add the following to the META-INF/MANIFEST.MF file:

```
Require-Capability:
 osgi.extender;
  filter:="(osgi.extender=osgi.serviceloader.registrar)"
```

This expresses a dependency on the OSGi Service Loader Mediator (provided by SPI-Fly). If this dependency is missing, the bundle will fail to resolve.

By default, all services under the `META-INF/services/` directory will be made available. If a single service type should be exported, it can be expressed with `Provide-Capability` on the `osgi.serviceloader`:

```
Provide-Capability:
 osgi.serviceloader;osgi.serviceloader=java.lang.Runnable
```

Multiple instances of the same interface need no extra configuration lines; all of the instances in the `java.lang.Runnable` file will be exported. If there are multiple service types (in other words, multiple files under the `META-INF/services/` directory), they can be represented as follows:

```
Provide-Capability:
 osgi.serviceloader;osgi.serviceloader=java.lang.Runnable,
 osgi.serviceloader;osgi.serviceloader=java.util.Comparator
```

Downloading the required bundles

To run the producer, some prerequisite bundles must be acquired. These can be downloaded from Maven Central or from the book's GitHub repository at `https://github.com/alblue/com.packtpub.e4.advanced/`.

The necessary bundles are as follows:

- `asm` (for byte-code weaving), which can be downloaded from `https://repo1.maven.org/maven2/org/ow2/asm/asm-all/4.0/asm-all-4.0.jar`
- `aries.util` (dependency for the `spifly` bundle), which can be downloaded from `https://repo1.maven.org/maven2/org/apache/aries/org.apache.aries.util/1.0.0/org.apache.aries.util-1.0.0.jar`
- `aries.spifly.dynamic` (provides the Service Loader Mediator), which can be downloaded from `https://repo1.maven.org/maven2/org/apache/aries/spifly/org.apache.aries.spifly.dynamic.bundle/1.0.0/org.apache.aries.spifly.dynamic.bundle-1.0.0.jar`

Import these into the Eclipse workspace by navigating to **File** | **Import** | **Plug-in Development** | **Plug-ins and Fragments**, and then choose the directory that the prerequisite bundles have been downloaded into, as illustrated in the following screenshots:

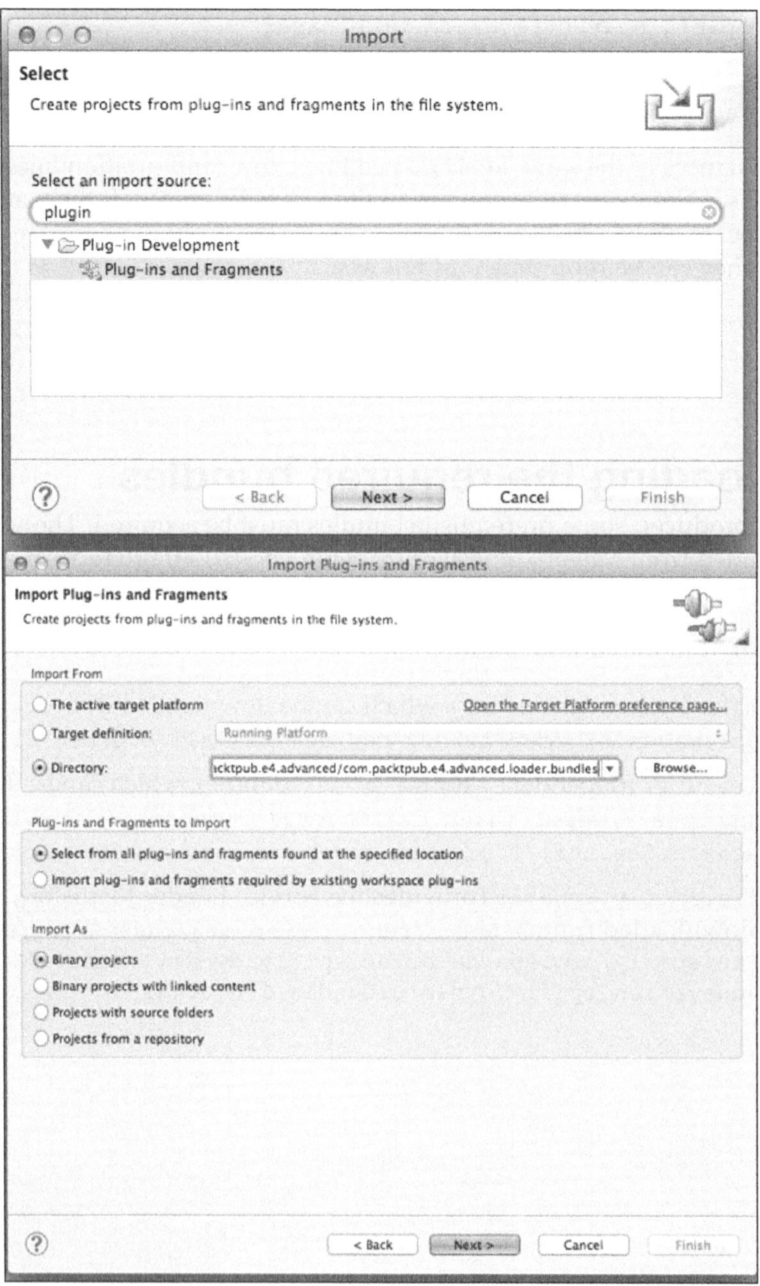

Click on **Next** and select all of the available bundles by choosing **Add All**, followed by **Finish**:

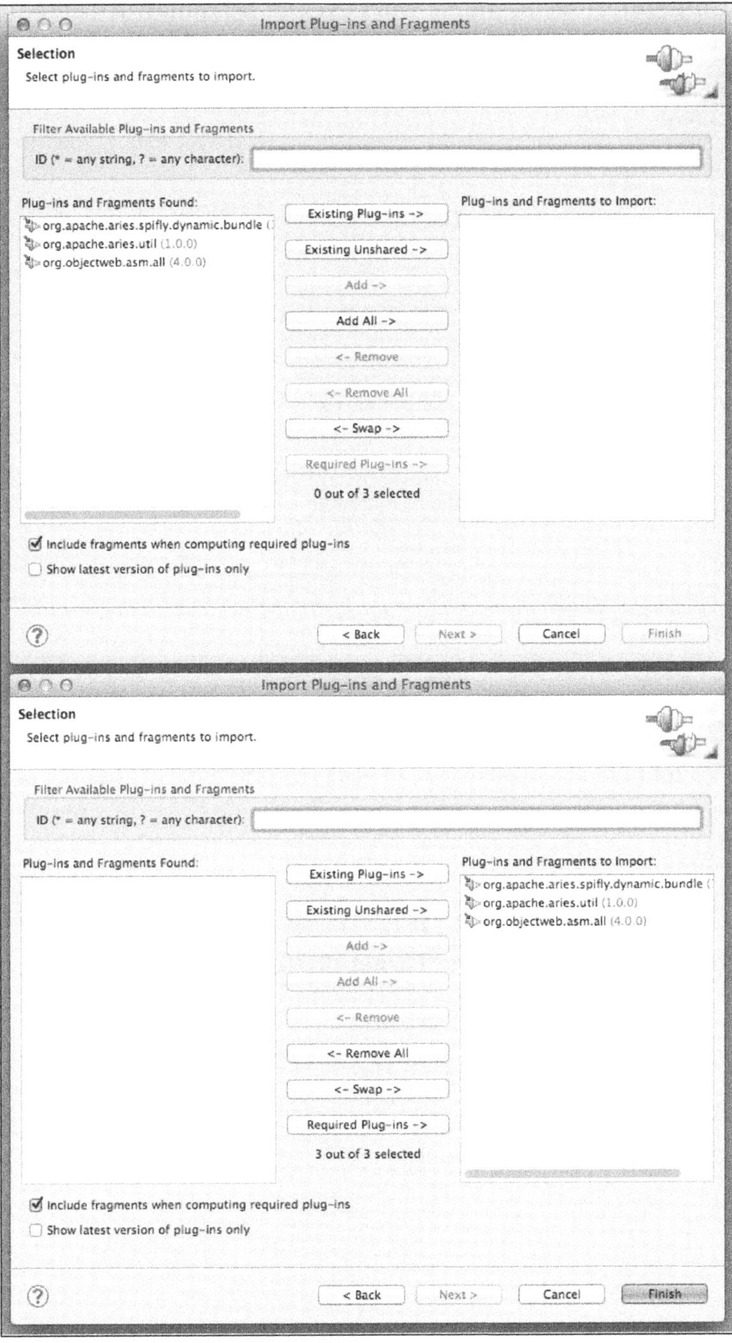

Running the producer

To run the producer, create a new Launch Configuration by navigating to **Run | Run Configurations ...** menu. Click on **OSGi Framework** and hit the **New** button to create a new configuration called `ServiceLoader Producer Only`:

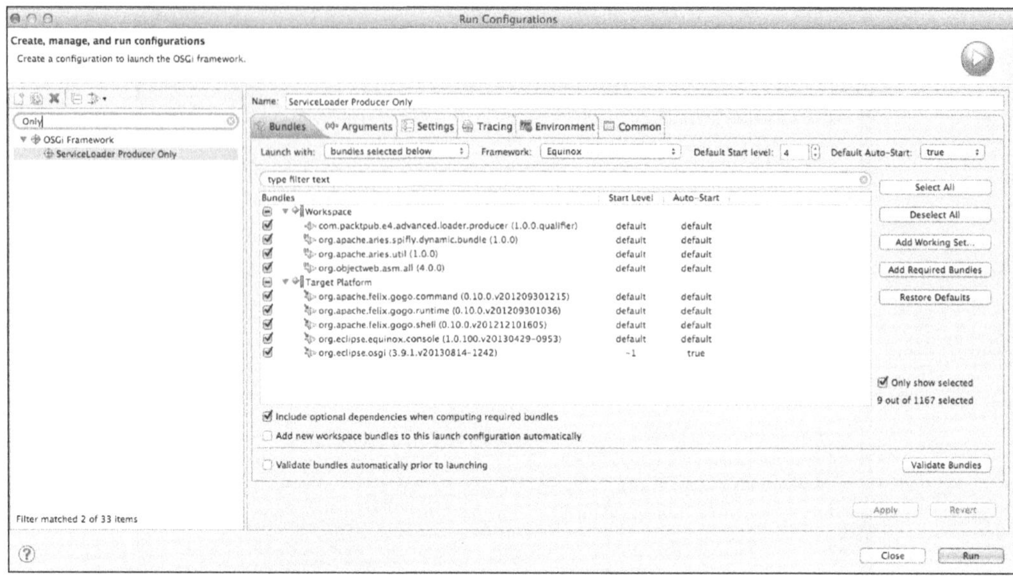

Add the following bundles from the **Workspace**:

- `com.packtpub.e4.advanced.loader.producer`
- `org.apache.aries.spifly.dynamic.bundle`
- `org.apache.aries.util`
- `org.objectweb.asm`

Add the following bundles from the **Target Platform**:

- `org.apache.felix.gogo.command`
- `org.apache.felix.gogo.runtime`
- `org.apache.felix.gogo.shell`
- `org.eclipse.equinox.console`
- `org.eclipse.osgi`

Run the framework by clicking on **Run**.

Using the console, look at the producer bundle. It should declare that it has registered the `Runnable` instance as an OSGi service:

```
osgi> ss | grep producer
4 ACTIVE com.packtpub.e4.advanced.loader.producer_1.0.0.qualifier
osgi> bundle 4
com.packtpub.e4.advanced.loader.producer_1.0.0.qualifier [4]
 Id=4, Status=ACTIVE
 "Registered Services"
 {java.lang.Runnable}={
  .org.apache.aries.spifly.provider.implclass=
  com.packtpub.e4.advanced.loader.producer.HelloWorldRunnable,
  serviceloader.mediator=7, service.id=46}
```

In this case, the `serviceloader.mediator` service property is `7`, and bundle `7` is the SPI-Fly implementation:

```
osgi> bundle 7
org.apache.aries.spifly.dynamic.bundle_1.0.0 [7]
```

Creating a service consumer

Create another plug-in project called `com.packtpub.e4.advanced.consumer`, this time with an `Activator` that looks like the following code:

```
package com.packtpub.e4.advanced.loader.consumer;
import java.util.ServiceLoader;
import org.osgi.framework.BundleActivator;
import org.osgi.framework.BundleContext;
public class Activator implements BundleActivator {
  public void start(BundleContext context) throws Exception {
    ServiceLoader<Runnable> sl=ServiceLoader.load(Runnable.class);
    Runnable runnable = sl.iterator().next();
    runnable.run();
  }
  public void stop(BundleContext context) throws Exception {
  }
}
```

When the bundle starts, the `Activator` will look for implementations of the `Runnable` interface, and then `run` them. The `iterator.next` method will fail if there are no implementations available, which will prevent the consumer bundle from starting if a `Runnable` instance cannot be found.

When run, the bundle fails because the client has not been processed to hook the `ServiceLoader.load` call to look for OSGi specific services.

To fix this, the consumer bundle needs to register the following as a generic capability in the `META-INF/MANIFEST.MF` file:

```
Require-Capability:
 osgi.extender;
  filter:="(osgi.extender=osgi.serviceloader.processor)"
```

This ensures there is a processor present, and calls to `ServiceLoader.load` will be replaced with a call to an appropriate OSGi handler routine. Now, when the client bundle is started, `Hello World` should be printed out when the framework starts up.

As with the producer, it is possible to constrain the consumer such that it only allows lookup for implementations of a specific interface:

```
Require-Capability:
 osgi.extender;
  filter:="(osgi.extender=osgi.serviceloader.processor)",
 osgi.serviceloader;
  filter:="(osgi.serviceloader=java.lang.Runnable)";
  cardinality:=multiple
```

Also, as with the producer, if multiple services are required, then these can be added by adding additional `osgi.serviceloader` capability requirements.

The filter should not be used to represent a disjunction or a conjunction of filters, which would either say "An instance that satisfies either X or Y" or "An instance that satisfies both X and Y."

Instead, there needs to be two separate requirement constraints, the bundle needs X and the bundle needs Y. For example, to require both a `Runnable` and a `List`:

```
Require-Capability:
 osgi.extender;
  filter:="(osgi.extender=osgi.serviceloader.processor)",
 osgi.serviceloader;
  filter:="(osgi.serviceloader=java.lang.Runnable)";
```

```
  cardinality:=multiple
 osgi.serviceloader;
  filter:="(osgi.serviceloader=java.util.List)";
  cardinality:=multiple
```

Should the bundle import and export individual constraints for each service? An argument against this is that it makes the bundle manifest more complex, and when adding additional services, the manifest needs to be updated as well.

On the other hand, if entries are added, then it is possible for a resolution tool to determine whether this code requires a `Runnable` instance, and this requires finding a bundle that explicitly provides a `Runnable` instance.

If there is only one service that is exposed or used by a bundle, having additional requirement constraints can be a good way of documenting the available services.

Running the consumer

To run the consumer, create a new Launch Configuration by navigating to **Run** | **Run Configurations ...** menu. Click on **OSGi Framework** and hit the **New** button to create a new configuration called `ServiceLoader Producer And Consumer`:

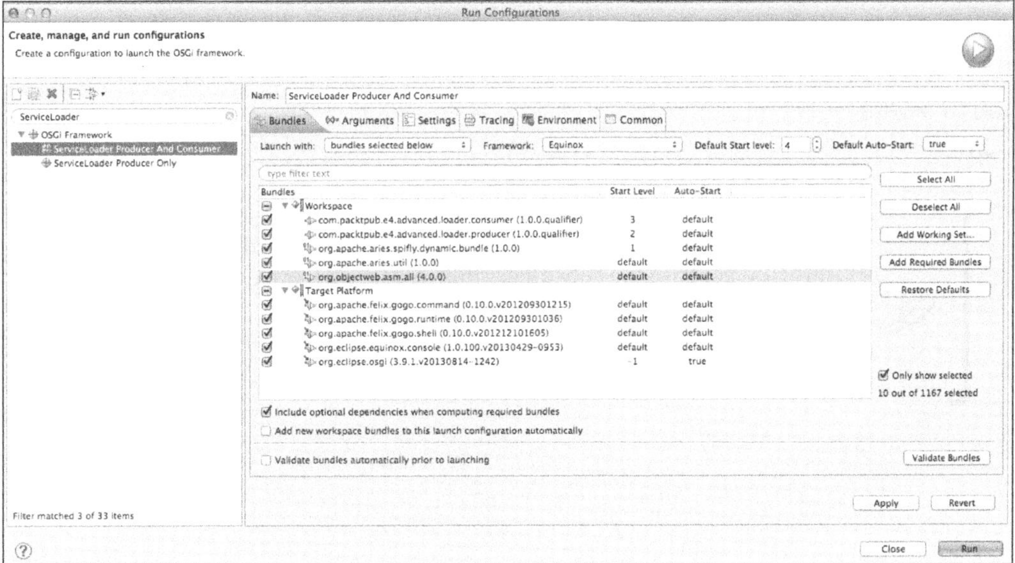

Add the following bundles from the **Workspace**:

- `com.packtpub.e4.advanced.loader.consumer` (start level 3)
- `com.packtpub.e4.advanced.loader.producer` (start level 2)
- `org.apache.aries.spifly.dynamic.bundle` (start level 1)
- `org.apache.aries.util`
- `org.objectweb.asm`

In this case, the producer is started first so that when the consumer starts, there is a `Runnable` instance to acquire. The `spifly` bundle needs to be started before the consumer so that it has the chance to rewrite the consumer's loading by replacing calls to `ServiceLoader` with the appropriate OSGi calls.

Add the following bundles from the **Target Platform**:

- `org.apache.felix.gogo.command`
- `org.apache.felix.gogo.runtime`
- `org.apache.felix.gogo.shell`
- `org.eclipse.equinox.console`
- `org.eclipse.osgi`

Run the framework by clicking on **Run**. It should display `Hello World` in the console as the client bundle is activated and acquires the registered producer service:

```
Hello World
osgi>
```

Unlike the standalone producer service, start levels are needed in this case because the consumer runs its service loader code at bundle start-up in the `Activator` class.

Depending on explicit start-ordering is not good practice in an OSGi runtime, and generally this represents a code smell.

OSGi upgrade strategies

While many open source libraries already natively support OSGi, there are still some that do not have the required metadata added by default. Fortunately, there are a number of strategies that can be used to enable the libraries to be used in OSGi runtimes such as Eclipse, or repositories such as Eclipse Orbit (`http://eclipse.org/orbit/`) that contain corrected bundles.

Embedding the library directly

If the library is only needed in one bundle, then the most expedient mechanism is to embed the JAR(s) into that bundle. Since all libraries in a bundle share the same classpath, this allows the library to run without being aware of the fact that it is running in an OSGi environment. This can be done by embedding the JAR into the bundle and using a `Bundle-ClassPath` header that refers to the library:

```
Bundle-ClassPath: .,lib/example.jar
```

Note that the dot (`.`) must be present if the bundle itself contains classes, or to enable other resources to be loaded. This approach works well for Hibernate (before version 4.2) or other ORM tools that do not work well with multiple ClassLoaders.

With an embedded library, it is also possible to export a subset of packages made visible by the library itself. This allows only the public API to be exposed while hiding the internal API from users.

Embedding a library is an expedient way of testing the bundle without having to rebuild the JAR. Sometimes, it is useful if the library is signed or cannot be changed, as mutating a signed JAR leads to problems in the Eclipse runtime.

Note that embedded JARs are slightly less performant, as the JAR needs to be extracted from the library at runtime and made available on the filesystem in order to load resources from it. As a result, this is not the preferred way to solve the problem.

Wrapping the library with bnd

An extension to merely embedding, wrapping the library also adds additional `Export-Package` and `Import-Package` headers to allow the library to resolve. This permits other bundles to import packages exported by the library bundle and use it as a standard library.

If the library is minimal, the bundle's manifest can be calculated manually. However, it is more efficient to use an automated tool such as **bnd**, which can be downloaded from Maven Central at `https://repo1.maven.org/maven2/biz/aQute/bnd/bnd/2.2.0/bnd-2.2.0.jar`.

The bnd tool allows a JAR to be processed and entries for the used `Import-Package` and `Export-Package` calculated based on the contents of the classes. It is used indirectly by most of the build tools to generate valid OSGi metadata.

As an example, consider upgrading `commons-logging-1.0.4`, available from `https://repo1.maven.org/maven2/commons-logging/commons-logging/1.0.4/commons-logging-1.0.4.jar`.

> Note that `commons-logging` Version 1.1 and above already have support for OSGi, and they should be used instead for Java applications. The older version is being used to demonstrate how to add OSGi metadata to a publicly available library that doesn't already have it.

The bnd tool provides a means to print an existing JAR's manifest:

```
$ java -jar bnd-2.2.0.jar commons-logging-1.0.4.jar
[MANIFEST commons-logging-1.0.4]
Ant-Version              Apache Ant 1.5.3
Created-By               Blackdown-1.3.1_02b-FCS
Extension-Name           org.apache.commons.logging
Implementation-Vendor    Apache Software Foundation
Implementation-Version   1.0.4
Manifest-Version         1.0
Specification-Vendor     Apache Software Foundation
Specification-Version    1.0
```

In this case, it can be seen that it does not have any OSGi data associated with it. There is no `Bundle-SymbolicName` or `Bundle-ManifestVersion`.

The bnd tool can calculate the set of required dependencies with the `wrap` command:

```
$ java -jar bnd-2.2.0.jar wrap
  --output commons-logging-1.0.4.osgi.jar
  --bsn commons-logging
  commons-logging-1.0.4.jar
-----------------
Warnings
000: Using defaults for wrap, which means no export versions
$ java -jar bnd-2.2.0.jar print commons-logging-1.0.4.osgi.jar
```

```
[MANIFEST commons-logging-1.0.4.osgi]
Ant-Version              Apache Ant 1.5.3
Bnd-LastModified         1390176259029
Bundle-ManifestVersion 2
Bundle-Name              commons-logging
Bundle-SymbolicName      commons-logging
Bundle-Version           0
Created-By               1.7.0_45
Export-Package
 org.apache.commons.logging,
 org.apache.commons.logging.impl;
  uses:="org.apache.avalon.framework.logger,
    org.apache.commons.logging,org.apache.log,org.apache.log4j"
Extension-Name           org.apache.commons.logging
Implementation-Vendor    Apache Software Foundation
Implementation-Version 1.0.4
Import-Package
 org.apache.avalon.framework.logger;resolution:=optional,
 org.apache.log;resolution:=optional,
 org.apache.log4j;resolution:=optional
Manifest-Version         1.0
Originally-Created-By    Blackdown-1.3.1_02b-FCS
Specification-Vendor     Apache Software Foundation
Specification-Version    1.0
Tool                     Bnd-2.2.0.20130927-173453
```

The generated bundle can now be installed in an OSGi environment. Although this provides a starting point for wrapping a non-OSGi bundle, typically the manifest will require additional adjustments. In this case, the `org.apache.log4j` package may be a non-optional dependency of the `commons-logging` interface and so should be updated; in addition, the `Bundle-Version` should really be `1.0.4` to correspond to the original version of the upstream JAR. Additional operations can be supplied on the `bnd` command line or by providing an additional `.bnd` configuration file. Documentation is available at the Bnd homepage at `http://www.aqute.biz/Bnd/Bnd`.

Bnd can also be used to add additional metadata to the bundle, such as headers to enable Declarative Services (covered in *Chapter 3, Using OSGi Services to Dynamically Wire Applications*) or service mediator requirements (see the *Java ServiceLoader* section earlier in this chapter).

Upgrading the library to use services

Many libraries are pure library code; they provide no implementation or services for consumers. These can often be wrapped/exported to provide packages for other bundles to depend upon.

However, if the library is expected to provide a service, there may be an advantage in exposing this as an OSGi service. That way, other OSGi bundles can depend on the service itself rather than a particular provider of that service.

The easiest way to publish services is to use either Declarative Services or Blueprint (see *Chapter 3, Using OSGi Services to Dynamically Wire Applications*, for more details). By adding the appropriate service XML files and adding the right manifest headers, no code needs to be written and the library can publish services automatically. When used in combination with Config Admin, the library can have new services published or updated as configuration data changes without needing to write any code.

Dealing with class resolution issues

Most libraries do not need to refer to class names directly. However, a subset of them will need to look up classes, typically if they are doing deserialization or parsing from a database or stream. There are four ways to handle this:

- Pass in `Class` instances instead of class names into the library. This is the most portable way of resolving the problem, and this works for many APIs, especially those using annotations to expose information.
- Pass in a `ClassLoader` along with the class names, which can be acquired from the calling bundle's context. This will allow the library to acquire classes from the correct `ClassLoader`.
- Wrap calls to the library with an appropriate `threadContextClassLoader` set. This is likely to be the least efficient way of solving the problem but may at least allow a library to work in some situations.
- Add `DynamicImport-Package:*` to the library. This will allow the library to wire up dependencies as it attempts to look them up. This will also prevent bundle re-loading in the same VM as it will pin the version of the client to the library. This is not recommended as a general practice; use this only as a last resort.

If none of the mentioned ways are appropriate, consider using a different library. Some libraries are sufficiently broken that they cannot be used in a dynamic environment such as Eclipse or OSGi. It is quite likely that the same problems will exist for these kinds of libraries in other multiple `ClassLoader` environments such as web application servers.

Summary

In this chapter, we looked at how OSGi's use of `ClassLoader`s permits bundle separation, and what effect that has on libraries that mistakenly assume there is only one `ClassLoader` per JVM. We also looked at how to upgrade such libraries so that they can run in an OSGi environment, and how to avoid such problems in the first place.

In the next chapter, we'll look at how to design applications in a modular way, building upon the material covered up to this point.

7
Designing Modular Applications

This chapter will present some common techniques and design patterns that are used to implement modular applications with OSGi. It starts by introducing the concept of semantic versioning, which is a key part of how bundles and packages are versioned, followed by how **baselining** can be used to enable automatic version incrementing. This is then followed by an overview of some of the **design patterns** common in OSGi applications, including the benefits they present, and finally finishes with a list of **best practices** in OSGi.

Semantic versioning

A key aspect of OSGi bundles and packages is that they are versioned using **semantic versioning**. This encodes compatibility into the version number so that clients can select an appropriately versioned component to build against or bind to.

Semantic versioning breaks down a number such as `1.2.3.RELEASE` into the following four parts:

- **Major version**: This is a number that indicates the major release (`1`)
- **Minor version**: This is a number that indicates the minor release (`2`)
- **Micro (or patch) version**: This is a number that indicates the micro (patch) release (`3`)
- **Qualifier**: This is a textual string that indicates the patch (`RELEASE`)

This version numbering scheme is used by every Java JAR in Maven Central and can be used to determine whether or not upgrading to a later version will be compatible. Numbers default to `0` if they are not specified, and the qualifier defaults to an empty string. In OSGi, numbers are sorted numerically and the qualifier is sorted alphabetically.

Changes in **major** version numbers are deemed to be **incompatible changes**. Thus, a client that depends on `commons-collections-1.0` might not be able to upgrade directly to `2.0`. In a major change, it is expected that there will be backward compatibility problems, such as renaming entire packages or removing methods or classes that used to exist.

Changes in the **minor** version are expected to be **backward compatible**, but with new functionality. For example, clients that are built and tested against `commons-collections-2.0` might expect to be able to upgrade to `commons-collections-2.1` without recompilation. Changes that are backward compatible include adding new classes or new packages, or for interfaces or classes that are not designed to be implemented or subclassed, adding new methods. In Java 8, adding new `default` methods is considered a backward compatible change.

Changes in the **micro** version are deemed to be backward compatible without any change in the API. These are incremented when bug fixes are performed. Note that a bug fix by definition includes user visible behavior (the bug existed before, but not afterwards), but this does not usually mean a change in the API or the contract. If the contract or API is changed to accommodate a bug fix, then the appropriate version numbers should be incremented.

Finally, the **qualifier** is used to encode optional metadata, such as the state or quality of the release (for example, `M1`, `RC2`, or `RELEASE`) or a date or timestamp (such as `201408171400`).

Semantic versioning also suggests that initial development starts with a major version of `0` and that until the major version reaches `1`, the content is in flux. Although not strictly recognized by OSGi, it is a common convention that others tend to use.

M1 stands for Milestone 1 and RC2 stands for Release Candidate 2. These can be compared lexicographically along with Release, since Mx < RCx < RELEASE.

Public APIs and version ranges

When making changes to a bundle, the appropriate segment of the version number should be incremented. If the API doesn't change, then clearly just the micro version should be updated. However, if there's new functionality, then the minor version should be updated, and the major version should be updated for backward incompatible changes.

But what is a backward incompatible change? It depends on what the change is. For example, a new method on an interface called by clients is a minor change since it's new functionality, the interface will be a subset of the previous version. However, if the client is expected to implement the interface, then adding a new method would cause a break in clients, because classes that implemented the interface would no longer compile.

This happens in Java periodically; for example, the JDBC `Connection` interface had a `createBlob` method added in Java 1.6 and a `getSchema` method added in Java 1.7. For clients that call the `Connection` class, the behavior remains the same, but for providers who must implement the class, the change requires more work.

> When a client is a **consumer** of an interface, it should import up to the next major version number such as `[1.2,2)`. When a client is a **provider** of an interface, it should import up to the next minor version `[1.2,1.3)`. This allows consumers to accept new functionality but requires implementors to verify and rebuild when the minor version changes.

Baselining and automatic versioning

There are several different implementations that allow version numbers to be automatically incremented. At its simplest, `maven-release-plugin` allows the micro version to be incremented on each release, with the expectation that the developer team will take care of incrementing minor and major version numbers as appropriate.

For automated semantic versioning, there has to be a way of performing a comparison against the prior release in order to know whether the public API has changed in any significant way. This generally takes one of two forms: either the version being built has to be compared against a "last known built" JAR or the latest version needs to be acquired from a repository automatically.

These versions are known as **baselines**, and the mechanism to acquire or refer to them is tool-specific. However, the general principle involves setting a baseline (if it can't be acquired automatically) and then, after each build, comparing the build with the baseline for any changes in the API.

> Note that processes that force you to decide/plan on the version number at the start of the cycle are flawed; you generally don't know until you near the end of the life cycle whether you should be releasing packages with a micro, minor, or major increment. You might plan to have just a micro release, but if it involves extending the API, then it should be promoted to a minor release instead. Such rigid processes are inherently flawed by design and violate semantic versioning by diktat.

Eclipse API baselines

Tools exist to help automate the management of versions based on the publicly exposed APIs of a project. Eclipse has the concept of an **API Baseline**, which can be created from a directory of a set of bundles.

Export the bundles in the `com.packtpub.e4.advanced.feeds` and `ui` projects by navigating to **File** | **Export** | **Plug-in Development** | **Deployable plug-ins and fragments** to a location on the filesystem. This will be used to record a baseline.

An API baseline can be created by navigating to **Preferences** | **Plug-in Development** | **API Baselines** and clicking on the **Add Baseline** button. This asks for the directory the bundles were exported to earlier, as shown in the following screenshot:

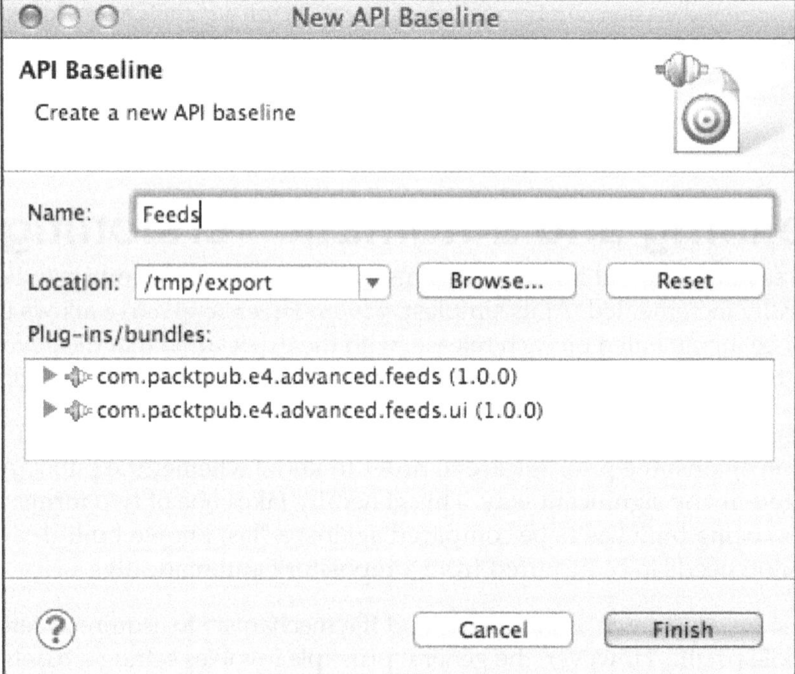

Clicking on **Reset** (to scan the directory) followed by **Finish** will set up the baseline:

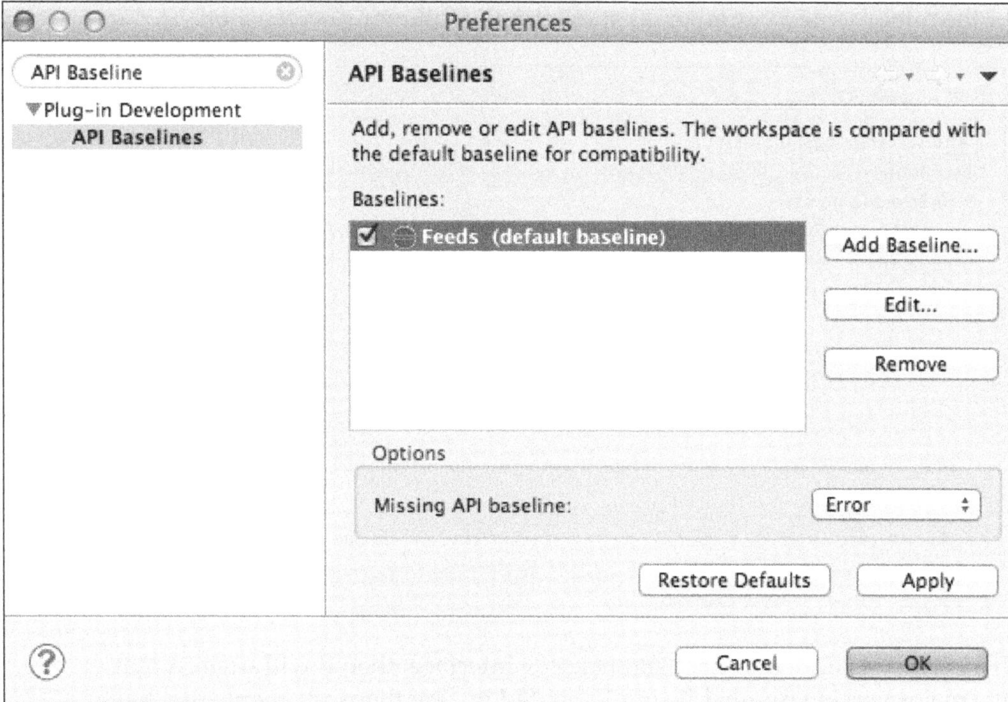

Once a baseline has been created, it can be associated with projects. Right-click on the `feeds` and `feeds.ui` projects, and navigate to **Plug-in Tools | API Tools Setup**. The `org.eclipse.pde.api.tools.apiAnalysisNature/Builder` will be added to the `.project` file, although the baseline itself will only be stored in the developer's workspace.

Now when methods are added to the existing classes or interfaces, the API tooling will suggest the addition of `@since` documentation tags and update the bundle version accordingly.

If methods are added to a class (such as the `newMethod` added to the `FeedParserFactory` class), then the API baselining will suggest a bump of the minor version number, as shown in the following screenshot:

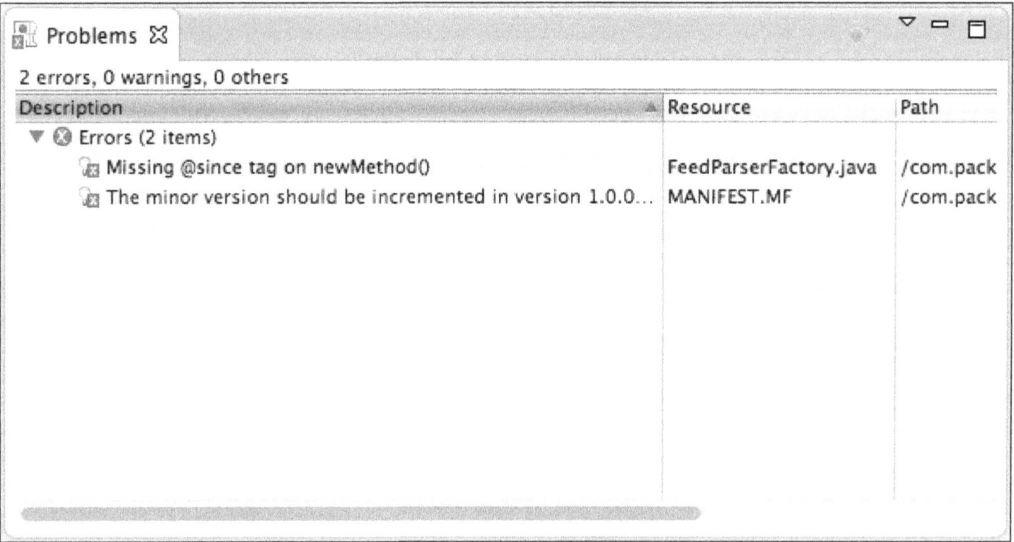

If a method is added to the `IFeedParser` interface, then it will suggest that the major version number be implemented in case there are clients that have implemented the interface:

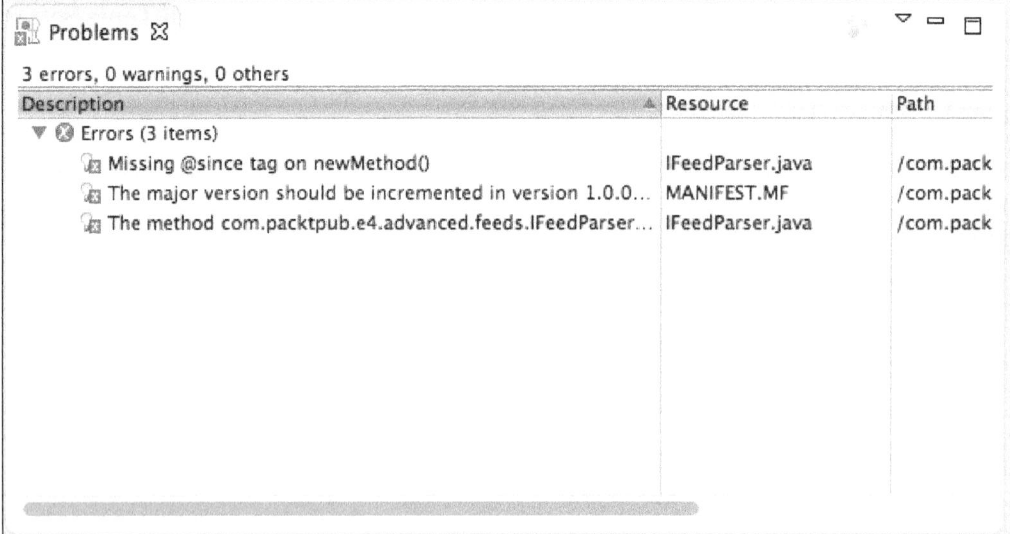

If the interface was intended as an API and not as a class that clients can implement, adding the Eclipse-specific `@noimplement` JavaDoc tag will suggest a minor version instead of a major version change.

Bnd baseline

The Bnd tool is a bundle processing tool written by Peter Kriens and is available both as a runtime class and an embeddable library. It has a means to perform baselining by comparing two JARs with each other and determining whether the publicly visible API has changed. It compares the version of the JAR with the previous version given:

```
$ java -jar bnd-2.2.0.jar baseline <newjar> <oldjar>
  Package                             Delta New   Old   Suggest
* com.packtpub.e4.advanced.feeds      MINOR 0.0.0 0.0.0 0.1.0
* com.packtpub.e4.advanced.feeds.ui   MAJOR 0.0.0 0.0.0 1.0.0
```

Note that Bnd will provide package-level versioning advice as opposed to bundle-level versioning. Generally, the bundle version should be incremented so that if a package's major version is changed, then the bundle's major version is incremented, and if a package's minor version is changed, then the bundle's minor version is incremented. The micro version should be incremented each time a change is made.

More information about Bnd can be found at the project's home page, which is at `http://www.aqute.biz/Bnd/`, as well as at the source repository at `https://github.com/bnd/`. The bnd baselining operation is also used by `baseline-maven-plugin` and `maven-bundle-plugin`.

Bndtools

Bndtools (hosted at `http://bndtools.org`) is an IDE plug-in for Eclipse that builds around the Bnd format. It creates projects and maps dependencies in a way that will be familiar to Eclipse users, but it does so using the `.bnd` file for dependencies and wiring instead of using the `.classpath` or `MANIFEST.MF` files.

In addition to compiling bundles, Bndtools automatically baselines bundles based on its internal repository. Bndtools creates a project called `cnf` (an abbreviation for `configuration`) which it uses to store the configuration and repository for the local workspace.

When a Bndtools release is performed, it will recommend any updates for the bundles, based on either the specified version in the .bnd file or the latest released version in the repository. Suggestions, if any, are given in the dialog when the release is performed:

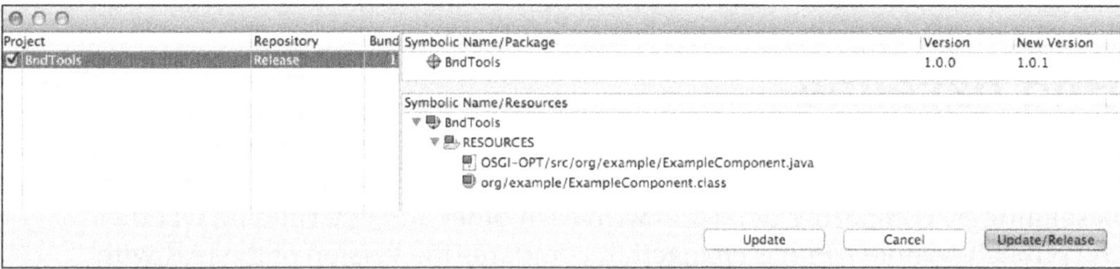

Maven baselining

A number of Maven plug-ins have been created to assist with incrementing the version number of a project based on the most recently released version. These usually take the form of a plug-in that is added to the pom.xml Maven build to automatically check whether the version number should be increased, similar to the way in which a JUnit test is used that runs and cause failures if the code is faulty.

The maven-bundle-plugin, a standard to build bundles with Maven, has been able to generate baselining reports since version 2.5.0. The baseline goal can be added to trigger a build failure if the version number needs to be incremented in comparison to the last published build. A baseline-report goal is also provided to show information about what needs to be updated.

To enable this for a Maven project, add the following to the pom.xml file:

```
<plugin>
  <groupId>org.apache.felix</groupId>
  <artifactId>maven-bundle-plugin</artifactId>
  <version>2.5.0</version>
  <extensions>true</extensions>
  <executions>
    <execution>
      <id>bundle</id>
      <phase>package</phase>
      <goals>
        <goal>bundle</goal>
      </goals>
   </execution>
```

```
      <execution>
        <id>baseline</id>
        <phase>package</phase>
        <goals>
          <goal>baseline</goal>
        </goals>
      </execution>
    </executions>
  </plugin>
```

When the Maven project is built, it will report any errors in comparison to the prior version available in the repository:

```
$ mvn install
$ mvn versions:set -DnewVersion=1.0.1
... make changes to Java files ...
$ mvn package
```

By default, any errors introduced by modifications to the baseline without a corresponding version number change will cause the build to fail, with output that looks like the following:

```
[INFO] --- maven-bundle-plugin:2.5.0:baseline (baseline) @ example
[INFO] Baseline Report - Generated by Apache Felix Maven Bundle Plugin
on 2014-07-06T20:43Z based on Bnd - see http://www.aqute.biz/Bnd/Bnd
[INFO] Comparing bundle example version 1.0.1 to version (,1.0.1)
[INFO]
[INFO] * com.packtpub.e4.advanced.baseline
 Delta Current Base  Recommended Warnings
 ===== ======= ====  =========== ========
 minor 1.0.0   1.0.0 1.1.0       Version increase required
[INFO]      < class com.packtpub.e4.advanced.baseline.Example
[INFO]          + method newMethod()
[ERROR] com.packtpub.e4.advanced.baseline:
 Version increase required; detected 1.0.0, suggested 1.1.0
[INFO] Baseline analysis complete, 1 error(s), 0 warning(s)
```

Changes to the class will cause a failure of the build, with a recommended version number change. The failure can be disabled with a `failOnError` plug-in configuration element or with the `baselining.failOnError` Java system property.

Design patterns

A **design pattern** is a reusable element of software architecture that can be applied to different situations. This section presents the two most common OSGi-specific patterns: whiteboard and extender.

The whiteboard pattern

The OSGi **whiteboard pattern** is one in which updates are communicated by bundles to a central location. This approach can be compared to that of a shared whiteboard where someone updates an entry on the whiteboard and others can come and have a look at it, without needing any direct connection or coupling between them, as illustrated in the following diagram:

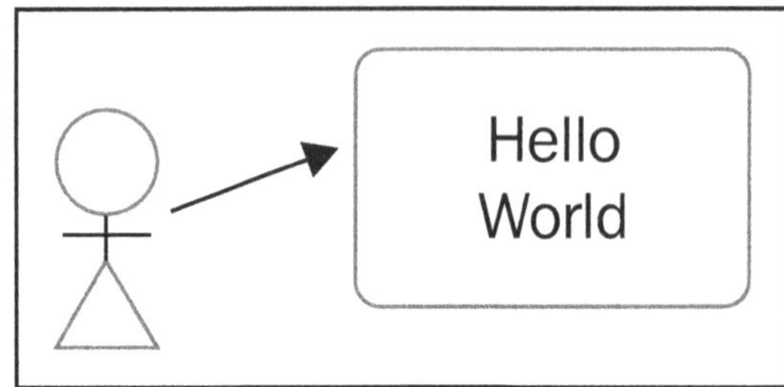

Provided that the individual has a reference to the shared whiteboard, they can add notes to it. This allows others to pick up the message without having any direct relationship with the individual who created it:

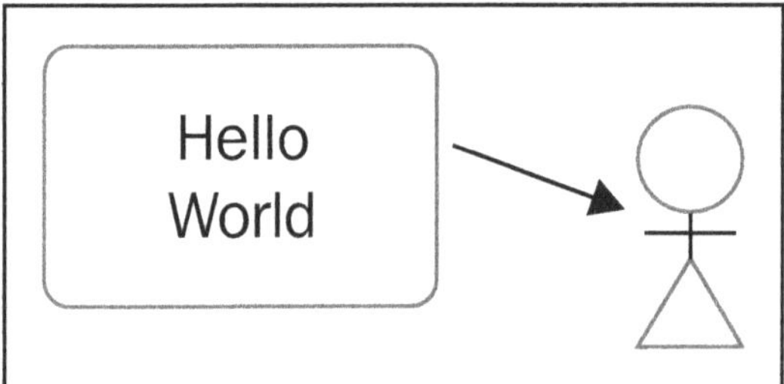

The OSGi Service Registry and OSGi Event Admin (covered in *Chapter 8, Event-driven Applications with EventAdmin*) are both examples of the whiteboard pattern. Here, bundles talk to the shared service (whiteboard) and post or receive events. Other bundles may then receive or post replies but are otherwise decoupled from each other.

One property of the whiteboard pattern is that the pattern can be **event-driven**; that is, when an event occurs, it can trigger a number of other behaviors. It also allows a many-to-many relationship to be defined; any number of producers can deliver content, and many consumers can receive it.

Although this pattern is seen in most message-driven systems where the shared whiteboard is known as the **broker**, this can apply to other kinds of patterns as well. In plain Java, the JDBC `Driver` class is an example of a whiteboard pattern, where driver classes are registered, and then subsequently the code looks up drivers based on an opaque string.

> Note that whiteboards do not necessarily need to be singletons. Although the `Driver` example is a global singleton, the `BundleContext` is something that can be instance-specific and delivers a filtered view of the available services.

The extender pattern

The OSGi **extender pattern** is one that allows a bundle to add additional data, functionality, or processing to another bundle at runtime. This is typically triggered by the presence of a header in a bundle's manifest to indicate that some kind of action should be taken.

Declarative Services, covered in *Chapter 3, Using OSGi Services to Dynamically Wire Applications*, is an example of the extender pattern. When a bundle is installed into the runtime, the Declarative Services bundle notes the presence of a specific header:

```
Service-Component: OSGI-INF/example.xml
```

If the Declarative Services bundle finds such a header, it takes additional action. If the header is not present, it takes no further action. The Declarative Services bundle *extends* the functionality of the client bundle, without the client bundle having any direct relationship with the Declarative Services bundle itself.

This pattern is used by a number of other bundles. The **Remote Services** specification allows a subset of services to be exported as remote APIs using web services or another means. Instead of the bundle having to provide its own mechanisms, the extender will generate remote proxies for the services and make them available on remote hosts.

The extender pattern is also used for **entity persistence**. JPA providers such as EclipseLink or Apache Aries can look out for bundles being installed with a `Meta-Persistence` header. If so, the persistence files are loaded and then automatically wired up to the proxy objects that provide the persistence services. In this case, the extender bundle will dynamically generate classes and inject them into the target bundle through the use of fragments or other delegated ClassLoaders.

The advantage of the extender pattern is that the bundle does not need to declare an explicit dependency on a specific provider. However, the disadvantage is that if the bundle is installed into a framework without an extender, then it may not function as expected.

The OSGi R6 Enterprise specification, due to be released in 2015, provides a means to use `Require-Capability` constraints to ensure that an extender is present before the bundle is activated. A bundle requiring Declarative Services could express a requirement:

```
Require-Capability: osgi.extender;
 filter:="(osgi.extender=osgi.service.component)"
```

Note that the syntax of the `osgi.extender` namespace is subject to change; see the OSGi R6 Enterprise specification and associated Declarative Services section for the correct requirement.

If designing an application that implements the extender pattern, look for a header in the manifest that can be used to trigger processing. Don't have it default to a value such as `**/*.xml`, as this will cause a performance problem in searching all bundles whether they have the feature or not. Blueprint makes this mistake: when Blueprint is installed into an OSGi runtime, every bundle installed is scanned for Blueprint configuration files, thus causing slowdown at boot. Detecting the existence of a header in a manifest file is much faster (since the manifest has already been loaded and parsed), and this can then trigger more expensive computation on bundles that need it.

Best practices

This section covers some of the best practices that can be applied when designing modular systems, and in particular, modular applications that are built on either OSGi or using the standard Eclipse extension mechanisms.

Separate API and implementation

It is very common for OSGi applications to have a separate API and implementation. This allows the API to be versioned independently from any implementations that may follow.

To implement this effectively, most APIs are specified in terms of pure Java interfaces. However, it is possible that classes are present as well; exceptions must be represented as classes, as are common POJO data structures.

Eclipse documents the interfaces that are not suitable to implement and the POJOs that are not suitable to subclass with the **@noimplement** and **@noextend** JavaDoc tags. These indicate to clients that the interface is not intended to be used outside of the API and that the classes are not designed to be subclassed. The annotations are not binding, but along with being good documentation, they give an idea of whether doing this is supported or not.

One way of separating an interface from implementation is to put all the publicly visible types in one package and have all the implementation details inside another package. Then, using the OSGi `Export-Package` manifest header, only the implementation package can be exposed. This technique is used by the Java libraries (particularly by AWT) where internal implementation classes are put in a `com.sun` package and end user APIs are put into `java.*` or `javax.*` packages. However, the disadvantage with this approach is that any client can become tightly bound to the implementation bundle and so, it cannot be replaced without refreshing/restarting the client bundle.

The reason this occurs is because a client becomes **tightly bound** to the APIs when they are resolved. The client bundle has a package dependency to the API classes, and this is not released until the bundle is refreshed (which implies a stop/start cycle). This prevents the API bundle from being replaced on the fly.

The solution to this problem is to put the API classes and interfaces in separate bundles. This way, clients only need to depend on the API bundle and acquire the implementation through another means (for example, looking up an OSGi service). This permits the client to only be tightly bound to the API but permit dynamic replacement of the implementation at runtime.

This technique is used by JDBC drivers, where the client depends on the `java.sql` package, but the implementation comes from elsewhere. It is also used to access the OSGi framework, where the client depends on the `org.osgi.framework.*` packages, not on the specific implementation provided by the framework itself.

> For convenience, it may be tempting to provide a factory instance in the API bundle, such as the `FeedParserFactory` from *Chapter 2, Creating Custom Extension Points*, and *Chapter 3, Using OSGi Services to Dynamically Wire Applications*. Care must be taken not to leak implementation details out to the client, as otherwise, the API bundle will end up being wired to the implementation bundle. The typical way to prevent this is to ensure that the implementation bundle depends on the API bundle, then a cyclic reference cannot occur.

The popular logging framework, **Simple Logging Facade for Java** (**SLF4J**), provides a separate versioned API to the implementations. This allows clients to depend at compile time only on the API and not on any implementation details, so at runtime, the appropriate implementation can be used and changed where necessary.

Decouple packages

An application that depends only on package dependencies might be seen as modular but might still run into modularity problems. For a start, multiple packages in the same bundle are visible to one another, so it may seem that the packages are loosely coupled but still have dependencies leak between them.

Building a system using multiple separate modules is the only way to enforce separation of implementation. Using OSGi to provide additional filtering/hiding of implementation packages can do this further.

At the extreme end, having one public package per bundle will allow an OSGi runtime to validate the set of dependencies completely. It is likely that this is not appropriate in many cases, but having a smaller number of public packages will allow better granularity than having all packages in one bundle.

> One advantage of using an OSGi-aware build system is that it can detect when private implementation classes are leaked, thereby preventing compilation from occurring when it happens. The ability to hide internal implementation packages and prevent their use outside of a bundle is one of OSGi's key strengths, and it aids in maintainability.

Decouple services

A better approach to having a pure package-level separation is to have a service-level separation. This allows an implementation to be substituted at runtime instead of having a fixed lifetime for the bundle itself.

An example of this is the Tomcat engine. When a web application is dropped into the `webapps` folder, the application is automatically deployed, and when it is removed, the web application is stopped. This allows a web application to be updated by simply dropping in a new version without having to restart the server.

Such decoupling comes from having a separation of API to implementation; in this case, the `javax.servlet.Servlet` API and the web applications as providers of the `javax.servlet.Servlet` service.

The OSGi HTTP service uses this technique along with the extender pattern to notice when `Servlets` are published, which are then wired up for incoming requests.

Using Dynamic Services requires a dynamic framework such as OSGi, and it also requires the clients to be aware of the services coming and going. This is typically achieved through the use of helper classes such as `ServiceTracker` or by extender patterns such as Declarative Services.

The concept of decoupled services has been around in Java for some time; JDBC has the concept of a `Driver`, which registers an implementation, and a lookup based on a string representation of the driver type. More generally, the `ServiceLoader` (added to Java in 1.6) provides a generic way of locating one or more implementations based on the name of an interface. This is used to provide a form of decoupling from the consumer to the provider; the consumer needs an implementation of a specific interface, and the provider offers an implementation of that specific interface.

As covered in *Chapter 6, Understanding ClassLoaders*, the `ServiceLoader` class is not well suited from a dynamic perspective though load-time weaving of classes can rewrite references to the `ServiceLoader` if necessary.

This pattern is often combined with the **Factory pattern** in which an interface of the desired type is used and in which a third party (such as a `Factory`, `ServiceLoader` or the Service registry) is used to obtain and return an instance of this interface. Typically, `Factory` implementations are configured to instantiate new services, but in OSGi's case, they can be used to return or select an existing instance.

Prefer Import-Package to Require-Bundle

A bundle can declare its dependencies using either `Require-Bundle` or `Import-Package`. The former allows the import of all exported packages while the latter allows packages to be imported individually (a more general form, `Require-Capability`, was added in OSGi R4.3; this allowed non-package dependencies to be expressed).

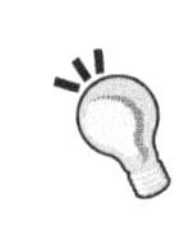

> Historically, the Eclipse platform used plug-in dependencies that required access to the entire content of the plug-in. When it migrated to OSGi in 3.0, the `Require-Bundle` was added to the OSGi R4 specification. Today, Eclipse PDE still prefers to generate dependencies with `Require-Bundle` as a result.

Typically, OSGi applications should prefer using `Import-Package` for the following reasons:

- It is possible to version packages independent of the version of the bundle
- It represents the bundle's requirements more accurately (the code depends on classes in the specified packages and not necessarily on any one named bundle)
- It permits the package to be moved to a different bundle should it be refactored in the future
- It allows a bundle to be replaced with a different or mock implementation without changing any consuming bundles or code

On the other hand, it's quite common for Eclipse bundles to use `Require-Bundle`. For example, the JDT UI bundle expresses a hard dependency on the JDT core bundle:

```
Bundle-SymbolicName: org.eclipse.jdt.ui; singleton:=true
Require-Bundle: …
 org.eclipse.jdt.core;bundle-version="[3.9.0,4.0.0)",
 …
```

Partly this is because the PDE tooling in Eclipse is set up with the expectation of writing the bundle's manifest by hand, and creating automated lists of imports/exports is best left to tooling. It's also historical as most dependencies in Eclipse are set up to use bundle versions instead of package versions, and so the tooling is optimized for the common case of Eclipse development.

It is possible to switch from using `Require-Bundle` to `Import-Package` in PDE; there is a somewhat hidden **Automated Management of Dependencies** section that allows candidate bundles to be specified. Clicking on the **add dependencies** hyperlink populates the list of dependencies as either a list of **Require-Bundle** or **Import-Package**, depending on which setting is used below the list.

To migrate the dependencies for the `feeds.ui` project, open up the `MANIFEST.MF` file and switch to the **Dependencies** tab. Expand the collapsible **Automated Management of Dependencies** section, and it will show an empty table:

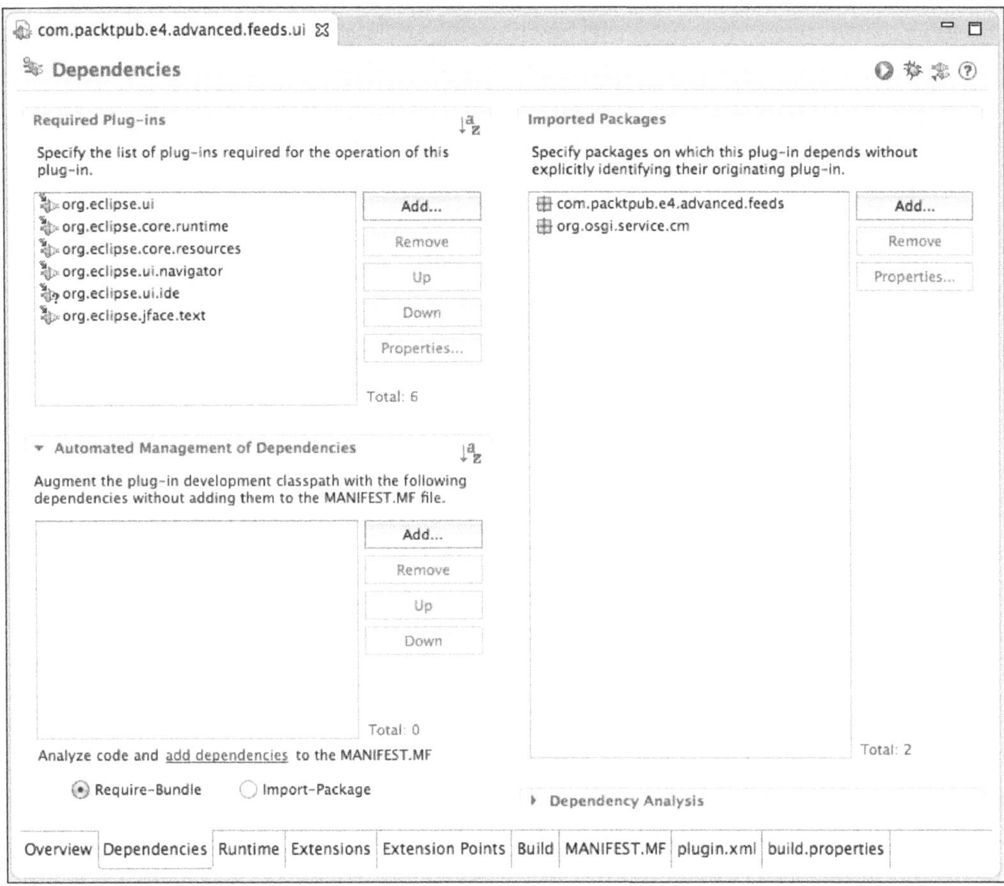

Now move the dependencies down from the **Required Plug-ins** section to the **Automated Management of Dependencies** section. To allow the existing packages to be automatically imported, add the `com.packtpub.e4.advanced.feeds` and `org.eclipse.osgi.services` bundles to the candidate list and remove them from the **Imported Packages** section:

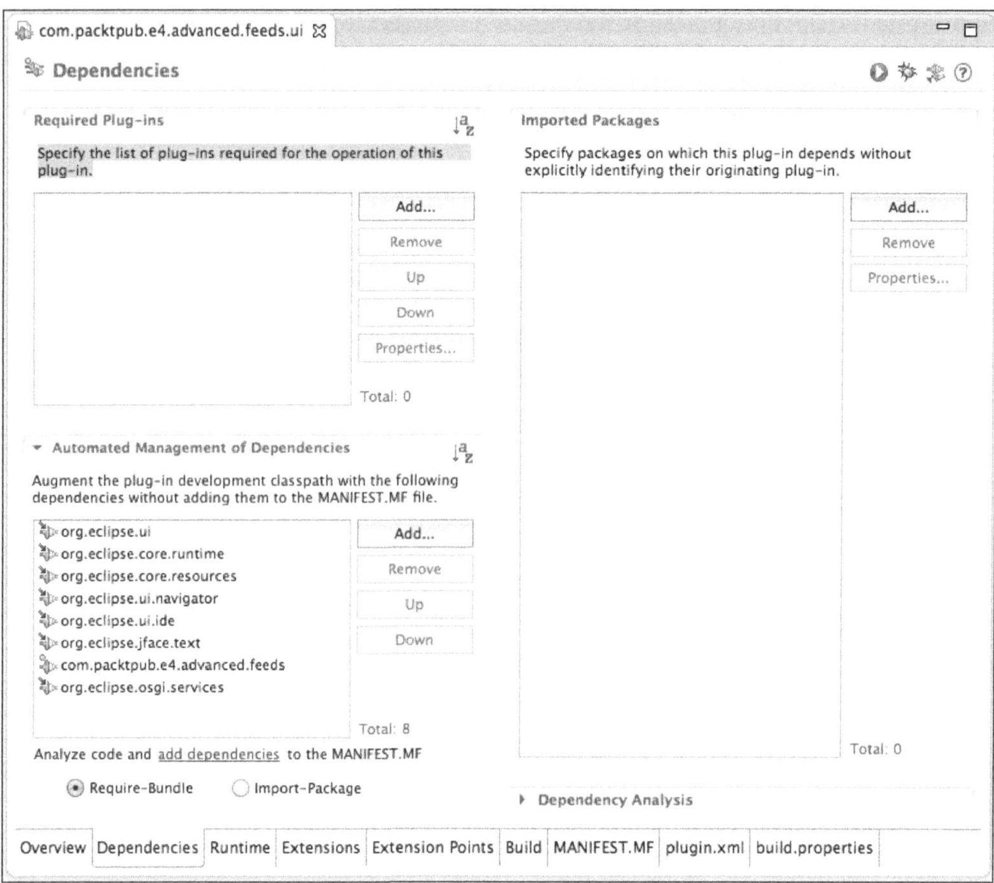

Now change the **Require-Bundle** at the bottom to **Import-Package**, and then click on the underlined **add dependencies** link. This will populate the **Imported Packages** list on the right-hand side with a full list of packages. Packages that have a versioned export are also imported with the version installed in the workspace:

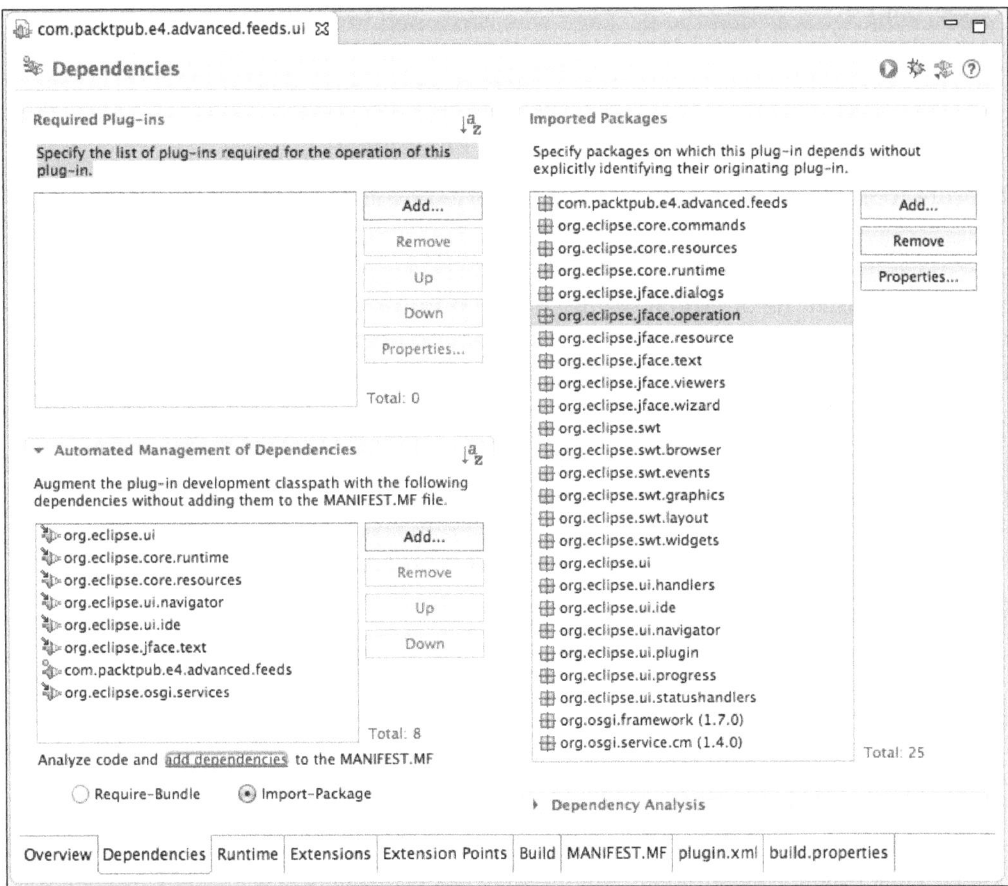

In this example, the `org.osgi.framework` package is imported with version `1.7.0`, which corresponds to the version in Eclipse 4.3. To support running on older versions of Eclipse, changing this to a lower value would be required. Of course, testing the bundle on older versions would still be required to make sure that the package does not take advantage of any newer features.

Version packages and bundles

In the previous section, the `Require-Bundle` was replaced with an `Import-Package`. This increased the number of dependencies added to the bundle; however, since these were automatically added, managing them becomes easier.

Another change was that the package was versioned instead of the bundle. A versioned package is declared by appending a `version` attribute to the package export:

```
Export-Package: org.osgi.framework;version="1.7"
```

In order to use this package, it must be imported by specifying the version as well:

```
Import-Package: org.osgi.framework;version="1.7.0"
```

This ensures that the bundle will bind to a minimum of version `1.7`. Note that the strings `1.7` and `1.7.0` are equivalent, as a version number component defaults to `0` if not specified.

The advantage of versioning specific packages is that they provide a finer level of granularity than the version level of a bundle. If a bundle exports many packages (such as the Eclipse Equinox kernel, `org.eclipse.osgi`), then it can only have a single version number at the aggregate level. In the case of Eclipse `4.3.2`, the bundle version is `3.9.2`. In the case of Eclipse `4.4.0`, the bundle version is `3.10.0`.

However, both versions of Eclipse export `org.osgi.framework.hooks.bundle` with version `1.1.0`. Clients that need to use this package only need to import it and don't have to worry that in Equinox, it comes from the `org.eclipse.osgi` bundle. In the case of Apache Felix, this package comes from the `felix` bundle and exports the same version.

If new functionality is required, such as depending on `CollisionHook` that was added in version `1.1.0`, then it would be an error to install it in an environment that did not provide a minimum of version `1.1.0`. If this functionality is installed in Eclipse in the `org.eclipse.osgi` bundle but in Felix as the `felix` bundle, then there is no consistent name or version of the bundle that could be used. If the bundle developer used `Require-Bundle: org.eclipse.osgi;bundle-version="3.9.0"`, then the bundle would not resolve in other OSGi frameworks such as Felix.

Using a versioned `Import-Package` allows the bundle to depend on the appropriate level of service, regardless of which bundles are installed in the system. In general, all OSGi framework packages are versioned, as are many of the Apache Felix bundles.

Note that most Eclipse-based OSGi bundles do not export package versions.

Avoid split packages

In OSGi terminology, a **split package** is one that is exported by several bundles. This leads to a more complex view of the environment as a whole and might lead to incorrect behavior if only part of the bundle is imported. When an `Import-Package` dependency is wired for a bundle, it is only wired to a single provider of that package. If there is more than one version of a package, the framework can choose to wire it to one or the other but not both.

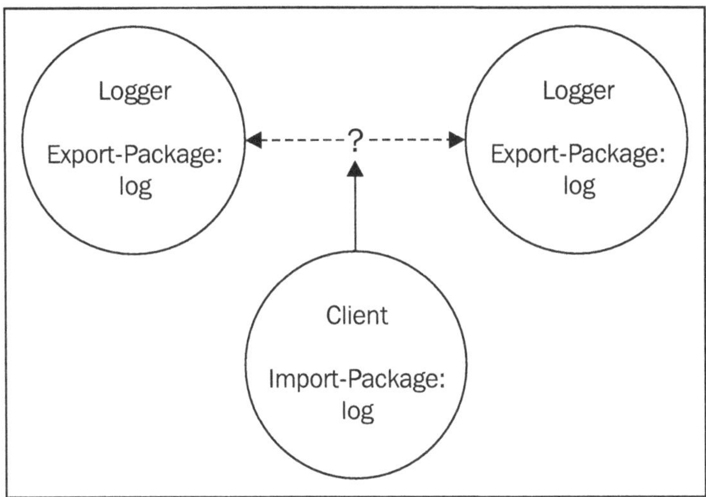

As a result, if a package is split between two or more bundles, then it cannot be imported by a single client with `Import-Package`.

> Note that JARs have the same concept of a single package coming from a single bundle, using **sealed packages**. This is achieved for plain Java with entries in the manifest such as the following:
>
> ```
> Name: com/example/pack/age/Sealed: true
> ```

Typically, split packages evolve by accident or through refactoring or evolution of a package where some functionality has been exported and made available elsewhere.

To allow packages with content to be imported from two or more split packages, an intermediary aggregator bundle needs to be used. This uses `Require-Bundle` to wire together the packages by a symbolic name while using `Export-Package` with the common package.

Using `Require-Bundle` to merge the dependencies together is easy, but it is also necessary to prevent bundles from depending on the original exported packages. To do this, add a **mandatory directive** to the split packages, which prevents the package from being imported unless it has a `Require-Bundle` or `Import-Package` with the appropriate attribute:

```
Bundle-SymbolicName: foo.logger
Export-Package: log;mandatory:=foo;foo=bar
```

This will prevent bundles from importing the `log` package unless they also add a `foo` attribute with a `bar` value:

```
Import-Package: log;foo=bar
```

Another way to get the `log` package is to use `Require-Bundle`:

```
Require-Bundle: foo.logger
```

The solution will look like the following `MANIFEST.MF` entries:

```
# logger.jar
Bundle-SymbolicName: com.packtpub.e4.advanced.log.logger
Export-Package: log;mandatory:=by;by=logger

# other.jar
Bundle-SymbolicName: com.packtpub.e4.advanced.log.other
Export-Package: log;mandatory:=by;by=other

# merge.jar
Bundle-SymbolicName: com.packtpub.e4.advanced.log.merge
Export-Package: log
Require-Bundle:
 com.packtpub.e4.advanced.log.logger,
 com.packtpub.e4.advanced.log.other

# client.jar
Bundle-SymbolicName: com.packtpub.e4.advanced.log.client
Import-Package: log
```

The relationships between the bundles are shown graphically in the following diagram:

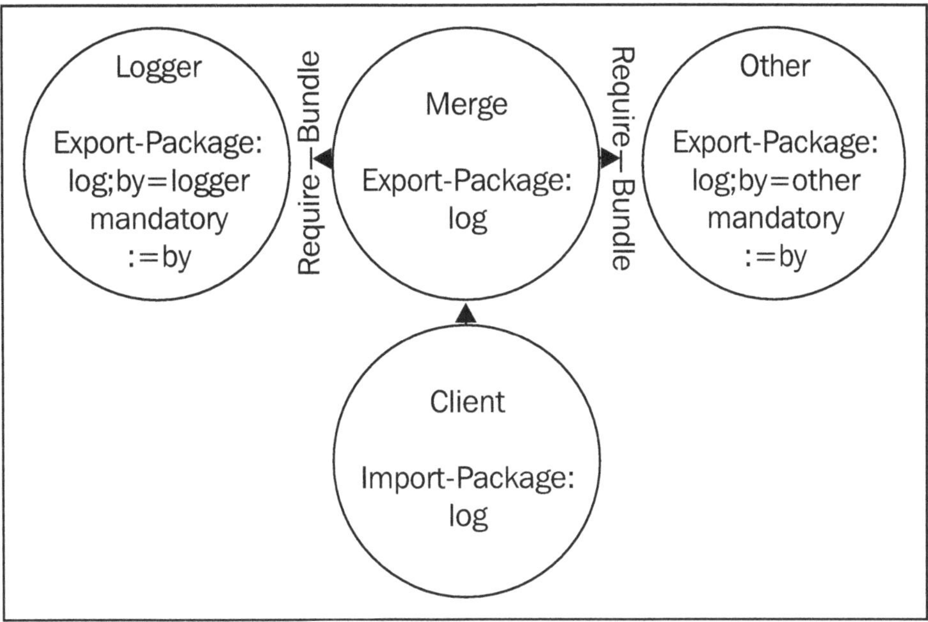

The `mandatory` directive is used to state that the package can only be imported using the `by` attribute, which allows a selection of a specific variant of the package. These can be merged with multiple `Require-Bundle` bindings. This is then transparent to the clients that can use the `Import-Package` to be wired to the merged bundle.

> Using split packages can cause problems at implementation and should generally be avoided. The only reason split packages should be used is when refactoring existing packages has meant that there is no alternative to having classes in more than one place. If split bundles are required, then it will be necessary to provide a combination bundle that knows of the components and has imported them; this is optional in the case of a component that is no longer required.

Import and export packages

In OSGi Release 3, an `Export-Package` implied an `Import-Package` of the package. In OSGi Release 4 (which is the version Eclipse started using), an `Export-Package` no longer implies an `Import-Package`.

Tools that use `bnd` to build bundles typically automatically add an `Import-Package` to every `Export-Package` that is generated. This includes tools such as Bndtools, Maven Felix, and the Gradle OSGi plug-in. As a result, a `foo` package that is exported will have the following in the `MANIFEST.MF` file:

```
Export-Package: foo
Import-Package: foo
```

However, bundles that are written by hand (such as used by PDE) tend to not do this and instead just export the package:

```
Export-Package: foo
```

What's the difference between both approaches and which is preferred? The OSGi specification (section 3.6.6) suggests that it is best practice to import packages that are exported, as long as the package does not use private packages and a private package uses an exported package. For example, it should also import it in a bundle that exports an API, as shown in the following diagram:

The reason to import a package that is exported is to allow the bundle to substitute the local package with one from a different bundle. For example, if two versions of `org.slf4j` API packages are installed and the package is imported from two bundles, the framework can upgrade the API package by importing the package from the more recent bundle. This allows a package to be substituted for a newer version if it becomes available. The following diagram illustrates this:

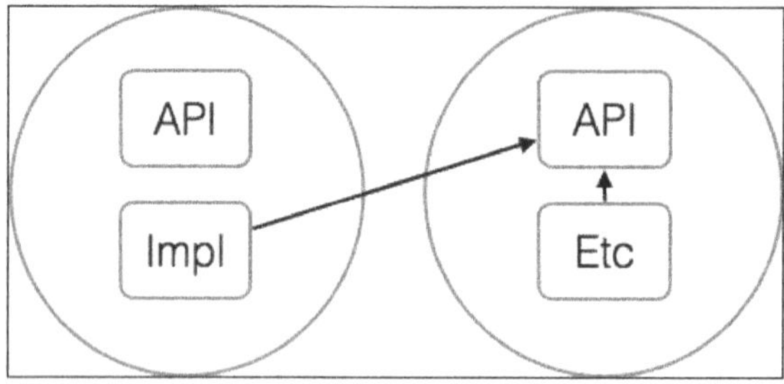

Substitutability only works if the exported package does not expose dependencies on internal packages. If the exported package has a dependency on an internal package (for example, a return type, argument type, annotation, or exception), then it cannot be substituted. Similarly, the bundle must internally depend on the package in order for it to be replaceable; if it doesn't depend on the package, then there is no need to import it.

Avoid start ordering requirements

The OSGi framework has a concept of a **start level**, which mirrors start levels in Unix. This is a positive integer that can be increased or decreased at runtime. The framework begins and ends at start level 0 and then progressively increments the start level until it reaches the initial start level (which is generally 4 for Eclipse and 1 for Felix).

Each time the start level increases, bundles that are defined to start at that level are started automatically. Similarly, each time the start level decreases, bundles that no longer meet the start level are stopped. Upon framework shutdown, the start level is progressively decreased until all bundles are stopped, and the start level goes to 0.

Relying on a particular start ordering generally indicates a fragile relationship between bundles. However, sometimes start ordering is necessary. It is used by Eclipse and Equinox to ensure that Declarative Services are started early so that any bundles subsequently started are able to take advantage of Declarative Services. Similarly, some **weaving hooks**, which are used to process class files, can only be used if the hook is installed prior to subsequent class files being loaded.

There are several ways to avoid start level-ordering problems:

- The first is to use a component model such as Declarative Services (see *Chapter 3, Using OSGi Services to Dynamically Wire Applications*, for more information). This will ensure that the services are registered and available for use but only instantiated once the services' dependencies are available. This will ensure that the system will wait until it is needed, and the services will be instantiated on demand.
- The second is to listen to bundle events (see *Chapter 8, Event-driven Applications with EventAdmin*). It is possible to listen to bundles coming and going and taking appropriate action when bundles are installed. This is used by bundles that implement the extender pattern (see the *The extender pattern* section earlier in this chapter) to process bundles as they are installed and started. Generally, the processing involves iterating through all the currently installed bundles followed by switching to a listener-based mechanism to pick up newer bundles. The `ServiceTracker` performs something similar to listen to services that are coming and going.

- The final option is to design the bundle or service in such a way that if dependent services are not available, the correct operation still occurs. For example, if a bundle depends on a logging service and it is not present, then the bundle could decide not to log information or substitute a default null logging system instead. Generally, in a dynamic framework such as OSGi, services may come and go at any time, and the client should be prepared to handle such cases.

Avoid long Activator start methods

At the start of the framework, the start level is increased (see the *Avoid start ordering requirements* section for more information). All the bundles in a given start level are started before moving to the next start level.

As a result, it's possible for a bundle to delay further bundles by taking a long time to return from a `start` method in a `BundleActivator`. Generally, the `start` method should return as quickly as possible and move processing to a different thread if computation will take a long time.

This is especially true if the bundle is started not through the framework start-up but through an automated start caused by a lazy bundle activation. If a bundle has a `Bundle-ActivationPolicy: lazy` manifest entry, then as soon as a class is requested from this bundle, it will be started automatically. If the bundle start-up takes some time (for example, interacting with an external resource or dealing with I/O), then it will delay the class being handed back to the caller.

Sometimes, it may be desirable to have a bundle start-up delayed until a particular resource is available. For example, if a bundle requires database connectivity, it might be the case that the activator verifies that the database is available before being started. An alternative is to let the bundle come up but only present the service after the database connection has been verified. Instead of treating the bundle as the atomic unit of start-up, using services is more flexible, and it means that the service can be implemented by a fallback or another bundle subsequently.

Use configuration admin for configuration

Configuration Admin, also known as **Config Admin**, is a standard OSGi service that can be used to supply configuration data to a bundle at start-up. Management agents can supply the configuration from a number of sources such as a property file in the case of Felix FileInstall or custom configuration bundles if desired.

By separating how the configuration information is passed (by defining a generic API) and how it is sourced, a bundle can be configured without needing to change anything about the system or code.

Reading configuration information directly from a `properties` file (a technique used by many Java libraries) can be problematic as it will require a filesystem and a hard-coded list of properties. If any configuration information needs to be changed (such as increasing the logging level for a particular component), typically, the file needs to be edited and the process restarted. Similarly, hard-coding system properties at start-up of the JVM suffers from the same problem; any changes made are not visible to the bundle at runtime.

Using Config Admin solves both of these problems. Config Admin uses a push mechanism—when either initial or new configuration is found, it is pushed to the component for configuration. As the component can already handle having configuration data set in this way, it will be able to dynamically react to configuration changes in addition to an initial static set of data.

Additionally, OSGi permits bundles and services to be instantiated multiple times within a JVM. Config Admin can configure each of these individually, whereas a system property or single file would not be able to distinguish between the two.

The only requirement to be usable by Config Admin is to either implement the `ManagedService` interface, which provides an `updated` method that takes a `Dictionary` of key/value pairs, or to use a component model such as Declarative Services, which is already integrated with Config Admin. As such, it is very easy to implement generic services that consume this configuration information.

> Why does `ManagedService` use an `updated` method and not use JavaBeans properties? Essentially, if many configuration values change at one time, it is desirable to commit this set of changes atomically and then restart whatever is required once all the changes are in place. If a set of changes were drip-fed into a service, one JavaBean setter at a time, it would not be possible to hook in the completion of all the changes in a standardized way.

Share services, not implementation

As OSGi is a dynamic environment, services can come and go after the system is started. Bundles that depend solely on implementation classes will not be dynamic; bundles that depend on services can be.

The corollary is that it makes sense to share behavior by exporting/registering services rather than exporting code. It is possible to provide helper methods in the API that perform the service lookup (similar to SLF4J's `Logger.getLogger` method), as the returned instance can be part of a well-known interface. It also allows the acquisition of that data object to be encapsulated inside a small but standard implementation that does not need to concern the caller.

To take full advantage of the dynamism that OSGi provides, these services should be registered and deregistered dynamically. The easiest way to achieve this is to use a component model such as Declarative Services or Blueprint, as both of these allow components to be defined externally to the code and then instantiated on demand. In this way, when the component is created (through access, configuration admin, or some other mechanism), it will be automatically registered as a service for other bundles to consume. If there are any required services that are not available, the creation of the component will be delayed until a time where the services are available.

Services also make it much easier to provide mock implementations. The bundle under test can be installed into a test runtime, along with a test bundle that provides a mock service for use by the main bundle. In this way, the service can be tested in isolation without requiring any additional data.

Loosely coupled and highly cohesive

Bundles should be designed so that they are loosely coupled and highly cohesive. **Loosely coupled** means that the bundle has limited dependencies on API classes (never implementation) and will dynamically acquire services when needed. **Highly cohesive** means that the bundle forms a united whole, and the contents cannot be split into logical subgroups. (If a bundle can be split into logical subgroups, then it indicates that a better approach would be to split the bundle into two or more bundles; one per subgroup and optionally, one overarching group).

Loose coupling is desirable as a function of modules in a complex system, because it means that it is unlikely that this module will depend on any specific set or emergent behaviors in the rest of the system. Instead, if the dependencies are cleanly exposed, then any refactoring required will be limited to the dependencies present.

Loose coupling is harder than it sounds in a large system. If a project in an IDE is loosely structured (such as having many logical packages) but is compiled with a project-wide classpath, then it's easy for unintended dependencies to creep in.

For example, in the Jetty project in version 6, the client implementation had an unintended dependency on the server implementation; this meant that all client code had to be shipped with a copy of the server code at the same time. This unintentional dependency crept in because the individual units were not separated on the filesystem, and the compiler transparently compiled the server classes at compile time.

Similarly, the JDK has unintended dependencies by virtue of the Java packages being compiled as a monolithic unit; the `java.beans` package depends on the `java.applet` package, which depends on the `java.awt` package. So, despite the fact that the `beans` package has no direct need for a GUI, any project that uses `java.beans` is implicitly drawing in GUI dependencies. Modularizing is hard; modularizing the JDK doubly so, although JEP 200 plans to split the JDK into separate modules and JEP 201 plans to enforce modularity at compile-time for the JDK..

One way of achieving loose coupling is to break down modules into smaller and smaller units, until they become indivisible units both logically and from an implementation perspective. By doing this, loose coupling will be an emergent property of the modules after the translation is complete. It will also highlight where there may be some dependencies that are not appropriate, and attention can be given to how to rectify the situation (such as deprecating the `java.beans.Beans.instantiate` method that takes an `AppletInitializer`). Often, the act of doing the modularization will be enough to highlight where these APIs require remediation. Separating the modules into their own classpaths (for example, separate Maven modules or Eclipse projects) will often immediately highlight where assumptions about a global classpath have been made.

Highly cohesive bundles have packages tightly grouped together. In other words, the packages form a tight knit group and don't expect to be split from each other. Typical anti-cohesive bundles are ones with a `util` in the name; they contain all manner of unrelated classes. The problem with such bundles is that they tend to accrete contents and make refactoring subsequently more difficult. Secondly, the accretion of contents often implies an accretion of dependencies; this makes the bundle a join in a many-to-many dependency wiring between bundles.

In most cases, the solution is to **minimize dependencies** and **maximize cohesion**. This is often a journey instead of a destination, as a bundle can keep being split until all the units meet the cohesion requirements.

Compile with the lowest level execution environment

OSGi bundles can specify a `Bundle-RequiredExecutionEnvironment`, which is the set of Java platforms that the bundle will work on. These include `CDC-1.0/Foundation-1.0`, `JavaSE-1.7` and `JavaSE-1.8`.

When installing, building, or running a bundle, the OSGi framework will ensure that the required execution environment is met. The bundle will not resolve unless the running environment is at least the minimum requirement. However, it is possible for a bundle to run on a higher version than it is expecting both at runtime and at compile time.

There is a risk when compiling on `JavaSE-1.8` but declaring a required execution environment of `JavaSE-1.7` that methods available in 1.8 but not in 1.7 are used. The compiler might not be able to tell whether new methods (such as `List.sort`) are present in older versions of Java and let the bytecode be compiled and work on an OSGi platform with a `JavaSE-1.8` runtime. If the bundle is subsequently run on a `JavaSE-1.7` platform, then silent runtime failures might occur.

The way to avoid this is to ensure that the bundles are built only using the specified version of Java declared in the `Bundle-RequiredExecutionEnvironment`. This is often done by server-side builds so that even if a single IDE does not have the correct JDK, then the server-side builds will pick up the error.

OSGi supports low-powered devices such as embedded routers and home automation systems. The APIs in OSGi therefore limit themselves to `OSGi/Minimum-1.2`, which might not include generics or the newer collections APIs added since Java 1.2.

As embedded systems become more powerful, the use of generics has started to creep in to OSGi runtimes. With Java 8 bringing lambdas and `default` methods, it is likely that bundles will transition to supporting a minimum of Java 8 in the near future, even if the traditional APIs do not.

Avoid Class.forName

Traditionally, Java applications have used `Class.forName` to dynamically load a class from a given name. This is often used in conjunction with externalized configuration such as a JDBC database driver or the name of a codec or charset encoding.

There are two problems with `Class.forName`, which means that it should be avoided wherever possible in an OSGi application.

First, it assumes a global visibility of classes such that any class will be available from any other class or `ClassLoader`. This works for monolithic Java applications (which only have a single application `ClassLoader`) or ones where class loaders and therefore classes are not shared (such as individual applications in a Tomcat container). As this may not always be the case, a lookup of a class becomes dependent upon where it was looked up from instead of being globally available.

Second, the result of the class is pinned both in the `ClassLoader` of the providing bundle and in the bundle of the requesting class. This would be fine if it were the interface or API class (as this will be pinned in the lifetime of the bundle anyway), but the implementation class is specifically supposed to be replaceable dynamically. Instead, once a `Class.forName` has been invoked, then the implementation class is permanently wired to the client bundle until the client bundle is refreshed (when it gets a new `ClassLoader` object).

The solution to both of these problems is not to call `Class.forName`. How then can bundles work with APIs where the classes are not known in advance? The obvious solution is to use services instead and have the bundle locate the service using the standard OSGi mechanisms. For situations where this is not possible, the `BundleContext` can be used to get the `Bundle`, which provides a `getResourceAsStream` method (for loading resources), and a `loadClass`, which does the right resolution for a specific implementation class.

If the `Bundle` isn't known, it is possible to use `ClassLoader.loadClass` instead by using the `ClassLoader` of the current class. This will then delegate to the right `ClassLoader` to find the implementation.

The best approach is not to use string names at all but pass `Class` instances instead, or if a string must be used, then pass it with the appropriate `ClassLoader` as well. Many database mapping tools will take a `Class` instance to perform mapping instead of a class name.

Avoid DynamicImport-Package

Along with using the `Require-Bundle` and `Import-Package` to wire dependencies, OSGi also provides a more general dynamic one called `DynamicImport-Package`. This can be used to provide a last attempt to find a class that is being requested from the bundle if it has not been found any other way.

The format of `DynamicImport-Package` is to specify a package name, optionally with a wildcard, that can be used to create an `Import-Package` wire on demand if a class is requested. Using a generic `*` for everything will result in dependencies being found automatically when they are looked up and not found in any other way:

```
DynamicImport-Package: com.example.*
```

When a class in the bundle attempts to find `com.example.One` or `com.example.two.Three`, then the framework will attempt to create a wiring for the `com.example` and `com.example.two` packages. If there are bundles in the system that export these packages, then wires will be added to the bundle, and the resolution will work as expected. If not, then the load attempt fails, as with other failed lookups, and an exception will be thrown.

When debugging failed lookups, the following two types of failures might occur:

- `ClassNotFoundException`: This is raised when the direct type cannot be found, for example, you have a typo in the class name (such as `omc.example.One`).
- `NoClassDefFoundError`: This is raised when an indirect type cannot be found; in other words, the JVM has found the class requested (`com.example.One`), but this class depends on another that cannot be loaded or found (`com.example.Two`). Exceptions thrown in a `static` initializer might also result in a `NoClassDefFoundError` being reported.

The problem with the use of `DynamicImport-Package` is that it will pin the dependency permanently for the lifetime of the requesting bundle. As such, even if this dependent bundle were to be stopped, the `ClassLoader` would be pinned to the wired dependency bundle. The only way the wire will be removed is if the requesting bundle is refreshed or stopped.

Generally, the use of `DynamicImport-Package` is a code smell in OSGi, and the underlying problem should be resolved (such as replacing lookups with services or with the explicit dependencies as required). It can be a useful diagnostic tool in the right use cases, but it should not be generally relied upon.

Avoid BundleActivator

`BundleActivator` is used in many cases where it is not necessary. Typically, the `BundleActivator` will store a `static` reference to the `BundleContext` and/or provide helper methods that look up platform services. However, this ends up being stored as an effective singleton with a `static` accessor to return the instance:

```
public class Activator implements BundleActivator {
  private static Activator instance;
  public static Activator getInstance() {
    return instance;
  }
  private BundleContext context;
  public BundleContext getContext() {
    return context;
  }
  public void start(BundleContext context) throws Exception {
    this.context = context;
    instance = this;
  }
  public void stop(BundleContext context) throws Exception {
  }
}
```

This is not necessary because the `Bundle` (and therefore, the `BundleContext`) can be acquired from any class in an OSGi runtime using `FrameworkUtil` and from that, any service of a given type.

The `BundleContext` only exists for bundles that are `ACTIVE` (have been started). If a bundle has not been started, then its bundle context will be `null`. Code should handle this and fail gracefully. Alternatively, the `Bundle-ActivationPolicy: lazy` manifest header can be added to the manifest, which will automatically start the bundle on access.

If a service is required, this method can be used to return an instance of a service:

```
public static <S> S getService(Class<S> type, Class<?> caller) {
  Bundle b = FrameworkUtil.getBundle(caller);
  if (b.getState() != Bundle.ACTIVE) {
   try {
      b.start(Bundle.START_TRANSIENT);
    } catch (BundleException e) {
    }
  }
  BundleContext bc = b.getBundleContext();
  if(bc != null) {
    ServiceReference<S> sr = bc.getServiceReference(type);
    S s = null;
    if(sr != null) {
      s = bc.getService(sr);
      bc.ungetService(sr);
    }
  }
  return s;
}
```

As it is possible to obtain an instance of a service given a caller class and a desired type, the majority of the use cases in a `BundleActivator` are no longer required. The only remaining use case is to start or register a service dynamically at bundle start-up, but this can be achieved through the use of Declarative Services or another component model instead.

Consider thread safety

Other than the `BundleActivator` and the `start` and `stop` methods, it cannot be guaranteed that any particular thread will be calling the bundle's code or, indeed, might be calling it at the same time. In particular, when processing events from Event Admin (covered in *Chapter 8, Event-driven Applications with EventAdmin*), the events might be delivered from different threads from the one they first posted.

If there are UI operations that are required and they need to obtain a lock or run on a particular thread, then care must be taken that when the UI is invoked, it is done from the correct thread. Generally, OSGi frameworks will use multiple threads, and so an incoming event or service call might not be on an appropriate thread for the service to process.

Thread safety should also be considered with regard to mutable data structures. For data structures that are highly volatile or might be mutated and read at the same time, suitable synchronization guards should be implemented to prevent unknown problems from occurring at runtime.

Test in different frameworks

Although an OSGi bundle might work correctly in the framework environment that the developer tested in, it might have problems if run in a different framework or a different environment.

One common cause for failure is not having the right dependent bundles in the target environment, such as having Declarative Services installed and running. In general, any extender pattern is only going to work if the extender is configured and running in the system.

Another problem is the different frameworks and their use of the boot delegation options. When a class is looked up from a bundle, if the package begins with `java.` or is listed as an entry in the `org.osgi.framework.bootdelegation` system property, it is delegated to the parent (JVM) `ClassLoader`. Otherwise, the package is selected from the `Import-Package` wiring (if present) or `Require-Bundle` (if present), followed by the embedded `Bundle-ClassPath` contents.

This presents a problem with testing bundles, particularly ones that look up classes in the `sun.*` or `javax.*` spaces. Code that appears to work correctly in Equinox will fail to work in Felix because the former is looser by default. To ensure that Equinox behaves in the same way as Felix, set `osgi.compatibility.bootdelegation=false` as a system property on the Equinox JVM. Although it talks about OSGi compatibility, in fact this is an Eclipse-specific behavior, and the default action of Eclipse is to use non-standard boot delegation. As this has not changed in over a decade, it is likely that it will not happen any time soon, and there might be misconfigured bundles that never show up in test failures because of this issue.

Generally, if a bundle works correctly in Felix, then it will work in other runtime engines. The reverse is not always true.

Summary

The key concept of bundle compatibility is managed with version numbers and version number ranges. Whether the major, minor, or micro version is changed, it indicates to the end consumer whether or not the change is backward compatible. Version ranges can be used to ensure that the appropriate version is selected at runtime.

Being able to design an Eclipse plug-in or OSGi application involves a repeated process of breaking down the components into smaller indivisible modules until they are loosely coupled to their neighbors and highly cohesive. Standard patterns help this, and following best practice allows for maximal flexibility.

The next chapter will present reactive applications based on the OSGi event bus.

8

Event-driven Applications with EventAdmin

The OSGi `EventAdmin` service provides a means to publish and receive events between bundles. This can be used to build applications that dynamically react to changes from external or internal sources.

This chapter will present the OSGi `EventAdmin` service and how it can be used to build decoupled applications. The `EventAdmin` service is an example of the **whiteboard** pattern, and therefore provides a means to **loosely couple** the components together.

Understanding the OSGi EventAdmin service

The OSGi `EventAdmin` service is described in the *OSGi Compendium* and *OSGi Enterprise* specifications in *Chapter 113, Event Admin Service Specification*. It provides a means to use a **publish** and **subscribe** mechanism to send **events** that may be targeted at a particular **topic** and may contain an arbitrary number of **event properties**.

Event topics are text names that are used to identify where the event will be delivered. They are represented with a slash (/) separating parts of the name, for example, `org/osgi/framework/ServiceEvent` or `org/osgi/service/log/LogEntry`.

An `Event` is an immutable object, initialized from a `Dictionary` or `Map`, which has a number of properties. These properties can store user-specific data, along with a number of other (potentially `null`) standard properties from the `EventConstants` class:

- `BUNDLE_ID` - `bundle.id`, the bundle's ID number
- `BUNDLE_SIGNER` - `bundle.signer`, the name of the signer of the bundle
- `BUNDLE_SYMBOLICNAME` - `bundle.symbolicName`, the symbolic name of the bundle
- `BUNDLE_VERSION` - `bundle.version`, the bundle's `Version` number
- `EXCEPTION` - `exception`, a `Throwable` object if the event was raised as an error
- `EXCEPTION_CLASS` - `exception.class`, the class name of the `exception` object (useful for filtering out types of exceptions such as `NullPointerException`)
- `EXCEPTION_MESSAGE` - `exception.message`, the message returned from the `exception` object if present
- `MESSAGE` - `message`, a human-readable message that is usually not localized
- `SERVICE_ID` - `service.id`, the ID of the service that generated the event
- `SERVICE_OBJECTCLASS` - `service.objectClass`, the class name of the service that generated the event (suitable for matching/filtering)
- `SERVICE_PID` - `service.pid`, the persistent identifier of the service that raised the event
- `TIMESTAMP` - `timestamp`, the time that the event was posted

Sending e-mails

The example in the next few sections will cover the case of components needing to send e-mails. A component may desire to send an e-mail when a particular condition occurs, such as if an error is received when processing an event, or if a user has feedback to submit.

Clearly, the component can be directly linked to an SMTP library such as `commons-email`. This requires some configuration in the component such as what the SMTP hostname is, what ports should be used, and whether there are any additional authentication details required.

Cleanly separating the e-mail generator (the component wishing to report an error) from the component that sends the e-mail is desirable, as this provides a loosely coupled system, as described in the *Loosely coupled and highly cohesive* section in *Chapter 7, Designing Modular Applications*. The configuration data of the generator component itself does not need to worry about how the e-mail is transmitted, while the component that sends the mail can be configured appropriately (or updated when the e-mail requirements are updated).

Although this can be implemented as an OSGi service, using the `EventAdmin` service allows the event to be handed off into the background, thereby not blocking the call site. The mail can also be created using properties in the `Event` object so that the clients can add whatever information is required in order to generate the e-mails.

Creating an event

The `org.osgi.service.event.Event` object is a standard class in the OSGi framework. It can be constructed from either a `Map` or `Dictionary` of standard key/value pairs, along with a topic (the intended destination of the event).

As e-mails have an `Importance` field, the topic name can be used to distinguish between low, normal, and high priority items with `smtp/low`, `smtp/normal`, and `smtp/high`. The e-mail's content can be stored as event properties using standard RFC 822 header names (`To`, `From`, and `Subject`):

```
import org.osgi.service.event.Event;
...
Map<String,String> email = new HashMap<String, String>();
email.put("Subject","Hello World");
email.put("From","alex.blewitt@gmail.com");
email.put("To","alex.blewitt@gmail.com");
email.put("Body","Sample email sent via event");
Event event = new Event("smtp/high",email);
```

When this event is created, a copy of the `email` map is made so that subsequent changes to the `email` map are not reflected in the `event` object.

If the map is complex, and it needs to be used for multiple events, consider converting it to an `EventProperties` object. This will still perform a one-off copy (at construction time) but the `EventProperties` object can be reused as is for multiple events.

Posting an event

The `EventAdmin` service is used to deliver events synchronously or asynchronously.

Synchronous delivery can be performed with the `sendEvent` method. The event may be posted on the same thread that the client code is running on, but will be blocked until the event has been delivered to all the registered listeners. This is useful when events require processing before they are committed, but using this pattern can lead to **deadlock** in the system. For example, if the posting thread has a lock on a critical section, and the event listener also requires that critical lock, then the listener may never receive that notification. Once a system is deadlocked, then it cannot make further progress.

Avoid using synchronous delivery, as it can lead to deadlock in a system.

Asynchronous delivery can be performed with the `postEvent` method. The `EventAdmin` service enqueues the event and then calls it back with a different thread than the caller. The asynchronous delivery is more performant than the synchronous one, because it needs to use less locking and internal bookkeeping to determine which listeners have seen which events.

Sending an event requires acquiring an `EventAdmin` instance followed by the `sendEvent` or `postEvent` methods. The `EventAdmin` instance can be injected via Declarative Services or acquired through the `BundleContext` via `FrameworkUtil` if necessary (see *Chapter 3, Using OSGi Services to Dynamically Wire Applications*, for more details on how to acquire services in this way):

```
EventAdmin eventAdmin = getService(EventAdmin.class);
eventAdmin.postEvent(event);
```

The `event` will be queued and delivered to the listeners at some point later. Listeners that subscribe after the event is posted/sent will not see that event, though they will see future events.

Note that there are no guarantees that the message will be sent; unlike an enterprise message queuing system, the message is not persisted to disk or replayed upon restart. It is stored in-memory only, and will be discarded when the JVM shuts down.

Additionally, there is no guarantee that a listener is present at the time an event is sent; it may just be silently discarded. `EventAdmin` does not guarantee consistency like a two-phase commit message store.

Receiving an event

`EventAdmin` is used to manage a set of listeners for particular events. Each event listener implements the `EventHandler` interface. However, instead of having an `addListener` such as the `Observable` class, `EventAdmin` looks for services published under the `EventHandler` interface. This allows listeners to come and go or be replaced with alternative (or mock) ones. These can be registered with all the usual service properties (such as `service.ranking`) or with Declarative Services:

```
package com.packtpub.e4.advanced.event.mailman;
import org.apache.commons.mail.*;
import org.osgi.service.event.*;
import org.osgi.service.log.*;
public class MailSender implements EventHandler {
  public void handleEvent(Event event) {
    String topic = event.getTopic();
    if (topic.startsWith("smtp/")) {
      String importance = topic.substring("smtp/".length());
      String to = (String) event.getProperty("To");
      String from = (String) event.getProperty("From");
      String subject = (String) event.getProperty("Subject");
      String body = (String) event.getProperty("DATA");
      try {
        Email email = new SimpleEmail();
        email.setHostName(hostname);
        email.setSmtpPort(port);
        email.setFrom(from);
        email.addTo(to);
        email.setSubject(subject);
        email.addHeader("Importance",importance);
        email.setMsg(body);
        email.send();
        log(LogService.LOG_INFO, "Message sent to " + to);
      } catch (EmailException e) {
        log(LogService.LOG_ERROR, "Error occurred" + e);
      }
    }
  }
  private void log(int level, String message) {
    LogService log = this.log;
    if (log != null) {
      log.log(level, message);
    }
  }
}
```

The code sample uses `commons-email` from the Apache project and `javax.mail:mail`, both of which are available at Maven Central. Copies of the JARs are also available in the book's GitHub repository at `https://github.com/alblue/com.packtpub.e4.advanced/`.

When an event is received, if the topic begins with `smtp/`, then the event is converted into an `Email` object and sent.

The rest of the topic is used as a field for the `Importance` value, described in RFC 4021, and can take the values `low`, `normal`, and `high` (this is a hint and is not displayed by all e-mail clients).

The `log` method is a simple wrapper around a `LogService`, which logs if the service is available and not otherwise.

The `log` is captured in a local variable to avoid threading issues; if the log were `unset` during the call, then it would result in a `NullPointerException` between the `if` test and the call. Instead, by capturing it in a local variable once, the log can never be `null` in the `if` block.

To allow the handler to receive events, it needs to be registered as a service with the `event.topics` service property. The topics can be specified with an exact name (so that different handlers can be used to send `smtp/low` and `smtp/high`), but it's also possible to use a wildcard at the end of the topic name to pick up all the events (such as `smtp/*`).

If registering the handler manually (such as in an `Activator`), it would look like the following:

```
Dictionary<String, String> properties
 = new Hashtable<String, String>();
  properties.put("event.topics","smtp/*");
  context.registerService(EventHandler.class, new MailSender(),
   properties);
```

However, it would be much cleaner to create a Declarative Services component to register the `EventHandler`; this will stay on standby and be created when first used, along with providing an easy way to acquire the `LogService`:

```
<scr:component xmlns:scr="http://www.osgi.org/xmlns/scr/v1.1.0"
 name="com.packtpub.e4.advanced.event.mailman.mailman">
```

```
    <implementation
     class="com.packtpub.e4.advanced.event.mailman.MailSender"/>
    <service>
      <provide interface="org.osgi.service.event.EventHandler"/>
    </service>
    <reference bind="setLogService" cardinality="0..1"
     interface="org.osgi.service.log.LogService" name="LogService"
     policy="dynamic"/>
    <property name="event.topics" value="smtp/*"/>
  </scr:component>
```

Another benefit of using Declarative Services is the ability to pick up the configuration information from Config Admin to set the various properties on the object, such as the hostname to send mails to and the from address of the sender.

Filtering events

The `EventAdmin` service provides a coarse way to filter events through the use of topics. The topic name is a path with segments separated by a slash `/`, which can either be exact, or with the last segment as a wildcard, such as `smtp/*`, as shown in the previous example.

However, this does not provide a means to filter specific events. If additional filtering is desired (for example, ensuring that only select mails are processed), then this would traditionally be done in the code:

```
if(to.equals("alex.blewitt@gmail.com")) {
  ...
}
```

Such hard-coded tests are difficult to debug or modify in the future.

The `EventAdmin` service provides a standardized way to filter events before they are delivered to the `EventHandler`. This allows more specific filters to be set as a way of reducing the volume of events that are handled for processing.

The filter is set by adding a service property `event.filter`, which contains an LDAP style expression. The expression can refer to any of the properties set in the event.

To add a filter equivalent to the previous e-mail filter, set the following to the Declarative Services component when registering the filter:

```
<property name="event.topics" value="smtp/*"/>
<property name="event.filter" value="(Subject=Hello World)"/>
```

If the value contains special characters including parentheses `()` or asterisk `*`, then they must be prefixed with an escape character, which is the backslash \ character. The LDAP filter semantics are defined in RFC 1960.

Now only e-mails with a specific subject will be matched. Other LDAP filters can be used including wildcards to match substrings. For example, to match the local domain, `(To=*@localhost)` could be used.

Using the `event.filter` is usually more efficient than hardcoding the logic in the `handleEvent` method, because the LDAP filter is optimized in OSGi and is translated to a highly performant match when the handler is installed.

Secondly, when using Declarative Services, the component is only enabled when a matching event is seen; if events that don't match the filter are received, then the component isn't enabled. This allows the system to start up quickly without needing to enable components until they are first needed.

Threading and ordering of event delivery

The `EventAdmin` specification ensures that events posted asynchronously will be delivered on a different thread than the one that posts it. It does not guarantee that a particular thread will be used for all the events; nor does it guarantee that for synchronous event delivery, the same thread will be used. Implementations are free to either reuse the delivery thread for synchronous events, or use a different thread, provided that the blocking/waiting synchronization primitives are obeyed.

What the `EventAdmin` specification does guarantee is that events delivered to a particular topic are delivered in-order to individual subscribers. This implies that for each topic there is a queue for delivery to subscribers. Some implementations use a single thread to enforce ordered event delivery.

If asynchronous event delivery does not need to be strictly in-order, there is an `event.delivery` property that can take the value `async.unordered` (or referenced via the constant `DELIVERY_ASYNC_UNORDERED` in the `EventConstants` type). If the strict ordered requirement is relaxed, the `EventAdmin` implementation may be able to take advantage of multiple threads for event delivery.

Apache Felix provides a configuration option that can control the number of threads that are used for the `EventAdmin` delivery process. The default size for the Felix `EventAdmin` is 10, specified in `org.apache.felix.eventadmin.ThreadPoolSize`. The Equinox implementation (as of Eclipse 4.4) does not support this property, nor does it support multiple threads for delivery to event clients.

> The limitation of threading in the `EventAdmin` means that it may not be suitable for high-performance applications or one where rapid or timely event delivery is required. For high-performing message delivery, using Reactive Java (also known as RxJava) may be more appropriate.

Comparison between EventAdmin and services

Another approach to sending e-mails would be to use an e-mail `Service`, with a `sendEmail` method taking a `Dictionary` or `Map` object. This would do the same thing as the `handleEvent` method in the `MailSender` class.

There are a few differences that are worth covering when deciding whether to use events or services:

- **Synchronicity**: The OSGi services approach will always be synchronous; the call will block until the recipient has processed the request and returned. On the other hand, event-based processing can either be synchronous or asynchronous depending on the client's calling convention.
- **Cardinality**: The OSGi services approach will (typically) return a single service to interact with, whereas the event-based mechanism is a broadcast to all listeners. It requires no extra code effort for the event-based processing to add an additional listener to process messages, whereas with the OSGi services, the client has to be explicitly coded to deal with multiple services.
- **Typed**: The OSGi services model allows a custom service for each type of action, using a number of different arguments with specified types. Clients are obviously compiled with those services in place and are therefore strictly typed. The event model uses the same interface for everything (`Event`) and essentially stores arbitrary untyped payloads.
- **Interface/Topic**: The OSGi services model is based entirely on an interface type, which means that clients need to know the interface in advance. The interface can also be (semantically) versioned to enable future growth. The event-based mechanism is topic based and so the topic name needs to be known in advance. The topic allows for wildcarding, so an event published to `com/example/event/bus` will be picked up by listeners for `com/example/event/*` as well as `com/example/*` or even `com/*`. These events could be mapped into other communication technologies such as JSON messages over WebSocket to a browser, or even hooked up to a traditional JMS-based messaging system.

There isn't a hard rule as to when it's appropriate to use services or topics. Because topics can be created on the fly, it can be useful to represent events being fired for individual data objects to notify listeners that a change has happened; in fact, this technique is used in E4 to notify view components when the underlying model has changed as well as when the selection has changed.

In general, for broadcast mechanisms and topics that need to be created on the fly, the event mechanisms may be more suitable. For library and functional services, especially where a return value or state is needed, OSGi services may be more appropriate.

Framework events

The OSGi framework also has a number of events that get fired to notify subscribers when state changes occur in the framework itself. For example, when a bundle transitions through its life cycle states (uninstalled, installed, resolved, starting, active, and stopping), an event will be sent to notify clients of the new value. The events are sent after the transition has occurred.

The framework also has events that represent the system as a whole (to indicate the system has started, packages are refreshed, and for startlevel modifications) as well as certain log message types (info, warning, and error).

Framework events are sent under the `org/osgi/framework/FrameworkEvent/` topic prefix and include:

- `STARTED`
- `PACKAGES_REFRESHED`
- `STARTLEVEL_CHANGED`
- `INFO`
- `WARNING`
- `ERROR`

Bundle events are sent under the `org/osgi/framework/BundleEvent/` topic prefix and include:

- `UNINSTALLED`
- `INSTALLED`
- `UNRESOLVED`
- `RESOLVED`
- `STARTED`
- `UPDATED`
- `STOPPED`

Service events are sent under the `org/osgi/framework/ServiceEvent/` topic prefix and include:

- `REGISTERED`
- `MODIFIED`
- `UNREGISTERING`

For framework events, the following information will be provided:

- `event`: The `FrameworkEvent` object sent to the framework listeners

For bundle events, the following information will be provided:

- `event`: The `BundleEvent` object sent to bundle listeners
- `bundle`: The `Bundle` object
- `bundle.id`: The source's bundle ID as a `Long`
- `bundle.signer`: The string or collection of strings containing the distinguished name of the bundle's signers, if signed
- `bundle.symbolicName`: The bundle's symbolic name if set
- `bundle.version`: The bundle version as a `Version`

For service events, the following information will be provided:

- `event`: The `ServiceEvent` object sent to the service listeners
- `service`: The `ServiceReference` of the service
- `service.id`: The service's ID as a `Long`
- `service.objectClass`: The array of strings of the object classes this service is registered against
- `service.pid`: The service's persistent identifier as a string or collection of strings

Along with delivery via `EventAdmin`, the framework supports several custom listeners that can be added via the `BundleContext` add listener methods:

- `FrameworkListener`: This is an interface to receive `FrameworkEvent` objects
- `BundleListener`: This is an interface to receive `BundleEvent` objects
- `ServiceListener`: This is an interface to receive `ServiceEvent` objects

Note that classes such as `ServiceTracker` (covered in *Chapter 3, Using OSGi Services to Dynamically Wire Applications*) subscribe to service events in order to determine when services come and go, and extender patterns such as Declarative Services listen to bundle events in order to process them when they are installed or removed. Implementing an extender pattern generally looks like the following:

```
context.addBundleListener(new BundleListener() {
  public void bundleChanged(BundleEvent event) {
    int type = event.getType();
    Bundle bundle = event.getBundle();
    String myHeader = bundle.getHeaders().get("X-MyHeader");
    if (type == BundleEvent.STARTED && myHeader != null) {
      addBundle(bundle);
    } else if (type == BundleEvent.STOPPED && myHeader != null) {
      removeBundle(bundle);
    }
  }
});
for (Bundle bundle : context.getBundles()) {
  if (bundle.getState() == Bundle.ACTIVE
    && bundle.getHeaders().get("X-MyHeader") != null) {
    addBundle(bundle);
  }
}
```

Note that the pattern is generally to add the bundle listener first, and then iterate through all the existing bundles. This way, there may be some duplicate calls to the `addBundle` method, but the bundles should not be missed. Generally, the extender pattern will maintain a list of bundles under management so that when the extender provider is stopped, the bundles can be appropriately released.

Also note that most patterns use the existence of a header in the manifest to determine whether or not the bundle should be extended. This allows for a cheap test to determine if the bundle has any contents, and also why headers such as `Service-Component` exist in the Declarative Services specification.

Events and E4

The E4 Eclipse application uses events internally to manage the state of the user interface. The decoupling allows the user interface mechanisms to be separated from the user interface renderer, which allows different user interfaces to be presented (such as JavaFX).

There is an E4-specific wrapper for the `EventAdmin` service called the `IEventBroker`. This provides a simple mechanism to `post` or `send` objects to a particular topic, as well as frontends to register event listeners. It has specific ties to E4 and is present in the UI package. Create a plug-in named `com.packtpub.e4.advanced.event.e4`.

To write portable code that processes events headlessly, consider using `EventAdmin` directly.

Sending events with E4

The `IEventBroker` can be injected into an E4 component using standard injection techniques, and from that, events can be posted synchronously or asynchronously. Create a class named `E4Sender` in the `com.packtpub.e4.advanced.event.e4` plugin.

Obtaining the service in E4 is done through injection. Since the sender requires this, it will be a non-optional component:

```
@Inject
IEventBroker broker;
```

Having obtained the broker service, it can be used to send the e-mail event, in the same way as the previous `EventAdmin` example:

```
public void send() {
  String topic = "smtp/high";
  String body = "Sample email sent via event at "
    + System.currentTimeMillis();
  Map<String, String> email = new HashMap<String, String>();
  email.put("Subject", "Hello World");
  email.put("From", address);
  email.put("To", address);
  email.put("DATA", body);
  broker.send(topic, email);
}
```

The `IEventBroker` has the same kind of event delivery as with the `EventAdmin` service; it can either be used to send events asynchronously with `post`, or synchronously with `send`.

There is a subtle difference between `EventAdmin` and `IEventBroker`. The former only accepts a `Map` or `Dictionary`, while the latter takes any object. If a `Map` or `Dictionary` is passed to `IEventBroker`, it will be passed straight through to the `EventAdmin` without modification. If the object passed is of another type, it will be wrapped in a `Map` with the key `IEventBroker.DATA` (`org.eclipse.e4.data`).

Receiving events with E4

Since the `IEventBroker` uses `EventAdmin` under the covers, it is possible to process an `Event` with the same mechanism as used earlier in the chapter. However, there is an easier way to receive events with E4 using the `@EventTopic` and `@UIEventTopic` annotations. Create a class named `E4Receiver` in the `com.packtpub.e4.advanced.event.e4` plugin.

A method in an E4 component can be annotated with the `@Inject` and `@Optional` annotations, and the argument can be annotated with the `@EventTopic` annotation.

If the argument is an OSGi `Event`, then it will be passed through as it is. This allows the complete set of properties to be pulled from the `Event` object and processed in one call:

```
@Inject
LogService log;
@Inject
@Optional
void receive(@EventTopic("smtp/*") Event event) {
  log.log(LogService.LOG_INFO,
   "Received e-mail to " + event.getProperty("To"));
}
```

If the argument type is not an OSGi `Event` and the type matches the value of the `IEventBroker.DATA`, then that is used directly. If not, the handler will be ignored. This allows `broker.send("topic","value")` to be received with an annotation `receive(@EventTopic("topic") String value)`.

The event will be delivered on a background thread. If the processing of the event requires UI interactions, then these will need to be remapped to run on the UI thread instead. E4 provides a `UISynchronizer` that allows code to run on the UI thread.

There is an alternative annotation that can be used to indicate that the event needs to run on the UI thread. Modifying the annotation to `@UIEventTopic` instead of `@EventTopic` will result in the code being automatically run on the UI thread:

```
void receive(@UIEventTopic("smtp/*") Event event) {
  ...
}
```

When setting up an event handler in E4 (whether `@UIEventTopic` or `@EventTopic`), the documentation suggests using a non-public method. The injector can call non-public methods, and by making the methods non-public, it is ensured that they are not called directly. However, marking them as `private` may result in the compiler or IDE eliminating the code. Therefore, a minimum of package-level or `protected` access should be used for such handler methods.

Subscribing E4 EventHandlers directly

It's possible to subscribe event handlers using the `EventAdmin` directly, but it's also possible to use the `IEventBroker` to `subscribe` (and `unsubscribe`) event handlers. As with `EventAdmin`, the subscription takes a topic and the handler. By default, calls will be run on the UI thread.

```
@Inject
IEventBroker broker;
public void subscribeUI(EventHandler handler) {
  // will be called on the UI thread
  broker.subscribe("smtp/*", handler);
}
```

This allows a custom-built handler to receive events and guarantee that they will be run on the UI thread. E4 uses an (internal) implementation of `EventHandler`, which delegates to the passed handler, optionally wrapping it in a `UISynchronizer`.

Create a class named `E4Subscriber` in the `com.packtpub.e4.advanced.event.e4` plugin. To use the `IEventBroker` class without taking the UI thread, or to pass in a filter, there is an alternative method that provides more options:

```
public void subscribe(EventHandler handler) {
  broker.subscribe("smtp/*", "(Subject=Hello World)",
   handler, true);
}
```

The final parameter is whether to run the method headlessly or not (in other words, do not run in the UI). In this case, the `true` value says that this event should **not** be run in the UI.

This API is mainly useful if a handler always needs to be run in the UI. Alternatively, the body of the handler can trivially wrap itself in a UI block, such as a `UIJob` or via the `UISynchronize` class.

For events that do not need the UI, it is generally more efficient to register them with `EventAdmin` directly.

Comparison between EventAdmin and IEventBroker

When writing code to handle events, either the `EventAdmin` or the `IEventBroker` can be used. Although it may appear that the `IEventBroker` isolates the caller from having to deal with OSGi classes, if there are several properties that need to be acquired, then casting to an OSGi `Event` is often necessary.

The other problem is that the `IEventBroker` has direct references to the `EventHandler` class in the `unsubscribe` and `subscribe` methods. So, any dependency on the `IEventBroker` will automatically have a dependency on the OSGi `EventAdmin` classes.

The `IEventBroker` adds two things that are useful in an E4 application:

- Wrapping in an appropriate E4 context. This allows the event handler to receive injectable content when an event is received, including being able to receive other E4 contextual information
- Wrapping in the UI thread, which allows the event handler to process or interact with UI components.

When writing a handler that needs UI or E4 injection, use the `IEventBroker` to register or use the `@EventTopic` or `@UIEventTopic` annotations.

Designing an event-based application

Firstly, decide if using an event-based paradigm for the application makes sense. Event-driven systems are very useful if they meet the following characteristics:

- Components are loosely coupled
- Operations can be processed asynchronously
- The state of an operation may be part of a transient (in-memory) workflow
- Events can be broadcast and received by multiple listeners
- There is a standard agreement for what details an event should have
- The event topics are (or become) known at development time

On the other hand, the following are not suitable for (OSGi) event-driven systems:

- Where the state of the workflow is not only UI-based but part of the domain
- Where the consumption of an event is handled transactionally
- Where large volumes of events can throttle single-threaded delivery
- Where there is a lack of event payload structure
- Where there is a requirement for a synchronous response to occur

Componentizing the application

The first step in designing an event-driven system is to create components out of the parts of the application that need to talk to each other. This might correspond with the natural boundary of OSGi bundles, or it may be more fine-grained. There may be other boundaries—such as package boundaries or Declarative Services components—that more naturally represent the components in the application.

Once the components are known, it becomes easier to track the relationships between them, including what the messages are that the various components will need to send to one another to work.

For each of the components, there should be one or more input events, and one or more output events (or other side-effect changes). These should be represented as entry and exit points of the components, with a separate input for each type of event that might flow in.

Identifying the channels

For each of the input and output channels of the components, the main purpose needs to be identified. In the first iteration, this can be as simple as a noun (such as "mouse event" or "mail message"). Subsequent iterations will fill out details on the channels that get passed.

The result of this should be a high-level event diagram of the system. It may not be as detailed or object specific as an object interaction diagram, but it should show the graph of input events, followed by the directed triggers that could flow from them. For example, an incoming mail message might trigger a mail processing script, which in turn fires more events to send auto-response mails or log the message to a database.

> Identify whether the channels are firing an event for the purpose of causing a downstream event to occur, or whether they may be firing events for informational purposes (such as logging). Having events fired at different points in a life cycle means that it is easier to add additional functionality afterwards.

Identifying the properties

For each of the events that are sent, there may be zero or more properties containing additional information regarding the event. In the case of an incoming mail message, this could include the sender of the e-mail, the subject, the time the mail was sent, the importance, and of course the e-mail body as well.

The first iteration of the properties is likely to be a rough cut, and will evolve over time. As the event system is fleshed out, it may be necessary to record additional details that weren't captured in the first place. This may include things such as the time zone of the sender, or what hosts it hopped through to be delivered. The flexibility of the event pattern is that it's easy to evolve by adding additional information in subsequent releases and clients who do not need to know this information can simply ignore it.

A similar mechanism for evolution exists in JSON messages. Provided that a client knows how to parse a JSON object and knows which fields to specifically look for, it is possible to add additional fields to the object without breaking backwards compatibility.

Mapping the channels to topics

Once the channels and event properties have been decided, the next step is to map these to topics so they can be used in `EventAdmin`. Topics are represented in slash-separated format, and this is important because the wildcard character `*` can be used to subsume additional levels in the topic hierarchy.

Typically, the event hierarchy is based on a reverse domain name style prefix. This allows events produced by one organization to not conflict with other events when installed into the same runtime. In the case of OSGi bundles, it is very often the case that the event topic prefix will be a variation on the bundle name itself.

The topic may then be further segregated by the sub-channel, depending on what level of granularity is needed. In the E4 model, the topics for items changing in the workspace model begin with `org/eclipse/e4/ui/model/` and then continue with a type such as `commands` or `application`.

Since topics can be matched with wildcards, it may make sense to add another name segment for an event channel (such as `application/ApplicationElement/*` instead of just `application/ApplicationElement`) as this will permit future partitioning of the event space. A terminal leaf node cannot be split down into more children, whereas a segment can have more segments added afterwards. This was a pattern identified by the E4 platform, which initially just used the terminal node but then subsequently switched to a more partitioned space so that changes in individual attributes could be nominated using a common prefix.

Simulating events

One advantage of an event-driven system is that it is very easy to test in isolation. Besides having events driven by the `EventAdmin` specification directly, it is also possible to simulate the arrival of an event by calling the method directly. It is thus possible to test individual components by setting up listeners looking for output events and simulating the incoming events.

This also helps to test the component in a black box manner. Provided that the events delivered are well formed, and the events generated have the correct data, it is possible to show that the component is operating as expected.

It may be necessary to set up other mock services, event sources, or event sinks in order to test the functionality of that component, but the principle of segregated components making it easy to test are still important.

Versioning and loose typing

Because event-based systems are inherently loosely typed, it is necessary to define both the values of event topics and the schema of those events in an external location. This may be part of the project's documentation, or there may be other systems that record this information externally to the project or with schemas such as RelaxNG (though that is more suited for XML documents).

Changing the event's properties or modifying the event's topics will not be picked up by a static compiler. This results in a higher testing requirement being placed on the system itself, but also gives it additional flexibility for being able to respond to changes in the future.

When the version of the API changes, it may be necessary to implement version numbering information in the payload of the event itself. This can be used to communicate the state of the API to clients at any time, and if backward compatible changes are required, then these can be brought into play. It may also be possible for the client and server to agree on the version number to use, even if it means degrading to a lower version.

Always design a version number in your message formats, be they OSGi Events, JSON messages, or even XML documents. The version number should be stored at the top level and revisions to this number may indicate different content elsewhere or in a child element of the message.

It may be desirable to store the version number as a single integer, or it may be a pair or triplet of numbers. Whatever value is chosen, it should be treated as a semantic version, with major digits indicating a backwardly incompatible change, and minor versions being backwardly compatible but with potentially new features being added.

Servers (or event sources) hardly ever get rolled back, so typically these numbers will be monotonically increasing. It is thus usually sufficient to represent just the major number, or possibly the major and minor number as part of the API definition. It is usually an error to include the micro/patch numbers in the public part of the API as this binds the client too tightly to the version of the API in use. The main reason for exposing the minor version is in case a client is implemented to selectively enable additions for newer functions; this comes in handy if the same client is exposed to both old and new versions for an extended period of time.

With a known version and a known set of event properties and types, it is possible to document changes and upgrade the API when necessary to add new features or to document backward compatibility issues.

Event object contents

Since the `Event` objects are an in-memory representation, and the map that is passed can store objects of any type, it is possible to put any kind of object into the event object itself. For example, the `Bundle` can be embedded in the `Event` object or UI-specific components such as `Color` or even open `InputStream` objects.

The OSGi specification suggests limiting the use of the `Event` properties to the set of primitive values such as `int` (or their object counterparts such as `Integer`) along with `String` and single-dimensional arrays of the same. In other words, although it is possible to store `URL` instances in the map directly, it is recommended that it be stored as a `String` and then converted on the client into a `URL` object.

The reason for this recommendation is that while `EventAdmin` is a system designed for use within a single VM, it is not limited to being used in a single VM. In fact, in conjunction with OSGi Remote Services, it is possible to set up a distributed `EventAdmin` fabric, where events generated on one node get transported over the network and then handled on a remote node. To make this possible, all the values in the `Event` object need to be `Serializable`, and because it may be the case that the events are processed in a different language (such as JavaScript or C), having a standard set of known datatypes facilitates that translation.

Similarly, objects placed into an OSGi `Event` should be immutable. If an object placed into an `Event` is not immutable (such as the old `Date` class), then it would be possible to dispatch an event, and later modify its contents before a consumer has time to process the original value. No runtime checks are made by `EventAdmin`, but violating this rule can lead to surprises.

Comparison with JMS

Designing an event-driven system looks very similar to designing a message-driven system using an API such as **Java Messaging Service (JMS)**. Both follow a similar paradigm for being able to build an application; the system is modeled as a set of state changes triggered by incoming events (messages), resulting in either system updates or subsequent events (messages) being fired.

The following differences are worth observing between the event-driven and message-driven systems:

- **No broker**: In a JMS system, there is an intermediary (broker) that runs in a separate process with memory separation between the clients. The lifetime of this process is orthogonal to the lifetime of the client, and in particular, there may not be a broker running at any point. On the other hand, with `EventAdmin`, there is no separate standalone broker process, although the `EventAdmin` service acts like a centralized in-process broker.
- **Transactional**: Probably the biggest single difference is that JMS systems are designed to be transactional in nature. If the message is not processed successfully on a node, then the intermediary broker can attempt to pass that message on to another subscriber for redelivery. The transactional support can also extend to other transactional resources (such as databases) for a clean separation. No such transactional support is available in `EventAdmin`.
- **Broadcast versus point-to-point**: JMS provides different types of message deliveries. In a broadcast mechanism, all subscribers are notified of a message (these are typically called *topics*), and this is the mechanism that `EventAdmin` uses for `Event` delivery. JMS also provides a point-to-point mechanism (called *queues*), which ensures that only one subscriber gets each message. Queues are often used to allow scaling by adding additional workers. The `EventAdmin` service does not have a concept of queues or single event delivery.
- **Persistent versus transient**: JMS can be configured to operate in a persistent mode (where all messages are written to disk) or in a transient mode (where messages are held in memory and lost upon system restart). `EventAdmin` only has transient support; if the OSGi runtime crashes, then all in-flight events are lost. For unimportant states (such as which button in a GUI was being clicked at the time), this may not be an issue, but for data-specific processing, this may be a problem.

- **Language bindings**: Typically, JMS systems support more languages since the intermediary broker provides a means to be able to convert the message types to different languages, provided that a standardized set of properties are used. The OSGi `EventAdmin` doesn't officially support other languages, but leaves it open to implementors of the frameworks to support them if desired. In practice, it is fairly easy to hook up a set of events to something like JSON messages, which are becoming the de facto interchange format between systems as well as between clients and browsers.

The advice is to use an in-memory system such as `EventAdmin` where the state of the workflow is transient or does not need transactional persistence, and use a more heavy-weight solution such as JMS when queues or transactional storage is required.

Summary

The OSGi `EventAdmin` service provides a simple means to implement an event-driven application model in an OSGi runtime, and uses topics made of string identifiers separated by slashes to partition the namespace for events. An `Event` contains a number of key/value pairs, using `String` keys and primitive or `String` values, which can then be received by `EventHandler` implementations.

Handlers are registered as standard OSGi services, and can take advantage of filtering based on event contents as well as topic names or prefixes. Events are used heavily within the Eclipse E4 platform, and there are E4-specific annotations `@EventTopic` and `@UIEventTopic` that can be used to invoke methods upon receipt of particular events.

Finally, the chapter presented how event-driven applications can be designed along with a comparison of event-driven and message-driven services. Although superficially similar, message-driven systems often deal with persistence, transactions, and queues as well as topics.

The next chapter will look at how Eclipse P2 is used to generate update sites and what additional information can be encoded into P2 installers.

9
Deploying and Updating with P2

As a modular end user application, Eclipse has always been able to update itself and install new content. Under the covers, Eclipse has always consisted of a number of **plug-ins** as well as a number of **features** (a way of aggregating plug-ins). The original update mechanism, the classic update manager, provided a simple way to install and update features and plug-ins (bundles). In Eclipse 3.4, a mechanism called P2 was created that allowed more powerful update mechanisms and included the ability to update native code and configuration files. P2 provides a means to provision, run, update, and configure Eclipse-based applications.

Eclipse P2

The "P2" of Eclipse P2 was derived from "provisioning platform", but it is generally referred to by its acronym. It was created to improve the provisioning story not only for features and bundles, but also for non-Java content such as native executables and configuration files.

> An overview of P2 and its history is available from the online Eclipse help, also visible at `http://help.eclipse.org/luna/topic/org.eclipse.platform.doc.isv/guide/p2_overview.htm`.

There are a few key concepts to understand in P2:

- **Artifact**: This is a collection of bytes, such as a plug-in, feature, or product
- **Metadata**: This is the information about artifacts, including versioning information and dependency information, which is referred to as **Installable Units (IUs)**

- **Repository**: This is a collection of artifacts (an artifact repository) or metadata (a metadata repository) that may be hosted on a remote site
- **Composite Repository**: This is a composition of one or more repository references
- **Agent**: This a provisioning agent that can perform P2 updates, such as the headless director application or the new update mechanism
- **Touchpoint**: This is a post-processing action, such as modification to the Eclipse properties file (`eclipse.ini`), other branding, or the installation or removal of native files
- **Profile**: This represents the currently installed software as a set of IUs

Provisioning with the P2 director

An Eclipse application can be provisioned with all of the installable units using an existing P2 install, or by using an Eclipse application called the **director**.

Applications are launched headlessly with Eclipse using the `-application` command-line argument. In addition, it is common for applications to supply the `-consoleLog` argument (which ensures that any error messages are printed to the console) and the `-noSplash` argument (to disable the splash screen from showing).

Eclipse applications are covered in more detail in chapter 7 of *Eclipse 4 Plug-in Development by Example Beginner's Guide, Packt Publishing*.

The director is launched with the `org.eclipse.equinox.p2.director` application. Arguments specific to the director application include the following:

- `-repository`: The URL of the repository to install the content from
- `-destination`: The location to write out the installed contents
- `-installIU`: The installable unit to install
- `-uninstallIU`: The installable unit to uninstall
- `-profile`: The name of the P2 profile
- `-profileProperties`: The properties of the profile; generally, it includes `org.eclipse.update.install.features=true` to enable feature support

To provision a new copy of Eclipse, the following command can be run:

```
$ /path/to/eclipse -consoleLog -noSplash
 -application org.eclipse.equinox.p2.director
 -repository http://download.eclipse.org/eclipse/updates/4.4/
 -profileProperties org.eclipse.update.install.features=true
 -installIU org.eclipse.sdk.ide
 -destination /path/to/newfolder
...
Installing org.eclipse.sdk.ide 4.4.0.I20140606-1215.
Operation completed in 135634 ms.
```

The new version of Eclipse will be installed into `/path/to/newfolder`.

If running on Windows, `eclipsec.exe` can be used to allow the program to be run without opening a new GUI window (the `c` suffix stands for console).

Installing content into existing applications

The director can be used to install content into an existing application. The same process is used (as described earlier) with an additional IU; for example, to provision EGit support into an Eclipse application, the following command can be run:

```
$ /path/to/eclipse -consoleLog -noSplash
 -application org.eclipse.equinox.p2.director
 -repository http://download.eclipse.org/egit/updates/
 -installIU org.eclipse.egit.feature.group
 -destination /path/to/newfolder
...
Installing org.eclipse.egit.feature.group 3.4.1.201406201815-r
Operation completed in 11295 ms.
```

To install a feature into Eclipse, the installable unit name must be known. Generally, this is of the form `org.eclipse.<project>.feature.group`. It's possible to find out what the installable unit name is from an existing Eclipse installation by navigating to **Window** | **Preferences** (**Eclipse** | **Preferences** on Mac OS X) and clicking on **Installation Details**:

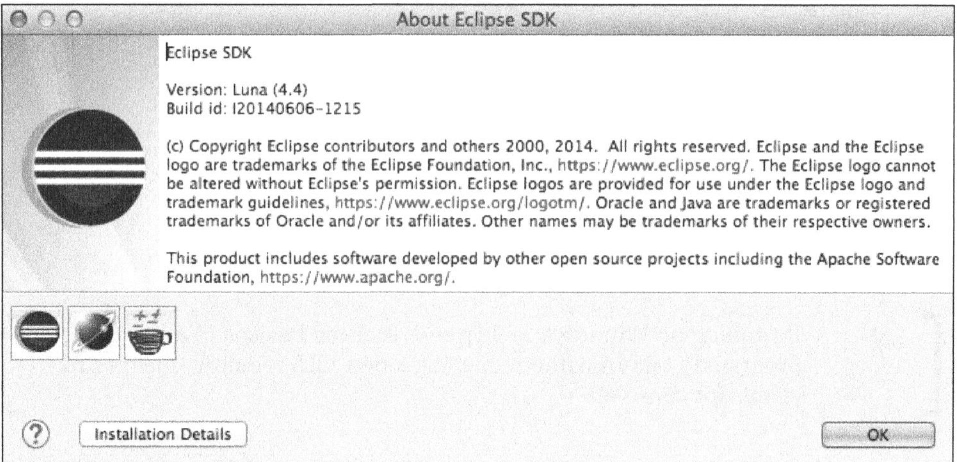

Navigate to the **Features** list, and the **Feature Id** will be shown. The name of the installable unit is the feature ID with a `.feature.group` suffix:

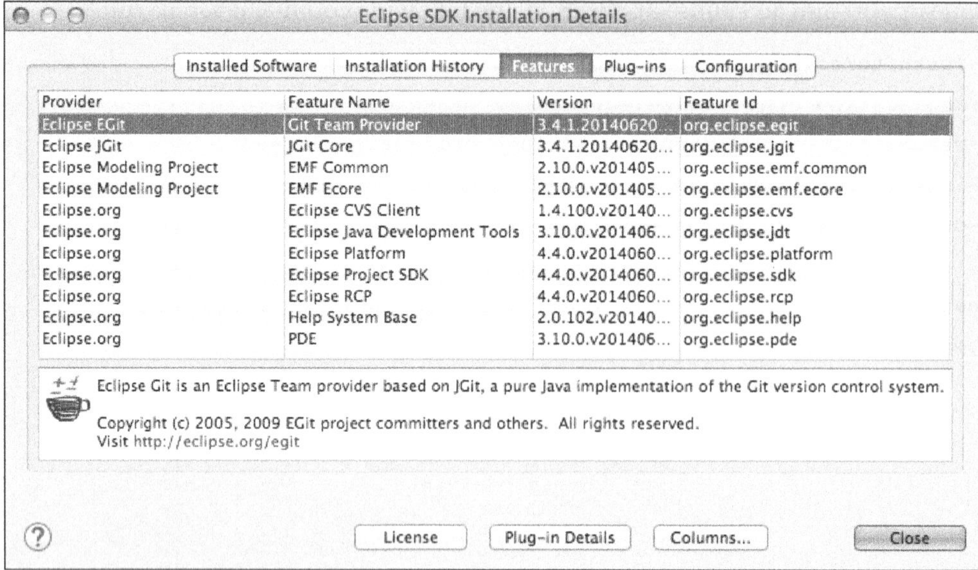

If the feature is not already installed in an Eclipse application, the feature ID can be discovered through the update manager. Navigate to **Help | Install New Software...** and then search for the feature to install:

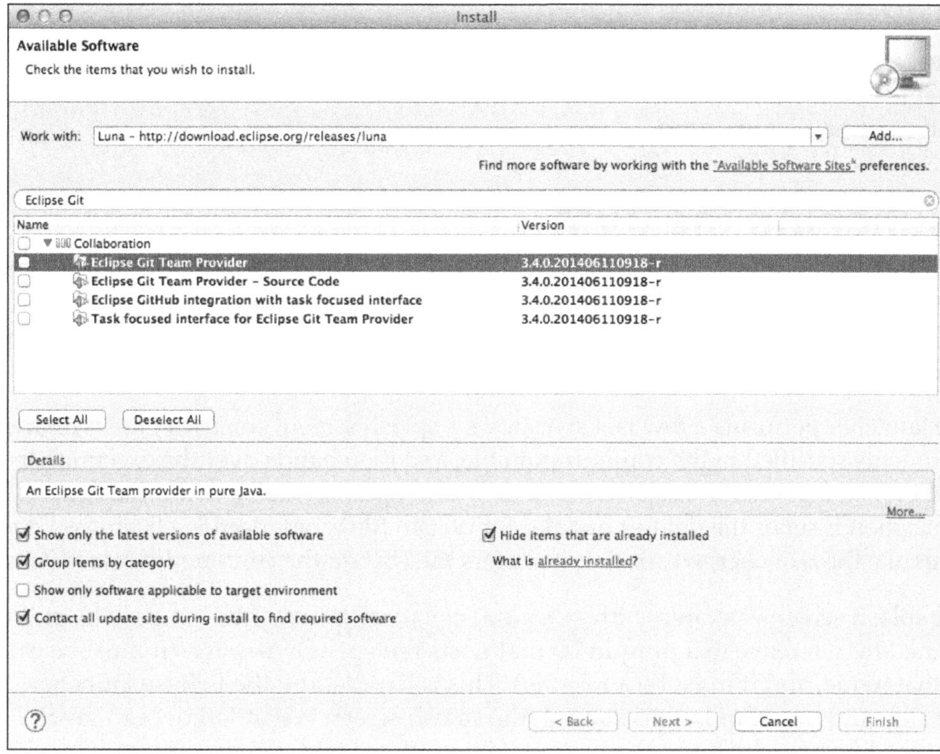

Select the feature and click on the **More...** link at the bottom-right corner of the details section, and a window will be shown with more information. The **General** page will have an **Identifier** label that contains the **Installable Unit** identifier, which for EGit is `org.eclipse.egit.feature.group`:

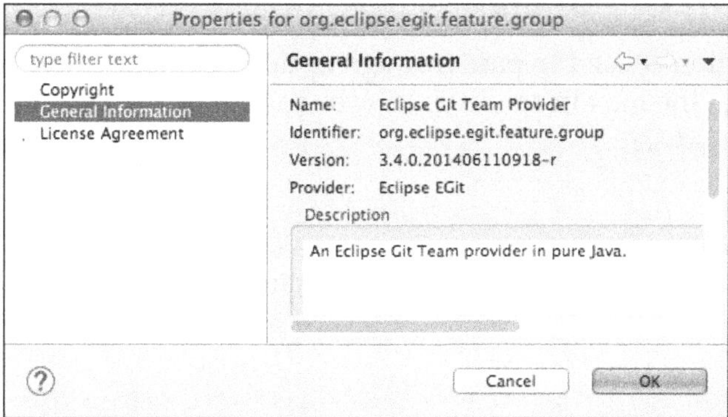

Running P2 applications

When a P2-managed application starts, a set of configuration files are read to determine which plug-ins and features to enable. Even though files may be present in `features/` and `plugins/`, they won't be installed into an Eclipse application unless the P2 configuration details refer to them. To understand how this works, it is informative to see how a modern Eclipse application launches and what configuration files are used.

Launching the JVM

The **launcher** is the `eclipse` executable (or `Eclipse.app` on Mac OS X). When run, the corresponding **eclipse.ini** configuration file is read. If Eclipse has been rebranded/renamed, then the executable will be called something else (`notEclipse`), and it will read the corresponding file (`notEclipse.ini`).

The launcher performs a few tasks; it shows a splash screen, creates a JVM with the arguments specified in the configuration file, and then hands over the execution to the Equinox launcher. It is also used to define an **open action** so that if the Eclipse application is set as the default handler for certain file types, double-clicking on it will re-invoke the launcher, which then transfers the URL to the running Eclipse instance.

The splash screen is shown with `-showSplash` (or hidden with `-noSplash`), and it is defined by reference to a plug-in ID that hosts the `splash.bmp` file (it must be called by that name, and it must be a `bmp` file). This is handled by the Eclipse launcher initially, and once Equinox is started, the splash screen is handed over to the SWT runtime library, which can then annotate it with text and progress bars.

The launcher creates an instance of the JVM based on the arguments specified. If a JVM is not given, it tries to find one using various heuristics (it checks whether `java` is on the path, whether `JAVA_HOME` has been set, and so on). However, it is possible to specify a JVM on the command line with the `-vm /path/to/bin/java` or `-vm /path/to/bin/` argument.

The `-vmargs` option is used to pass through options to the JVM itself. This can be used to set the max heap size (`-Xmx`) or configure the **PermGen** space (`-XX:MaxPermSize`).

Note that OpenJDK 8 removes the need to configure the PermGen space directly, and not all JVMs have the option.

The launcher provides an additional option, `--launcher.XXMaxPermSize`, which performs some heuristics to see whether the `-XX:MaxPermSize` is understood by the JVM being used, and adding the argument if it is understood.

> Generally, the `--launcher.XXMaxPermSize` argument should be preferred in order to avoid problems with JVMs that do not support this option.

Any arguments specified after the `-vmargs` option are passed through to the JVM, and not to the Equinox runtime. So, given `eclipse a b c -vmargs d e f`, the `a b c` options will be handled by the launcher and passed through to Equinox, while the `d e f` options are passed to the JVM. When adding command-line options to the end of either the configuration file or the command line, ensure that they are added in the right place.

> When specifying options on the command line with `-vmargs`, it will override any elements in the `eclipse.ini` file, unless the `--launcher.appendVmargs` argument is given. Using `--launcher.appendVmargs` is recommended for all Eclipse applications, and it is added by default to standard Eclipse packages.

Any system properties can also be specified on the command line, after `-vmargs`, using the standard `-D` options. There is a list of such options described in the online Eclipse help under *Eclipse runtime options*, but particular ones of note are as follows:

- `-Dosgi.requiredJavaVersion=1.6`: This is the minimum Java version required in order to launch the platform
- `-Dorg.eclipse.swt.internal.carbon.smallFonts`: Use smaller fonts when running on Mac OS X
- `-Xdock:icon=/path/to/Eclipse.icns`: Use the given icon as the dock icon on Mac OS X
- `-XstartOnFirstThread`: This allows SWT applications to run on Mac OS X

Many other arguments, such as `-clean` and `-data`, can also be specified as system properties such as `osgi.clean` and `osgi.instance.area`.

Starting Equinox

Once the launcher hands control over to Equinox (specified with the `-startup` and `--launcher.library` arguments), the process moves into Java code. It is also possible to run Equinox with `java -jar plugins/org.eclipse.equinox.launcher_*.jar`. Arguments are still passed through to the underlying application.

Equinox reads the `configuration/config.ini` file, which defines a set of system properties for the application. In particular, the default workspace is defined in a property `osgi.instance.area`, and allows substitution of property values such as the user's home directory with `@user.home`.

The `config.ini` file contains the initial bundle set to bring up the framework, which includes the `simpleconfigurator` bundle. This reads the contents of the `org.eclipse.equinox.simpleconfigurator/bundles.info` file, which is the set of bundles to be loaded into the framework. This list represents the last known state of the framework, but its history is managed through P2 profiles.

The `config.ini` file looks like the following:

```
eclipse.p2.profile=epp.package.standard
eclipse.p2.data.area=@config.dir/../p2
eclipse.product=org.eclipse.platform.ide
osgi.bundles=reference\:file\:org.eclipse.equinox.simple...
```

From a P2 perspective, there are two things of interest here. The first is the P2 profile name (`epp.package.standard`) and the second is the P2 data area (usually `p2` at the top level of the Eclipse install). The `p2` data area is used to store all P2 data, which includes the following:

- `org.eclipse.equinox.p2.core/cache/`: This is used to store cached copies of the root feature installs
- `org.eclipse.equinox.p2.engine/profileRegistry/`: This is the location of the P2 profiles
- `org.eclipse.equinox.p2.repository/cache/`: This is used to store a copy of the `artifacts.xml` and `content.xml` downloads from remote update sites

P2 profiles are sets of enabled features and plug-ins that are available in a running Eclipse framework. P2 allows for different profiles to be concurrently installed in an Eclipse install, and switch between them at launch time using a command-line argument. It is possible to have, for example, an Eclipse application configured for C development and an Eclipse application configured for Java development in the same install, and then at launch time switch between them using `-Declipse.p2.profile=epp.package.cpp` or `-Declipse.p2.profile=epp.package.standard`

Each profile is given a separate directory underneath `profileRegistry`; for example, .../`profileRegistry/epp.package.standard.profile/` is used for the EPP standard profile. Underneath the profile directory is a set of compressed timestamped files that use the time in milliseconds, which represent the state of the Eclipse platform's installed features and plug-ins at that point in time. When a new installation occurs (such as adding new features), a new timestamped profile is generated. When Eclipse starts, it looks for the largest numerical value that ends in `.profile.gz` (or `.profile`) and uses that as the boot profile.

The profile itself contains an XML file that contains `properties`, `units`, and `iuProperties`. It looks like the following:

```
<profile id="epp.package.standard" timestamp="1395612330274">
  <properties size="7">
    <property name="org.eclipse.update.install.features"
     value="true"/>
    …
  </properties>
  <units size="1564">
    <unit id="org.eclipse.jdt.feature.group"
   version="3.9.2.v20140221-1700" singleton="false">
      <properties size="12">
        <property name="org.eclipse.equinox.p2.name"
         value="%featureName"/>
        …
      </properties>
      <provides size="3">
        <provided namespace="org.eclipse.equinox.p2.iu"
         name="org.eclipse.jdt.feature.jar"
         version="3.9.2.v20140221-1700"/>
      </provides>
      <filter>(org.eclipse.update.install.features=true)</filter>
      <artifacts size="1">
        <artifact classifier="org.eclipse.update.feature"
         id="org.eclipse.jdt"
         version="3.9.2.v20140221-1700"/>
      </artifacts>
    </unit>
    …
  </units>
  <iuProperties size="1564">
    …
  </iuProperties>
</profile>
```

There are some top-level properties associated with the profile as a whole (whether features are enabled, where the cache locations are, and so on) as well as a set of installable units and installable unit properties. The installable units include plug-ins, features, configuration settings, and sets of dependencies that are required for the platform.

Each installable unit has a name and a version, which almost always correspond to a binary on disk. There is also a namespace, which is used to partition the installable units into different groups:

- `java.package`: This is the name of a Java package, to enable `Import-Package` resolution
- `osgi.bundle`: This is a dependency on a specific bundle name, to enable `Require-Bundle` resolution
- `osgi.ee`: This is the execution environment (such as `JavaSE-1.8`)
- `osgi.fragment`: This defines additional requirements for fragment bundles on their fragment host
- `org.eclipse.update.feature`: This gives information about features to enable feature dependencies
- `tooling*`: These are custom-created properties to enable specific entries to be added packages, such as `toolingorg.eclipse.platform.sdk` and `toolingepp.package.standard`

When items are installed into an application, the profile records what the additions or removals were and then regenerates the `bundles.info` file. This ensures that when the framework restarts, the profile is brought up in the correct state. Similarly, feature uninstallation will remove the entries from `bundles.info` and write out a new profile state.

Note that P2 manages more than just `bundles.info`; it can append entries to the `eclipse.ini` file, replace the application launcher itself, unpack and extract certain files from the runtime, and create directories. It is also used to calculate which additional features are required when installing new content. For this, the boolean satisfiability library SAT4j is used to determine whether there are any conflicts or whether there are any missing dependencies.

Once the P2 profile is activated, the bundles are installed and started if necessary, and then control is handed over to the Eclipse product or application, such as `org.eclipse.platform.ide` or `org.eclipse.ui.ide.workbench`.

P2 repositories

Repositories consist of a set of installable units, which are built from a set of features and plug-ins, optionally organized into categories. In Eclipse, a special **Update Site** project can be used to represent the set of features in a development environment, or it can be used as the source for a Tycho `eclipse-repository` build. An **Update Site** project can be created by navigating to **File** | **New** | **Other** | **Plug-in Development** | **Update Site Project**:

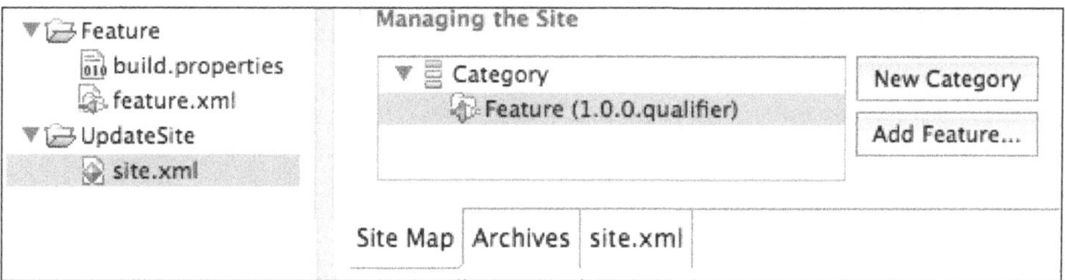

A feature can be built by clicking on the **Build All** or by highlighting the feature and clicking on **Build**:

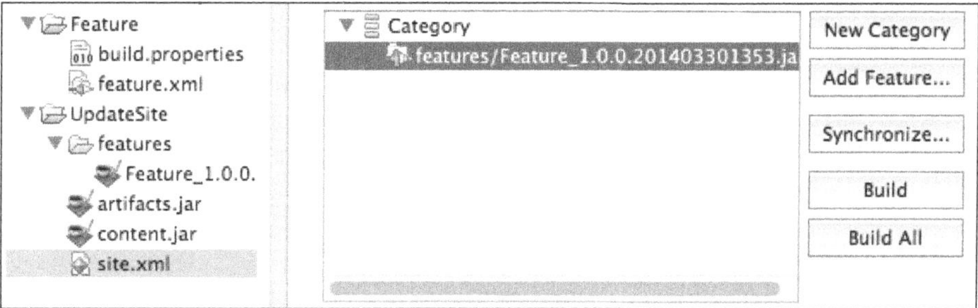

The feature will be named `features/name_version.timestamp.jar`, along with two files, **artifacts.jar** and **content.jar**. These two files are generated by the export mechanism and contain the set of P2 data that is required for the content to be visible to P2 installers. A similar option is presented if the feature is exported on its own via the **Generate P2 repository** checkbox; for this, navigate to **File** | **Export** | **Plug-in Development** | **Deployable features** to view the option:

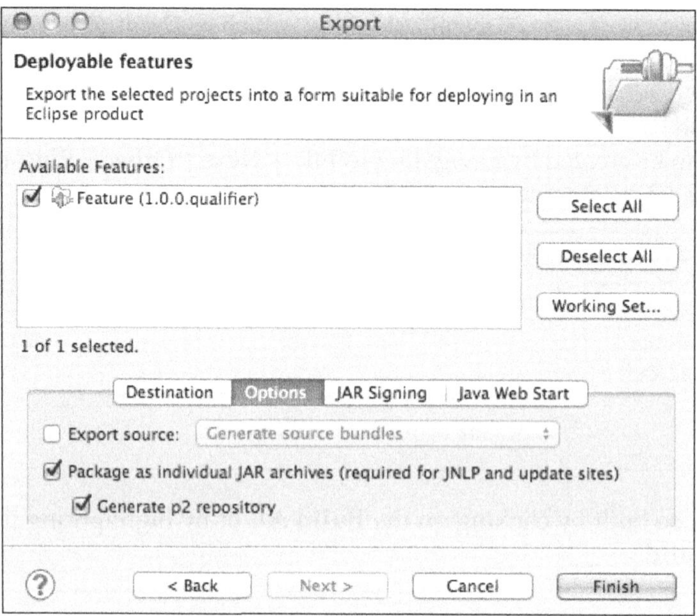

The contents of these files describe the individual downloadable files (`artifacts.jar`) and the metadata of each file (`content.jar`). The files themselves just consist of a single XML file, `artifacts.xml`, and `content.xml`.

P2 artifacts and contents files

The P2 artifacts file provides a way to bind an installable unit to a downloadable file. Given a triplet of `classifier`, `id`, and `version`, the artifacts file allows an installable unit's URL to be calculated. It also provides some additional information such as what the expected download type of the file is, its size, and optionally an MD5 checksum.

A repository has a human-readable name, a type, and a version. Underneath it are three sections; a list of properties, a list of mappings, and finally a list of artifacts. The following XML shows an example of a repository called `Update Site`:

```
<?xml version='1.0' encoding='UTF-8'?>
<?artifactRepository version='1.1.0'?>
```

```
<repository name='Update Site' type='org.eclipse.equinox.p2.artifact.
repository.simpleRepository' version='1'>
  <properties size='2'>
    <property name='p2.timestamp' value='1396184010474'/>
    <property name='p2.compressed' value='true'/>
  </properties>
  <mappings size='3'>
    <rule filter='(&amp; (classifier=osgi.bundle))'
     output='${repoUrl}/plugins/${id}_${version}.jar'/>
    <rule filter='(&amp; (classifier=binary))'
     output='${repoUrl}/binary/${id}_${version}'/>
    <rule filter='(&amp; (classifier=org.eclipse.update.feature))'
     output='${repoUrl}/features/${id}_${version}.jar'/>
  </mappings>
  <artifacts size='1'>
    <artifact classifier='org.eclipse.update.feature'
     id='Feature' version='1.0.0.201403301353'>
      <properties size='2'>
        <property name='download.contentType'
         value='application/zip'/>
        <property name='download.size' value='338'/>
      </properties>
    </artifact>
  </artifacts>
</repository>
```

The properties are used to provide additional information about the artifacts; in this case, the timestamp at which the content was last generated and whether the content of the repository should be compressed into an `artifacts.jar` file.

The properties can also contain a mirror reference with the `p2.mirrorsURL`. This allows a set of mirrors to be queried for an artifact instead of just the originating server; the Eclipse infrastructure uses this to share the load between mirror sites when new versions of Eclipse are released. When an artifact needs to be downloaded, the mirrors URL will be hit, and an XML file will be returned.

For Eclipse Luna, the mirror URL is `http://www.eclipse.org/downloads/download.php?format=xml&file=/eclipse/updates/4.4/R-4.4-201406061215`.

This is encoded in the `artifacts.xml` file as follows:

```
<property name='p2.mirrorsURL'
 value='http://www.eclipse.org/downloads/download.
php?format=xml&amp;file=/eclipse/updates/4.4/R-4.4-201406061215'/>
```

Because XML files cannot contain ampersands (&) without escaping, the XML file has `&` to separate parameters. The returned XML file looks like the following:

```
<mirrors>
  <mirror
   url="http://www.mirrorservice.org/sites/download.eclipse.org/"
   label="[United Kingdom] UK Mirror Service (http)"/>
  <mirror url="http://ftp.snt.utwente.nl/pub/software/eclipse/"
   label="[Netherlands] SNT, University of Twente (http)"/>
  <mirror url="http://eclipse.mirror.triple-it.nl/"
   label="[Netherlands] Triple IT (http)"/>
  ...
</mirrors>
```

Although the Eclipse servers generate the request dynamically with a PHP script, this could be provided with a static XML file or another automatically generated mechanism.

The Eclipse servers send out both HTTP and FTP mirrors; for sites that have firewalls that don't support FTP, it's possible to add `&protocol=http` to get just a list of HTTP mirrors.

If the `p2.mirrorsURL` is not present on the remote server, or it returns an empty list, the P2 mechanism will fall back to the originally requested URL.

The contents file contains much more information and records properties extracted from the bundle, such as the license, the copyright, and vendor, and for OSGi bundles, what packages are imported and exported along with other generic require-capability elements. There is a one-to-one mapping between entries in the artifacts file with entries in the content file.

Binary and packed files

Along with JARs hosted on an update site, other binary content can be stored and served. There are two categories for non-JAR content:

- Binary assets such as the Eclipse executable or configuration files
- Packed JARs using the `pack200` compression mechanism

Both of these can be stored either as top-level files in the `binary` directory or in a special `.blobstore` folder.

The **blobstore** is a means of allowing arbitrary content to be stored without the file extension causing problems for the update site server, by creating randomized filenames to distinguish between assets. Because the names of the files in the blobstore do not correspond to any well-known algorithm (such as `md5` or `sha1`), the names of the files give no information about its content. This can be used for storing binary executables as well as packed JAR files.

The blobstore causes problems for some webservers that don't know or expect a particular type of data. As a result, it is often desirable for a P2 repository to store `pack200` files next to the JARs instead of the blobstore. This is achieved by storing a property `packFilesAsSiblings` with the value `true` in the `artifacts.xml` file of the destination repository:

```
<property name='publishPackFilesAsSiblings'
 value='true'/>
```

This will ensure that the blobstore is not used for writing out the content of pack files, but they will be put next to the JAR files instead.

Note that an empty `artifacts.xml` file with the property needs to be created first, followed by running the mirror operation in order to take advantage of the update.

Creating P2 mirrors

Although a direct file or rsync copy will allow a set of artifacts to be mirrored, it is possible to use built-in functionality in Eclipse to allow P2 repositories to be mirrored. This will ensure that the contents listed in the remote update site are transferred as expected, and the metadata files are updated correctly.

Mirroring is done separately for artifacts and metadata, but they both follow the same structure. One mirrors the `artifacts.jar` files, and the other mirrors the `content.jar` files.

To mirror Luna's artifacts, use the following command:

```
$ /path/to/eclipse -consoleLog -noSplash -application
   org.eclipse.equinox.p2.artifact.repository.mirrorApplication
 -source http://download.eclipse.org/releases/luna/
 -destination file:///path/to/luna-mirror
 -verbose
 -raw
 -ignoreErrors
```

The `-verbose` flag tells the mirroring process to print out what is being copied at each point and is an optional argument.

The `-raw` flag tells the mirroring process to copy as is without translating or rebuilding the metadata from the original bundle. This is faster, but it can sometimes cause problems when mirroring from old-style update sites. This only has an effect on artifact mirroring and is an optional argument.

When the `-ignoreErrors` flag is given, any errors seen during the mirroring operation are ignored, causing the mirroring to continue. If not specified, then any error will terminate the mirroring process. This only has an effect on artifact mirroring and is an optional argument.

To mirror Luna's metadata, use the following command:

```
$ /path/to/eclipse -consoleLog -noSplash -application
   org.eclipse.equinox.p2.metadata.repository.mirrorApplication
 -source http://download.eclipse.org/releases/luna/
 -destination file:///path/to/luna-mirror
 -verbose
```

The previous two commands are almost identical; the only difference is the application name.

> Note that the destination must begin with `file:/` and thus be an absolute path, even though only `file:/` URLs are allowed to be used in the destination argument.

While mirroring, P2 will take advantage of any mirrors found. If the remote site lists a set of mirrors, then P2 will consult the mirror lookup and download assets from mirrors in order to spread the load.

> This can sometimes cause problems because mirrors are randomly switched between HTTP and FTP sites; if using a proxy that doesn't support FTP or are behind a misconfigured NAT router, then these connections will silently fail. To disable this, pass `-vmargs -Declipse.p2.mirrors=false` as the last entry on the command line.

The mirroring process can also verify the MD5 signatures of the files when they are being mirrored. This can be disabled by passing the command-line arguments `-vmargs -Declipse.p2.MD5Check=false`.

Generating P2 metadata

Some old update sites do not have P2 metadata generated; instead, they just have a `site.xml` file as a classic update site. While this works in older versions of Eclipse, it may cause errors with a new Eclipse install (or a Tycho build) with a cryptic error message that reads **Update site contains Partial IUs and cannot be used**.

To generate P2 metadata from a folder that contains `features/` and `plugins/` directories, the following Eclipse command can be run. Given a directory *DIR*, the following command will generate the `content.jar` and `artifacts.jar` files:

```
$ /path/to/eclipse -consoleLog -noSplash -application
   org.eclipse.equinox.p2.publisher.FeaturesAndBundlesPublisher
 -source DIR
 -metadataRepository file:/DIR
 -artifactRepository file:/DIR
 -compress
```

Note that *DIR* must be a filesystem, but the `-metadataRepository` and `-artifactRepository` arguments require URLs with a `file:/` prefix.

The `-compress` argument tells the P2 publisher to generate an `artifacts.jar` that contains the `artifacts.xml` file; similarly, the `content.jar` contains `content.xml`. While the standalone XML files are more human-readable, they are often between two and ten times smaller when compressed.

Unless using the P2 applications for learning exercises, the `-compress` argument should always be used.

The previous command will generate the `artifacts.jar` and `content.jar` files in the same location as the `features/` and `bundles/` directories, which is often what is required. However, if the output directory is in a different location, then only the `artifacts.jar` and `content.jar` files will be generated. To copy the features and plug-ins from the old location to the new location, use the `-publishArtifacts` argument as well:

```
$ /path/to/eclipse -consoleLog -noSplash -application
   org.eclipse.equinox.p2.publisher.FeaturesAndBundlesPublisher
 -source INDIR
 -metadataRepository file:/OUTDIR
 -artifactRepository file:/OUTDIR
 -compress
 -publishArtifacts
```

This will copy the features and bundles from *INDIR* to *OUTDIR* as well as generating the P2 metadata.

Note that these commands will overwrite the existing metadata, and in the case of the `-publishArtifacts` option, will overwrite existing features and plugins.

To add data to the existing repository instead of overwriting, use the `-append` argument. This will allow multiple updates to be mirrored into a single location.

Categorizing update sites

Updates and installations in Eclipse are usually feature based. Features are logical groupings of plug-ins and other features; for example, the Java Development Tools core feature consists of 24 individual plug-ins. Instead of showing the 24 plug-ins separately in the update site, only the JDT feature is shown.

There are also some other grouping features that do not necessarily need to be shown to the user. For example, JDT depends on Platform; Platform depends on P2, Help, and RCP; and RCP depends on E4.

All of these features can be shown to the user when the **Group items by category** checkbox is unselected, which can be found under **Help** | **Install New Software...**:

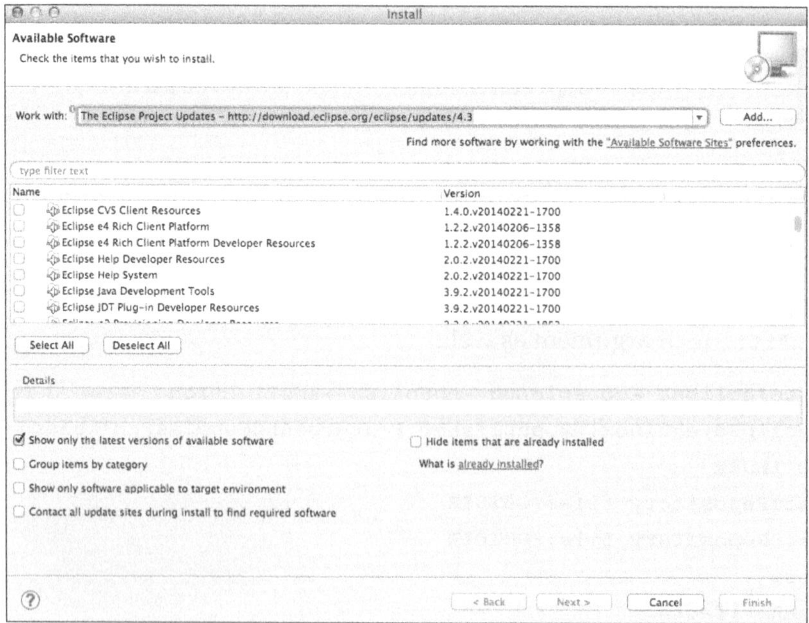

Showing the user all of these options may be confusing. Instead, they can be categorized to provide one level of grouping if the **Group items by category** checkbox is selected:

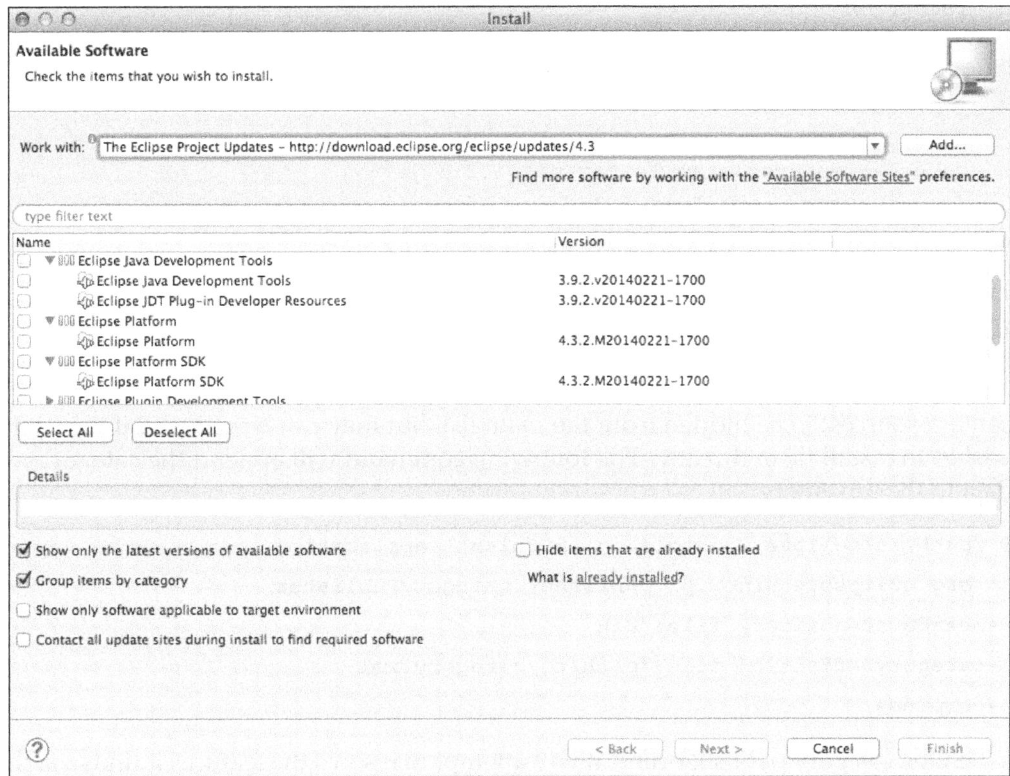

These categories are published as P2 metadata and presented to the user. Typically, these are published in conjunction with the artifacts, but the Eclipse update mechanisms allow for composite update sites, including the ability to publish the category information to a separate site.

To generate category information for an update site, a `category.xml` or `site.xml` file can be used. These files have identical contents and tags, but the `category.xml` file is intended to be used solely as an input for generating P2 data and not consumed at installation time, whereas the `site.xml` file was used to publish and consume updates in pre-Eclipse 3.4 days.

PDE provides both a `site.xml` **Update Site Map** editor and a `category.xml` **Category Definition** editor. While both can define categories and referenced features, the latter can also refer to plug-ins directly. An example category file looks like the following:

```
<site>
  <category-def name="cat.id" label="Text name">
    <description>Description of the category</description>
  </category-def>
  <feature id="example.feature" version="1.2.3"
   url="features/example.feature_1.2.3.jar">
    <category name="cat.id"/>
  </feature>
</site>
```

With an appropriate `category.xml` (or `site.xml`) file, the `CategoryPublisher` application can be used to generate P2 metadata to display the groups in the **Install New Software** dialog. This allows additional or helper features (or those that just contain sources) to be hidden from the main list, but they can be exposed if the user wishes to install them directly. The following command will append the category data to the repository:

```
$ /path/to/eclipse -consoleLog -noSplash -application
   org.eclipse.equinox.p2.publisher.CategoryPublisher
 -metadataRepository file:/DIR
 -categoryDefinition file:/path/to/category.xml
 -compress
```

When the category publisher runs, it will attempt to resolve the features it finds via the URL; if it cannot find the referenced feature or plug-in, it will silently ignore the entry.

The entries are written into the metadata with the ID defined in the category (in the example previously, it was `cat.id`). To disambiguate different categories, an additional argument can be specified to prefix the category IDs with a value. By adding `-categoryQualifier example.prefix` to the command, the category ID will become `example.prefix.cat.id` in the P2 metadata.

Composite update sites

So far, the examples have all used a single repository for hosting data. This may be useful for building small or medium-sized sites, but the ability to aggregate many update sites is useful in a number of circumstances.

P2 provides a mechanism called **composite update sites**, which allows a set of update sites to be aggregated by the client when installing. This provides a means to aggregate the content together without having to duplicate the binary data between them.

Composite update sites can also be used to provide a consistent top-level site while aggregating the results of multiple release, milestone, nightly, or continuous integration builds. This technique is used in the Eclipse release process, where the point releases are represented as separate child locations. For example, the Kepler update site is `http://download.eclipse.org/eclipse/updates/4.3/` and is a composite site.

Composite sites contain `compositeArtifacts.jar` and `compositeContent.jar` files, which contain `compositeArtifacts.xml` and `compositeContent.xml` files. These are almost identical, with the repository type being the only difference. Here are the Kepler SR2 `compositeArtifacts.xml` and `compositeContent.xml` files:

```
<?xml version='1.0' encoding='UTF-8'?>
<?compositeArtifactRepository version='1.0.0'?>
<repository name='The Eclipse Project repository'
 type='org.eclipse.equinox.internal.
  p2.artifact.repository.CompositeArtifactRepository'
 version='1.0.0'>
  <properties size='3'>
    <property name='p2.timestamp' value='1393595881853'/>
    <property name='p2.compressed' value='true'/>
    <property name='p2.atomic.composite.loading' value='true'/>
  </properties>
  <children size='3'>
    <child location='R-4.3-201306052000'/>
    <child location='R-4.3.1-201309111000'/>
    <child location='R-4.3.2-201402211700'/>
  </children>
</repository>

<?xml version='1.0' encoding='UTF-8'?>
<?compositeMetadataRepository version='1.0.0'?>
<repository name='The Eclipse Project repository'
 type='org.eclipse.equinox.internal.
  p2.metadata.repository.CompositeMetadataRepository'
 version='1.0.0'>
  <properties size='3'>
    <property name='p2.timestamp' value='1393595881941'/>
    <property name='p2.compressed' value='true'/>
    <property name='p2.atomic.composite.loading' value='true'/>
  </properties>
```

```
    <children size='4'>
      <child location='categoriesKepler'/>
      <child location='R-4.3-201306052000'/>
      <child location='R-4.3.1-201309111000'/>
      <child location='R-4.3.2-201402211700'/>
    </children>
  </repository>
```

The `location` can be a relative URL (which is taken to be relative to the current location) or an absolute URL (such as to another site).

It is possible to refer to a ZIP file as a child site using the standard Java `jar:` protocol. For example, to install Drools from Maven Central, an absolute URL `jar:https://repo1.maven.org/maven2/org/drools/org.drools.updatesite/6.0.0.Final/org.drools.updatesite-6.0.0.Final.zip!/` can be used as a child site.

Note the `jar:` prefix as well as the `!/` suffix of the URL. Using this is not generally recommended as it can be slow, but for small sites or places where an expanded file cannot be hosted, this approach may be useful.

In Kepler's case, the composite repository consists of four child repositories:

- `R-4.3-201306052000`
- `R-4.3.1-201309111000`
- `R-4.3.2-201402211700`
- `categoriesKepler` (content metadata only)

When Eclipse looks at `http://download.eclipse.org/eclipse/updates/4.3/` as an update URL, it will discover the child repositories and then subsequently hit:

- `http://download.eclipse.org/eclipse/updates/4.3/R-4.3-201306052000/`
- `http://download.eclipse.org/eclipse/updates/4.3/R-4.3.1-201309111000/`
- `http://download.eclipse.org/eclipse/updates/4.3/R-4.3.2-201402211700/`
- `http://download.eclipse.org/eclipse/updates/4.3/categoriesKepler/`

It is possible to have composite sites pointing to composite sites, allowing for any number of update sites to be chained together.

Given that there are multiple different types of P2 repository available, as well as the fallback `site.xml`, what is the order of the network requests? The following steps are taken by P2 when downloading a site for the first time:

- Download `<url>/p2.index` (if available)
- If `p2.index` is available, look for the files directed such as `compositeArtifacts.jar` or `artifacts.jar`
- Otherwise, look for `artifacts.jar`, then `artifacts.xml`, then `compositeArtifacts.jar`, then `compositeArtifacts.xml`, and finally `site.xml`

A similar thing happens for consulting the `content` files. Note that the `p2.index` file is repeatedly asked for, even if it hasn't changed, and so it should be as small as possible.

The content of a `p2.index` file for a composite update site should look like the following:

```
version=1
metadata.repository.factory.order=compositeContent.xml,\!
artifact.repository.factory.order=compositeArtifacts.xml,\!
```

The content of a `p2.index` file for a standalone update site should look like the following:

```
version=1
metadata.repository.factory.order=content.xml,\!
artifact.repository.factory.order=artifacts.xml,\!
```

Although the files specify `content.xml`, it will actually always look for `content.jar` first, followed by `content.xml`. Always compress P2 repositories and include one of the two `p2.index` files mentioned to avoid many spurious HTTP 404 errors in web server logs.

The classic update manager

When Eclipse was first created, the update manager was relatively simplistic. An update site would have a simple **site.xml** file that listed the available features, and the update manager would use that to determine if a newer feature was available.

> The classic update manager (`org.eclipse.update.*`) was deprecated in Eclipse 3.4 and removed in Eclipse 4.2, as described in the release notes at `http://www.eclipse.org/eclipse/development/porting/4.2/incompatibilities.html#update-manager`.

The following is a snippet of the update `site.xml` file that was used for Eclipse 3.0:

```
<site>
  <description url="index.html">
    The Eclipse Update Site contains feature and
    plug-in versions for Eclipse project releases.
  </description>
  <feature url="features/org.eclipse.jdt_3.0.0.jar"
   patch="false" id="org.eclipse.jdt" version="3.0.0">
    <category name="3.0"/>
  </feature>
  ...
</site>
```

When a newer version of a feature was available, the update manager would download the `feature.jar` file and display information, including copyright notices, and determine which dependencies were required. The `feature.jar` file contains the `feature.xml` file, along with a small amount of other information such as the list of included plug-ins:

```
<feature id="org.eclipse.jdt" version="3.0.0"
 label="%featureName" provider-name="%providerName">
  <description>%description</description>
  <license url="%licenseURL">%license</license>
  <url>
    <update label="%updateSiteName"
     url="http://update.eclipse.org/updates/3.0"/>
    <discovery label="%updateSiteName"
     url="http://update.eclipse.org/updates/3.0"/>
  </url>
```

```
    <requires>
      <import plugin="org.eclipse.platform" version="3.0.0"
       match="compatible"/>
    </requires>
    <plugin id="org.eclipse.jdt" version="3.0.0"/>
    ...
  </feature>
```

The `feature.properties` is used to substitute the percent values (such as `%description`) in the `feature.xml` file:

```
featureName=Eclipse Java Development Tools
providerName=Eclipse.org
description=Eclipse Java development tools.
updateSiteName=Eclipse.org update site
```

The `feature.xml` file thus forms a directed graph to a set of feature requirements and plug-in requirements. In the previous example, the JDT feature depended on the `org.eclipse.platform` plug-in, but `import` suggests that this plug-in is found in a different feature. On the other hand, `plugin id=org.eclipse.jdt` indicates the plug-in is part of this feature, and so it will be found on the same site as the JDT feature.

Although `site.xml` points to the feature by URL, there is no such URL referenced from the feature to the plug-in. Instead, the location of the plug-in is calculated as relative to the feature `../plugins/id_version.jar`.

When the old update manager ran, it would traverse the `site.xml` file of all the registered update sites. If changes were seen, it would download all the features, followed by all the necessary plug-ins.

There were several problems with the update manager, including having to download a lot of extra content in order to determine if there were any updates or incompatibilities. This led to a reduced user experience as failures would not occur until runtime. In addition, the update mechanism was only capable of updating the plug-ins, and not the other content (such as an embedded JRE or the `eclipse.exe` launcher).

For compatibility reasons, old update sites are still understood by P2, but this functionality may be removed in the future.

Touchpoints

A touchpoint is a P2 configuration option that specifies an action to be performed when a feature is installed/configured or unconfigured/uninstalled. This can be used to add additional flags to the Eclipse configuration file, making directories, updating permissions on files, as well as installing bundles and features.

There are two default categories of touchpoint actions:

- `org.eclipse.equinox.p2.touchpoint.natives`, which mainly operates on files, permissions, and copying or creating directories and ZIP files
- `org.eclipse.equinox.p2.touchpoint.eclipse`, installing bundles, features, source references, repositories, and modifying the JVM start-up or system properties

Touchpoints are stored in touchpoint advice files called `p2.inf` that can be stored in one of the following three locations:

- Inside the `META-INF` directory of a bundle
- Next to the `feature.xml` file in a feature
- Next to the `.product` file in a product

The touchpoint advice is added to the bundle, feature, or product when it is installed. The format of the touchpoint file looks like a properties file with dot-separated property values.

Categorizing features with P2

Although the `category.xml` (or `site.xml`) file(s) can be used to create categories for a feature, it is possible to add a category with a `p2.inf` file in the feature. This is processed by the category generator and allows the categories to be described by the features themselves.

To associate a feature with a category using P2, add a `p2.inf` file next to `feature.xml`. This will contain a set of installable units that are represented as a series of property keys beginning with `unit.1`, `unit.2`, `unit.3`, and so on.

Since the properties file doesn't provide a way of implementing an array, using an incrementing numeric suffix is common in `p2.inf` files.

Each installable unit has an `id` and a `version`. The `version` can be derived from the enclosing feature by using the value `$version$`:

```
units.1.id=com.packtpub.e4.advanced.p2.touchpoints.category
units.1.version=$version$
```

Each unit has a number of properties, requirements, and provisions. The properties allow arbitrary key/value pairs to be stored, which in this case say that it's a category, and has the name `Touchpoints Examples`:

```
units.1.properties.1.name=org.eclipse.equinox.p2.type.category
units.1.properties.1.value=true
units.1.properties.2.name=org.eclipse.equinox.p2.name
units.1.properties.2.value=Touchpoints Examples
```

As with the units, the properties are grouped with an incrementing number to provide a way of associating the otherwise separate name and value pairs.

The units also provide an identifier, which can be used as a reference elsewhere:

```
units.1.provides.1.namespace=org.eclipse.equinox.p2.iu
units.1.provides.1.name=\
 com.packtpub.e4.advanced.p2.touchpoints.category
units.1.provides.1.version=$version$
```

Finally, the category's content is defined in terms of needing one or more features; in this case, by declaring a `requires` dependency:

```
units.1.requires.1.namespace=org.eclipse.equinox.p2.iu
units.1.requires.1.name=\
 com.packtpub.e4.advanced.p2.touchpoints.feature.feature.group
units.1.requires.1.range=[$version$,$version$]
units.1.requires.1.greedy=true
```

Note that features in P2 are always suffixed with `.feature.group`, so if the feature already ends in `.feature`, then it will be `.feature.feature.group` in the P2 installable unit identifier.

When exported as a deployable feature, the category will be shown. If multiple features are desired, then additional features can be added using `units.1.requires.2`, `units.1.requires.3`, and so on. If a second category is required, then they would be specified as `units.2.requires.1` and so on.

The format of the `p2.inf` file can be thought of as a logical JSON file, but flattened to a property list format. An equivalent JSON file would look like the following:

```
{units:[
  { id:com.packtpub...,
    version:1.2.3,
    properties:[
      {name:category,value:true},
      {name:p2.name,Examples}
    ],
    requires:[
      {namespace:iu,name:feature,range:
       [1.2.3,4.5.6],greedy:true}
    ],
    provides:[
      {namespace:iu,name:category,version:1.2.3}
    ],
  }]}
```

Note that JSON is not a supported format for `p2.inf`, but this structure may help to visually demonstrate the data encoded in the properties file.

Adding update sites automatically

To add an update site when a bundle is installed, create a `p2.inf` file with the following content:

```
instructions.install=\
 addRepository(\
  type:0, name:EGit Update Site,\
  location:http${#58}//download.eclipse.org/egit/updates/);\
 addRepository(\
  type:1, name:EGit Update Site,\
  location:http${#58}//download.eclipse.org/egit/updates/);
instructions.uninstall=\
 removeRepository(\
  type:0, name:EGit Update Site,\
  location:http${#58}//download.eclipse.org/egit/updates/);\
 removeRepository(\
  type:1, name:EGit Update Site,\
  location:http${#58}//download.eclipse.org/egit/updates/);
```

Certain characters are not allowed in `p2.inf` files, including `$,:;{}` characters. These need to be replaced with a decimal character value of the form `${#nnn}`; so in this case `${#58}` is the escape character for `:` in the `http` URL. The \ is used to continue the property value across multiple lines, although the `instructions.configure` can be on one line if desired.

The `type` values are `0` (metadata) and `1` (artifacts). For a repository to be added successfully, it has to be added as both a metadata and artifact repository. A name is optional, though special characters must be encoded.

When the bundle is configured, it will add the repository to the update site list in the host Eclipse runtime. If the bundle is unconfigured later, the repository will be removed.

Registering touchpoint actions

The `addRepository` touchpoint action corresponds to an entry defined in `plugin.xml` of the `org.eclipse.equinox.p2.touchpoint.eclipse` plug-in. It has a fully qualified ID of `org.eclipse.equinox.p2.touchpoint.eclipse.addRepository`, which is associated with the class in the extension point.

It is possible to add additional touchpoint actions, but they need to either be imported or use a fully qualified name instead. For example, to add a repository, the following are equivalent:

```
instructions.install=\
 addRepository(\
  type:0, name:EGit Update Site,\
  location:http${#58}//download.eclipse.org/egit/updates/);
instructions.install.import=\
 org.eclipse.equinox.p2.touchpoint.eclipse.addRepository

# or with fully qualified name
instructions.install=\
 org.eclipse.equinox.p2.touchpoint.eclipse.addRepository(\
  type:0, name:EGit Update Site,\
  location:http${#58}//download.eclipse.org/egit/updates/);
```

Actions in `org.eclipse.equinox.p2.touchpoint.eclipse` and `org.eclipse.equinox.p2.touchpoint.native` are imported by default and do not need to be explicitly imported. However, custom actions need to be imported explicitly or use the fully qualified name instead.

Adding JVM or program arguments

To add JVM or program arguments to the `eclipse.ini` file at installation time, `addJVMArg` or `addProgramArg` can be used. These are typically added to a feature or a product rather than individual bundles. The modifications affect the `eclipse.ini` file and take effect at the next reboot.

To add additional memory, or to increase PermGen, the following can be used:

```
instructions.install=\
 addJVMArg(jvmArg:-Xmx2048m);\
 addJVMArg(jvmArg:-XX:MaxPermSize=512m);
instructions.uninstall=\
 removeJVMArg(jvmArg:-Xmx2048m);\
 removeJVMArg(jvmArg:-XX:MaxPermSize=512m);
```

OpenJDK 8 no longer requires the PermGen to be explicitly managed and will be a no-op on OpenJDK 8. It may be an error to pass the `-XX:MaxPermSize` argument in future.

It's worth noting that there is a better way to handle JVM arguments. Firstly, the launcher has specific knowledge of whether `XX` is needed for any given JVM (it's non-standard and so some JVMs do not support it).

Add the program argument `--launcher.XXMaxPermSize 512m`, and the launcher will determine whether or not the property setting is required. So, instead of adding it as a JVM argument, add it as a program argument:

```
instructions.install=\
 addJVMArg(jvmArg:-Xmx2048m);\
 addProgramArg(\
  programArg:--launcher.XXMaxPermSize,programArgValue:512m);
instructions.uninstall=\
 removeJVMArg(jvmArg:-Xmx2048m);\
 removeProgramArg(\
  programArg:--launcher.XXMaxPermSize,programArgValue:512m);
```

This is now more stable; if the JVM understands the `XX` flag, it will be added automatically, and if not, it will work the same. This allows for future proofing for current and future JVMs that may no longer understand the `-XX` flags.

Custom touchpoints

It is possible to add custom touchpoints to process additional data when a plug-in is installed. For example, it's possible to execute a custom license check when a feature is added.

To create a custom touchpoint, create a plug-in and add the following dependencies:

- `org.eclipse.equinox.p2.engine`
- `org.eclipse.core.runtime`

Now add an extension point, `org.eclipse.equinox.p2.engine.actions`:

```
<plugin>
  <extension point="org.eclipse.equinox.p2.engine.actions">
    <action name="licenseCheck" version="1.0.0"
    class="com.packtpub.e4.advanced.p2.touchpoints.LicenseCheck"/>
  </extension>
</plugin>
```

The class extends `org.eclipse.equinox.p2.engine.spi.ProvisioningAction` and implements the `execute` and `undo` methods, which return an `IStatus` object indicating success or failure:

```
public class LicenseCheck extends ProvisioningAction {
  public IStatus execute(Map<String, Object> parameters) {
    if (isLicensed((String) parameters.get("licenseFile"))) {
      return Status.OK_STATUS;
    }
    return new Status(Status.ERROR,
     "com.packtpub.e4.advanced.p2.touchpoints",
     "The plug-in is not licensed");
  }
  private boolean isLicensed(String file) {
    return file != null && new File(file).exists();
  }
  public IStatus undo(Map<String, Object> parameters) {
    // NOP
    return Status.OK_STATUS;
  }
}
```

The `LicenseCheck` class looks for a file that can be supplied as an argument, and if not found, throws an error. A real system might use a URL instead of a file and would check for more than just the existence of the file.

To use this in a plug-in, create a `p2.inf` file and an `instructions.install` that refers to the `licenseCheck` along with a `licenseFile` argument. Either the fully qualified name can be used or the fully qualified extension point can be imported:

```
instructions.install=\
 licenseCheck(licenseFile:/tmp/license);
instructions.install.import=\
 com.packtpub.e4.advanced.p2.touchpoints.licenseCheck
```

To ensure that the `licenseCheck` plug-in is enabled, a `metaRequirement` can be added. This tells P2 that in order to install the bundle with the `p2.inf` file, the `com.packtpub.e4.advanced.p2.touchpoints` installable unit (bundle) has to be installed. If additional `metaRequirements` are needed, creating properties with `metaRequirements.1` and `metaRequirements.2` is possible:

```
metaRequirements.0.name=com.packtpub.e4.advanced.p2.touchpoints
metaRequirements.0.namespace=org.eclipse.equinox.p2.iu
metaRequirements.0.range=[1,2)
```

The `metaRequirements` don't add any runtime requirements to the bundle itself; they are only used during the P2 processing phases.

Finally, install the licensed bundle into a runtime. If the license file exists (specified as `/tmp/license` in the example bundle), then the plug-in will be installed as expected. If the bundle does not exist, then an error will be displayed:

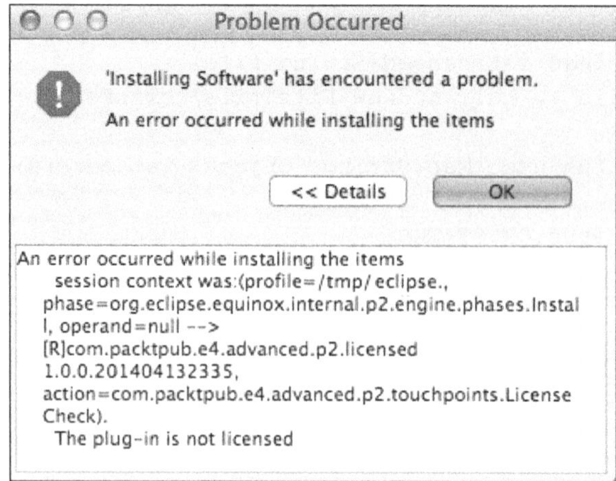

> This is not the best user experience for displaying licensed features. It is better to allow the feature to be installed and then provide information (including an ability to acquire a license) or to have some kind of live demo feature if it is not present. This example is used to demonstrate the ability of P2 to run custom code when installing the code.

Summary

P2 is used as the provisioning and updating engine for Eclipse and is used to install features, plug-ins (bundles), and native components such as the launcher and associated libraries.

The configuration is extensible, both by embedding references into plug-ins, features, and products, and also to define additional metadata and handlers to install content. Command-line utilities can be used to generate and mirror update sites, as well as provision instances of applications and manage the content headlessly.

The final chapter presents how to write help documentation for Eclipse to provide a comprehensive product.

10
User Assistance in Eclipse

This chapter presents the options for providing **user assistance** in Eclipse, including how to write **help pages**, how to run an external **help server**, how to **embed help** in an RCP application or run it as standalone, and how to write **cheat sheets** to allow the user to step through standard operations. By the end of this chapter, you will know about the different aspects to the user assistance options in Eclipse and be able to contribute plug-ins that add an interactive documentation to a standalone Eclipse environment, an RCP application, or via a website.

Help pages in Eclipse

Eclipse help pages are XHTML documents that are indexed with Apache Lucene and served over a web server either externally or as part of an Eclipse-based runtime. The pages are written in XHTML and have a table of contents that aggregates them together in a view known as a **table of contents** (**toc**). The table of contents may be **primary**, in which case it shows up as a closed book icon in the help pages; otherwise, it is shown as an open book icon and plugged in elsewhere.

This chapter will use the plug-in `com.packtpub.e4.advanced.doc` to act as the placeholder for documentation. This can be created from the extension point wizard by clicking on **Add...** in the **Extensions** tab of the `plugin.xml` file and choosing the `org.eclipse.help.toc` extension point, along with sample help contents:

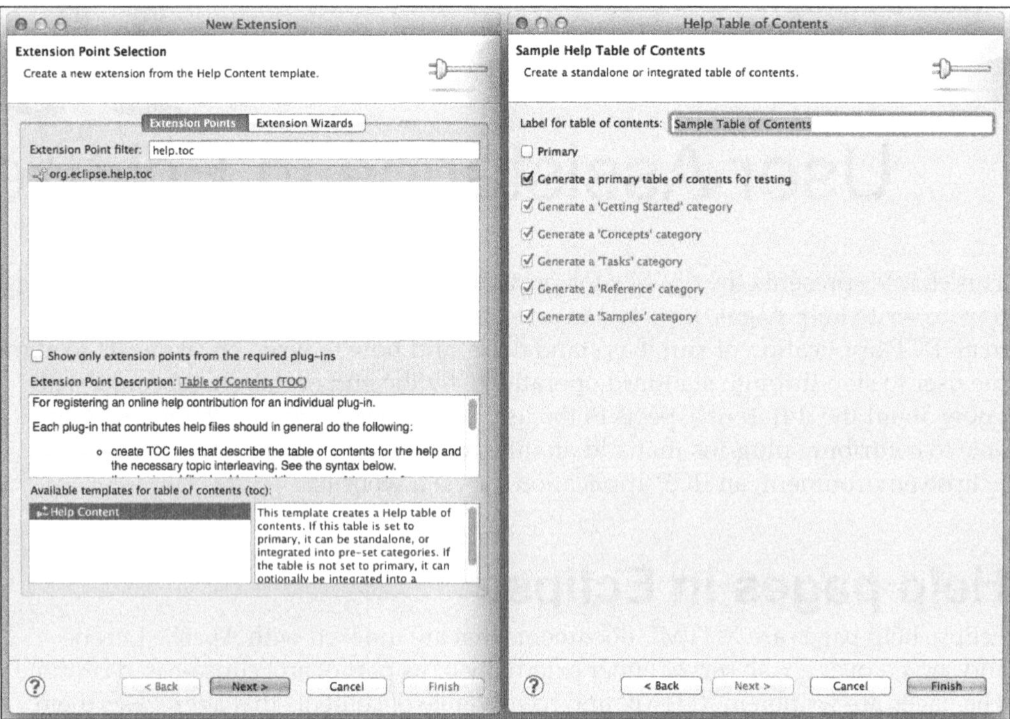

Adding help pages

Help pages are contributed through an extension point, which registers a table of contents that refers to individual help pages. The help pages are typically provided in a separate plug-in to the one they are documenting; this keeps the binary small for environments that don't need documentation, and permits the help pages to be translated into different languages.

The help pages are written in (X)HTML. Conventionally, they are stored under a directory `html/` in the plug-in, but this is not a requirement. Whatever folder name is used, `build.properties` needs to be updated to ensure that the documents are part of the generated documentation JAR file. Typically, a help or documentation plug-in will include a dot (`.`) as the `bin.includes` property to include everything.

Create an index file, `html/index.html`, with the following content:

```
<!DOCTYPE html>
<html>
<head>
<title>Help Contents</title>
</head>
<body>
  <h1>This is the help contents file</h1>
</body>
</html>
```

A table of contents (`toc.xml`) file must be created, which references the HTML file:

```
<?xml version="1.0" encoding="UTF-8"?>
<toc label="Book">
  <topic href="html/index.html" label="Topic"/>
</toc>
```

Finally, the table of contents needs to be registered as an extension point within the `plugin.xml` file of the enclosing plug-in:

```
<?xml version="1.0" encoding="UTF-8"?>
<?eclipse version="3.4"?>
<plugin>
  <extension point="org.eclipse.help.toc">
    <toc file="toc.xml" primary="true"/>
  </extension>
</plugin>
```

Note the `primary=true` attribute; without this, the book will not be shown in the **top-level** of the Eclipse help page.

Now, run an Eclipse application and navigate to **Help** | **Help Contents**. A browser will open up with the help documentation. The previous XML content will be shown as a standalone book called **Book**.

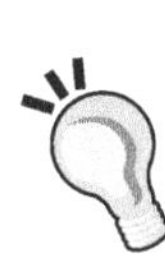

Make sure that the `toc.xml` file is marked as primary, and that the `toc.xml` file points to at least one topic with a page. If a `toc.xml` file is non-primary, it will not show up in the top-level list and, if it has no topics, then it will be hidden.

Check that `build.properties` is updated to include all the help and `toc.xml` files as applicable.

Nested table of contents

It is possible to build up a nested table of contents, which appears in the help browser as a series of nested books. If a table of contents is marked as primary, it will show up as a top-level book; otherwise, the table of contents must be referenced from another file. Most table of contents files are not primary.

The Eclipse JDT documentation is split into two plug-ins: one that provides end user documentation on how to use the Java tools (`org.eclipse.jdt.doc.user`) and one that provides programming APIs for developers wanting to extend or integrate with JDT (`org.eclipse.jdt.doc.isv`).

The **ISV** stands for **Independent Software Vendor**, and was designed to allow Eclipse to be used as the base of commercial IDEs such as IBM's WebSphere.

Inside each of the Eclipse books, there is a standard series of tables of contents, including **Getting started**, **Concepts**, **Tasks**, **Reference**, **Tips and Tricks**, and **What's New**. In addition, there are **Overview** and **Legal** standalone help pages:

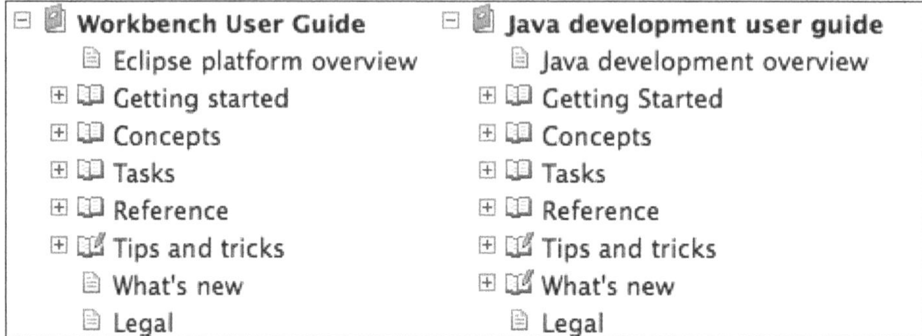

These pages and groups are not mandatory, but these have been conventionally provided across all of the traditional Eclipse features. It is recommended that developers creating language-specific extensions to Eclipse follow the same format.

This is achieved with several different table of contents files (as shown in the following list), each corresponding to the previous book icons:

- `topics_GettingStarted.xml`
- `topics_Concepts.xml`
- `topics_Tasks.xml`

- `topics_Reference.xml`
- `topics_Tips.xml`

Each topic XML file contains content similar to the `toc.xml` file shown earlier. They are referenced in the `plugin.xml` file as before, except that the `primary="true"` attribute is not present (and therefore defaults to `false`).

The top-level (primary) `toc` is an aggregation of all of these topics; for example, the JDT plug-in development guide help documentation contains a `toc.xml` that looks like the following:

```
<toc label="JDT Plug-in Developer Guide">
  <topic label="Programmer&apos;s Guide" href="guide/jdt_int.htm">
    <link toc="topics_Guide.xml" />
  </topic>
  <topic label="Reference">
    <link toc="topics_Reference.xml" />
  </topic>
  ...
</toc>
```

Since this is an XML file, the apostrophe is represented with `'` instead of `'` in the label of the topic.

This provides the top-level book and creates an aggregated list of the topic entries.

Note that the topic (book icon) can have an optional HTML page, which contains the help documentation for the topic as a whole. In this case, clicking on **Programmer's Guide** in the **JDT Plug-in Developer Guide** link will show a custom overview along with some background. If a page is not given, such as the **Reference** page, then an automatically generated table of contents will be listed instead.

Anchors and links

It is possible to generate a fixed list of contents using the help contents described previously. This works when the list of topics is known in advance and can be packaged into a single plug-in. However, if the documentation is more complex, it may need to be split across multiple plug-ins.

The references in the `href` attribute must be local files in the same plug-in as the table of contents file. This can be limiting, especially if a plug-in contains extension points that may be provided by other plug-ins.

Instead, the table of contents file can define an **anchor**, which is an extension location for help pages. For example, a help page may have a `Contributions` anchor, which is the place any contributed documentation will go to, or an `Examples` page, which can be appended by others.

Such an anchor is represented in the `toc.xml` file as follows:

```
<toc label="Anchor Examples">
  <topic label="Overview" href="html/overview.html">
    <link toc="topics_Overview.xml" />
  </topic>
  <anchor id="contributions" />
</toc>
```

This provides a placeholder which allows others to contribute items to. This is achieved by specifying a `link_to` attribute in another `toc` file:

```
<toc label="Contribution1" link_to="toc.xml#contributions">
  <topic label="Contribution 1" href="html/contribution1.html"/>
</toc>
```

Now when the help page is rendered, the contribution will show up as if it had been in place of the anchor. This can be used to add other contributions from other `toc` files:

```
<toc label="Contribution2" link_to="toc.xml#contributions">
  <topic label="Contribution 2" href="html/contribution2.html"/>
</toc>
```

Note that the contribution topics will all be rendered at the top level in a list:

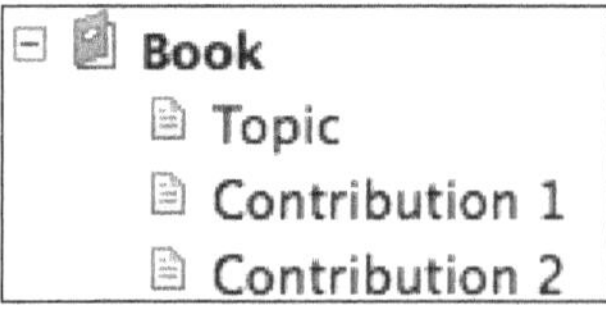

Although this works for some kinds of content, it may make sense to wrap an element in a topic so that when they are presented in the list, they are clearly distinguished. This also allows the automated table of contents to be generated based on the child topics. It is possible to contribute to a set of examples using the following:

```
<toc label="Grouped Examples">
  …
  <anchor id="contributions" />
  <topic label="Examples">
    <anchor id="examples" />
  </topic>
</toc>
```

Now examples can be contributed with the following:

```
<toc label="Examples" link_to="toc.xml#examples">
   <topic href="html/example1.html" label="Example 1"/>
</toc>

<toc label="Examples" link_to="toc.xml#examples">
   <topic href="html/example2.html" label="Example 2"/>
</toc>
```

When rendered, the content will show up with a group and an automatically generated index:

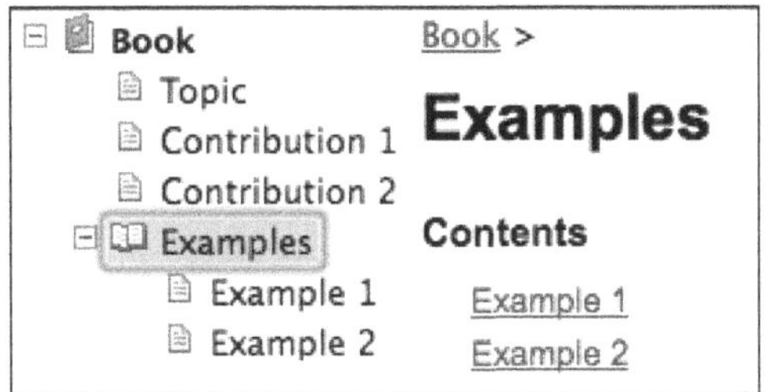

Linking to anchors in other plug-ins

Along with contributing to anchors in the current plug-in, it is also possible to contribute to anchors defined in other plug-ins. The `link_to` in this case points to the file with a prefix of `../` and the plug-in name.

To contribute an example page to the Java Development Toolkit documentation, consult the table of contents provided by the JDT. In the `org.eclipse.jdt.doc.user` plug-in, the `toc.xml` topic contains a `jdt_getstart` anchor:

```
<toc label="Java development user guide">
  <topic label="Java development overview"
   href="gettingStarted/intro/overview.htm"
```

```
      <topic label="Getting Started">
        <link toc="topics_GettingStarted.xml" />
      </topic>
      <anchor id="jdt_getstart" />
      …
    </topic>
  </toc>
```

This allows other plug-ins to contribute to the anchor, using an `href` of the form `../org.eclipse.jdt.doc.user/toc.xml#jdt_getstart`. To see how this works, create a new contribution with a topic, as follows:

```
<toc label="JDT extension"
 link_to="../org.eclipse.jdt.doc.user/toc.xml#jdt_getstart">
  <topic href="html/jdt.html" label="JDT Help Extension"/>
</toc>
```

Running the Eclipse instance and opening the help documentation shows the page merged into the JDT documentation:

Conditional enablement

Help documentation is often directly associated with the plug-in that it is describing. It may not make sense, therefore, to show the help documentation if the corresponding plug-in is not installed.

Although one way of doing this would be to place a dependency from the help bundle to the bundle it describes, this does not necessarily make sense. Instead, the help extension point has an **enablement condition**, which can be used to selectively show parts of the documentation or even exclude it completely. This uses the Eclipse **core expression** syntax.

To add an enablement condition to determine whether JDT is installed or not, add the following code to a node in the `toc`:

```
<toc label="Book">
  ...
  <topic label="Examples">
    <anchor id="examples"/>
    <enablement>
      <with variable="platform">
        <test args="org.eclipse.jdt.ui"
         property="org.eclipse.core.runtime.isBundleInstalled" />
      </with>
    </enablement>
  </topic>
</toc>
```

This condition is evaluated and the book is shown (and included in the search) if the condition is true. In this case, it is true if the `org.eclispe.jdt.ui` is installed.

If multiple conditions are required, they can be listed as siblings. An `<or>` or `<and>` element can be used to explicitly group conditions together.

The help documentation can also be conditionally included depending on the operating system:

```
<toc label="Book">
  ...
  <topic label="OSX specific help" href="html/osx.html">
    <enablement>
      <systemTest property="osgi.os" value="macosx"/>
    </enablement>
  </topic>
  <topic label="Linux specific help" href="html/linux.html">
    <enablement>
      <systemTest property="osgi.os" value="linux"/>
    </enablement>
  </topic>
  <topic label="Windows specific help" href="html/win.html">
    <enablement>
      <systemTest property="osgi.os" value="win32"/>
    </enablement>
  </topic>
</toc>
```

Valid values of the `osgi.os` system property are described in the Eclipse help pages.

Note that the HTML help pages can also be selectively filtered based on the enablement conditions. This requires that the help documentation be written in XHTML; the processor is only enabled if the source document is valid XML. For example, to tell the user to run an application, there is a difference in the prompt depending on the operating system, which can be shown as follows:

```
<?xml version="1.0" encoding="UTF-8"?>
<!DOCTYPE html PUBLIC "-//W3C//DTD XHTML 1.0 Transitional//EN"
 "http://www.w3.org/TR/xhtml1/DTD/xhtml1-transitional.dtd">
<html xmlns="http://www.w3.org/1999/xhtml">
  <head>
    <title>Example 1</title>
  </head>
  <body>
    <h1>Example 1</h1>
    <p>To run the program, execute:</p>
    <p>
      <code>c:\&gt;java -cp lib\a.jar;lib\b.jar example</code>
      <enablement>
        <systemTest property="osgi.os" value="win32" />
      </enablement>
    </p>
    <p>
      <code>$ java -cp lib/a.jar:lib/b.jar example</code>
      <enablement>
        <not>
          <systemTest property="osgi.os" value="win32" />
        </not>
      </enablement>
   </p>
  </body>
</html>
```

When the help page is shown to the user, it will show the correct form based on the platform's content:

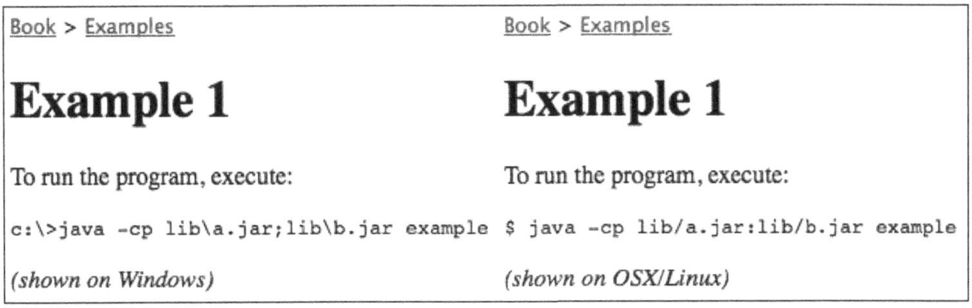

Book > Examples

Example 1

To run the program, execute:

`c:\>java -cp lib\a.jar;lib\b.jar example`

(shown on Windows)

Book > Examples

Example 1

To run the program, execute:

`$ java -cp lib/a.jar:lib/b.jar example`

(shown on OSX/Linux)

This can also be used to customize the names of key presses, for example, on Windows and Linux, the primary modifier is Control, whereas on Mac OS X, it is Command:

```
<p>
  To copy the information, press
  <span>Command + C
    <enablement>
      <systemTest property="osgi.os" value="macosx" />
    </enablement>
  </span>
  <span>Control + C
    <enablement>
      <not>
        <systemTest property="osgi.os" value="macosx" />
      </not>
    </enablement>
  </span>
</p>
```

On Windows or Linux, this will show **To copy the information, press Control + C**, whereas on Mac OS X, it will show **To copy the information, press Command + C**.

Context-sensitive help

In order to provide **context-sensitive help** for the Eclipse platform, a **help context** can be associated with a view, part, command, or any other widget. The `IWorkbenchHelpSystem` provides a means to associate help context IDs with widgets, which is a concatenation of the enclosing plug-in ID and a text identifier.

The **Dynamic Help** view updates its content based on the help context of the currently selected widget or view. The help view can be accessed by navigating to **Help** | **Dynamic Help**, or **Window** | **Show View** | **Other** | **Help** | **Help**.

For example, if the **Project Explorer** view has focus, then the **Help** view will look like the following screenshot:

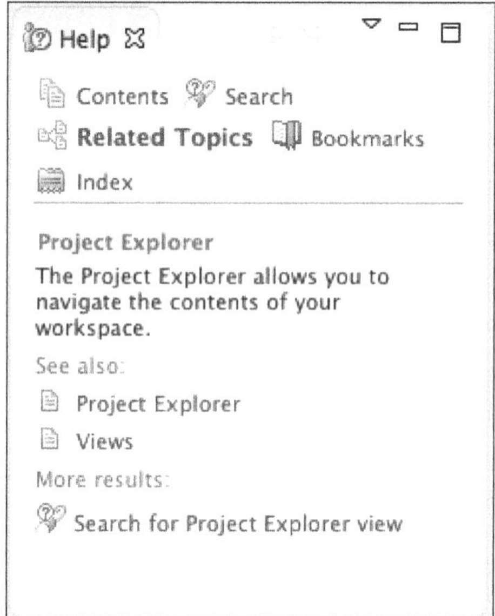

The `title` and `description` of the **Project Explorer** help is specified in the help context. This uses the fully qualified context ID `org.eclipse.ui.project_explorer_context` in this case. The `contexts_Platform.xml` file contains:

```
<contexts>
  <context id="project_explorer_context"
   title="Project Explorer Additional">
    <description>The project explorer allows projects to be
     explored.</description>
  </context>
</contexts>
```

This file is referenced from the `plugin.xml` file, which allows the contexts to be associated with a specific plug-in (or the current plug-in if not specified):

```
<extension point="org.eclipse.help.contexts">
  <contexts
   file="contexts_Platform.xml"
   plugin="org.eclipse.ui"/>
</extension>
```

Now, when **Project Explorer** is selected, the alternative description will be shown instead:

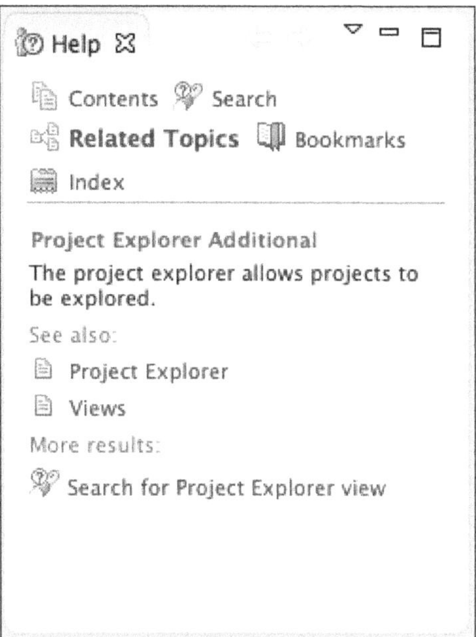

The help context can also refer to other help topics; in this case, the **See also** section contains the **Project Explorer** and **Views** help pages. Other pages can be contributed here by adding topic references to the context:

```
<contexts>
  <context id="project_explorer_context"
   title="Project Explorer Additional">
    <description>The project explorer allows projects to be
     explored.</description>
    <topic href="html/contribution1.html" label="Contribution 1"/>
    <topic href="html/contribution2.html" label="Contribution 2"/>
  </context>
</contexts>
```

Now the help page will look like the following screenshot:

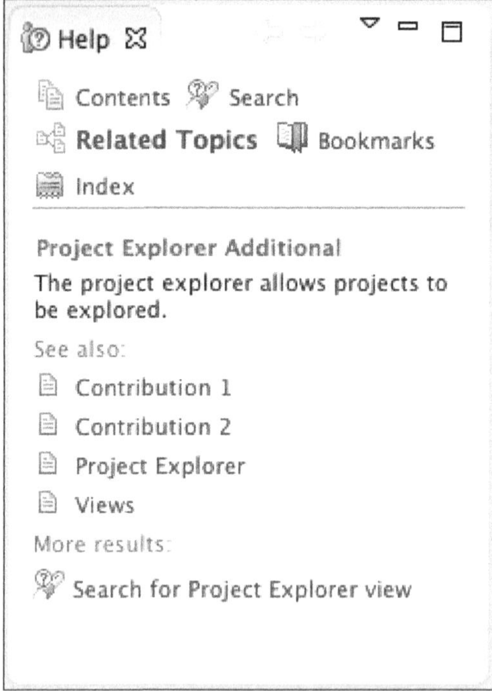

The `title` and `description` are optional if contributing to an existing context in another plug-in. The `label` is also optional; if not specified, it will inherit the `title` from the topic.

Active help

A JavaScript library (`org.eclipse.help/livehelp.js`) facilitates communication with the host Eclipse workbench to execute commands on the user's behalf. This is added by default to all Eclipse help pages served from an Eclipse workbench, and is known as **active help**.

To execute a command, the same serialization framework is used as with the cheat sheets, which is described later in this chapter in the *Adding commands* section. The format is `commandId(key=value,key1=value)`; for example, `org.eclipse.ui.newWizard(newWizardId=org.eclipse.jdt.ui.wizards.JavaProjectWizard)` will launch the **New Java Project** wizard.

The JavaScript function `executeCommand` takes a string containing the serialized command. This can be called via a `javascript:` URL, or by using an `href` attribute with a value `#` and an `onClick` handler to invoke the code:

```
<p>You can run the
<code>org.eclipse.ui.newWizard(
 newWizardId=org.eclipse.jdt.ui.wizards.JavaProjectWizard)</code>
command by clicking on <a class="command-link" href='#'
 onClick='executeCommand("
  org.eclipse.ui.newWizard(
   newWizardId=org.eclipse.jdt.ui.wizards.JavaProjectWizard)
  ")'>show the new Java Wizard</a>
</p>
```

Along with the references to commands, the help server can also be used to access content inside other plug-ins. The plug-ins are referenced by the plug-in ID, followed by the path of the resource inside the plug-in itself. As a result, hyperlinks to sample files, other references to different topic files, or images for icons can be used to improve the quality of the documentation.

To add an icon to the help documentation for the new Java wizard, add the following:

```
<img width="16" height="16" alt="New Java wizard"
 src="../org.eclipse.jdt.ui/icons/full/etool16/newjprj_wiz.gif"/>
```

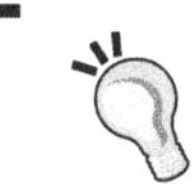

Note that the relative path will be relative to the location of the HTML file itself. If all of the HTML files are in the `html` directory, then additional `../` prefixes may be needed.

DocBook and Eclipse help

DocBook is a means to write technical documentation, and is described at `http://www.docbook.org`. DocBook documents are written in XML and can be transformed into a number of output formats, including Eclipse help. The XML files are typically translated with an XSL file, and the same source document can be processed with many XSL stylesheets to give different output types, such as PDF, HTML, or EPUB.

The standard DocBook stylesheet release, which is available on the project home page at `http://docbook.sourceforge.net/release/xsl/current/eclipse/`, contains stylesheets that can be used to generate Eclipse help documentation.

This approach is used by the WebTools project, which stores the help documentation as a DocBook source with the `org.eclipse.wst.xsl.doc` bundle.

> The source for the WebTools help documentation can be seen at the project's Git repository: `https://git.eclipse.org/c/sourceediting/webtools.sourceediting.xsl.git/tree/docs/org.eclipse.wst.xsl.doc`.
>
> This sample can also be seen at the GitHub repository for this book at `https://github.com/alblue/com.packtpub.e4.advanced/tree/master/com.packtpub.e4.advanced.docbook/`.

A simple DocBook `book.xml` document looks like the following:

```
<!DOCTYPE article PUBLIC "-//OASIS//DTD DocBook XML V4.5//EN"
 "docbook-xml-4/docbookx.dtd">
<book>
  <title>Sample DocBook</title>
  <bookinfo>
    <title>DocBook Intro</title>
  </bookinfo>
  <chapter>
    <title>Generating Help plug-ins</title>
    <section>
      <title>Generating Eclipse Help from DocBook</title>
      <para>
        The first step in generating Eclipse Help is to download
        DocBook templates from http://docbook.org, and styles from
        http://sourceforge.net/projects/docbook/files/docbook-xsl/
      </para>
    </section>
  </chapter>
</book>
```

The `book.xml` file can be translated with the `docbook-xsl/eclipse/eclipse3.xsl` stylesheet. A standalone program, `xsltproc`, can be used to do this:

```
$ xsltproc docbook-xsl/eclipse/eclipse3.xsl book.xml
```

This will generate a separate file for each chapter, and a table of contents file. It can also generate `MANIFEST.MF` and `plugin.xml` files.

Alternatively, an `ant` build file can be created to perform the translation with `xslt`:

```
<project name="DocBook to Eclipse Help" default="docbook-help">
  <target name="docbook-help">
```

```
    <xslt style="docbook-xsl/eclipse/eclipse3.xsl" destdir=".">
      <include name="book.xml" />
    </xslt>
  </target>
</project>
```

If using the `ant` and `xslt` task, a `NullPointerException` may occur in the `referenceToNodeSet` method. This can be fixed by adding `Xalan` to the `ant` classpath, as the version built into Java contains bugs. The easiest way is to add all of the `plugins/org.apache.x*` JARs to the **External Tools Configuration** dialog, as follows:

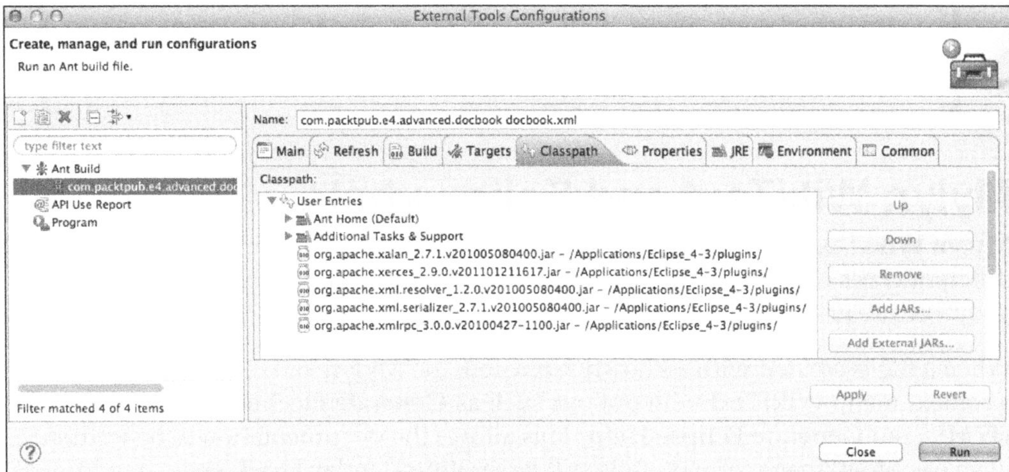

There are a number of optional parameters that can be used to configure the way that the help pages are generated. These can be passed with `--param` to `xsltproc`, or with a `<param>` element to the `xslt` task. The optional parameters are described in the following list:

- `eclipse.plugin.provider`: This sets the name of the `Bundle-Vendor`
- `eclipse.plugin.id`: This sets the `Bundle-SymbolicName`
- `eclipse.plugin.name`: This sets the `Bundle-Name`
- `suppress.navigation`: This turns the `Prev/Up/Next` links off (`0`) or on (`1`)
- `html.stylesheet`: This is the location of the CSS file to be used
- `create.plugin.xml`: This either creates the `plugin.xml` file (`1`) or doesn't (`0`)
- `eclipse.manifest`: This either creates the `MANIFEST.MF` file (`1`) or doesn't (`0`)
- `generate.index`: This either creates the index (`1`) or doesn't (`0`)

Note that the standard Eclipse help style can be enabled using a link for the `html.stylesheet` with `../PRODUCT_PLUGIN/book.css`. Additionally, since the Eclipse help system provides navigation, it is not needed in the individual HTML files:

```
<xslt style="docbook-xsl/eclipse/eclipse3.xsl" destdir=".">
  <include name="book.xml" />
  <param name="html.stylesheet"
   expression="../PRODUCT_PLUGIN/book.css"/>
  <param name="suppress.navigation"
   expression="1"/>
</xslt>
```

More information about authoring Eclipse Help using DocBook is described at `http://wiki.eclipse.org/Authoring_Eclipse_Help_Using_DocBook`.

Mylyn WikiText and Eclipse help

Mylyn WikiText can also be used to author help documentation. There are several different types of WikiText supported by Eclipse: `textile`, `mediawiki`, `confluence`, and `trac` are just some of them.

When a file is created with a known extension, the Mylyn WikiText provides a context menu **WikiText** with options such as **Generate Docbook**, **Generate HTML**, and **Generate Eclipse Help**. This allows the documentation to be written in an easy-to-manage format while still generating standard back-ends. In addition, the Mylyn WikiText can also be extended in future to support other wiki dialects, such as Markdown or AsciiDoc.

When generating Eclipse Help with Mylyn, the file is converted into HTML and a corresponding `toc.xml` file is created as well.

In addition to the user interface, Mylyn also provides `ant` tasks (defined in the `org/eclipse/mylyn/wikitext/core/util/anttask/tasks.properties` file) that can be used to convert documentation into the right format. The tasks are as follows:

- `wikitext-to-eclipse-help`: Used to generate Eclipse help documents
- `wikitext-to-html`: Used to generate standalone HTML documents
- `wikitext-to-docbook`: Used to generate DocBook documents
- `wikitext-to-dita`: Used to generate DITA documents
- `wikitext-to-xslfo`: Used to generate `xsl:fo` objects to create PDFs
- `html-to-wikitext`: Used for conversion of HTML to WikiText

There are two additional tasks (defined in the `org/eclipse/mylyn/internal/wikitext/mediawiki/core/tasks/tasks.properties` file) that can be used to acquire the contents of a MediaWiki server and generate help pages automatically:

- `mediawiki-to-eclipse-help`: Used to download MediaWiki pages and create Eclipse help pages
- `mediawiki-fetch-images`: Used to download MediaWiki images

These tasks are used by the EGit project to create documents automatically from the EGit wiki page at `http://wiki.eclipse.org/EGit`. The `ant` build file looks like the following:

```
<project name="org.eclipse.egit.doc" default="all">
  <path id="wikitext.tasks.classpath">
    <pathelement path="${compile_classpath}"/>
  </path>
  <taskdef classpathref="wikitext.tasks.classpath"
   resource="org/eclipse/mylyn/internal/wikitext/
    mediawiki/core/tasks/tasks.properties"/>
  <taskdef classpathref="wikitext.tasks.classpath"
   resource="org/eclipse/mylyn/wikitext/core/util/
    anttask/tasks.properties"/>
  <target name="all">
    <mediawiki-to-eclipse-help
     validate="true"
     wikiBaseUrl="http://wiki.eclipse.org"
     failonvalidationerror="true"
     prependImagePrefix="images"
     formatoutput="true"
     defaultAbsoluteLinkTarget="egit_external"
     dest="help"
     navigationimages="true"
     title="EGit Documentation"
     helpPrefix="help"
     generateUnifiedToc="true">
      <path name="EGit/User_Guide" title="EGit User Guide" />
      <path name="JGit/User_Guide" title="JGit User Guide" />
      <path name="EGit/Git_For_Eclipse_Users"
       title="Git for Eclipse Users" />
      <stylesheet url="book.css" />
      <pageAppendum>
= Updating This Document =
This document is maintained in a collaborative wiki.
If you wish to update or modify this document please visit
```

```
{url} </pageAppendum>
    </mediawiki-to-eclipse-help>
  </target>
</project>
```

To run this `ant` file, the `org.eclipse.mylyn.wikitext` plug-ins need to be on the classpath. This is launched from a Maven/Tycho build in the EGit distribution, which takes care of assembling the classpath from the bundle dependencies specified in the `pom.xml` file. Alternatively, the conversion can be performed by running the `ant` build file manually, provided that the classpath is correctly set up to resolve Mylyn dependencies.

Help Server and RCP

It is possible to include the help server and system in an RCP application, or to host the help server as a standalone application. The help system is made up of a number of separate plug-ins:

- `org.eclipse.help.webapp`: This serves the HTML pages and provides the web API to search and navigate (needs `org.eclipse.equinox.http.jetty` to run)
- `org.eclipse.help.ui`: This provides actions/commands for the help pages and the help browser view, along with preference pages
- `org.eclipse.help`: This provides the extension points for indexes and table of contents
- `org.eclipse.help.base`: This provides the InfoCenter application and index searching ability

There are of course a number of dependencies such as the core expressions that are used to provide content filtering, and the Jetty server which is used to provide the web application. When adding help to an RCP, ensure that the optional dependencies of the aforementioned plug-ins are included in order for it to work as expected.

Help and Eclipse 3.x

The `org.eclipse.help.ui` bundle is needed to integrate into the Eclipse 3 workbench. For Eclipse 3.x RCP applications, it should be added.

The `ApplicationActionBarAdvisor` is used to add workspace-wide menu additions, and this is the best place to add the Eclipse 3.x RCP help. When running in a hosted IDE mode, this function is performed by the workbench, which adds the actions programmatically.

> Actions have been deprecated for some time and new applications should use commands and handlers. The help system predates commands and handlers and has not been migrated to the new system. For more information about commands and handlers, see chapter 4 of *Eclipse 4 Plug-in Development by Example Beginner's Guide, Packt Publishing.*

The `org.eclipse.ui.actions.ActionFactory` is used to create instances of standard platform actions, such as copy/paste, undo, and so on. It can also be used to create the help menu actions. There are three of them, which are used for different purposes:

- `HELP_CONTENTS`: Used to create the **Help Contents** menu
- `HELP_SEARCH`: Used to create the **Search** menu
- `DYNAMIC_HELP`: Used to create the **Dynamic Help** menu

These actions are created in the `makeActions` method and then added to the menu items with `fillMenuBar`. The code to add the **Help** menu to an Eclipse 3.x RCP application is as follows:

```
public class ApplicationActionBarAdvisor extends ActionBarAdvisor{
  private IWorkbenchAction helpContents;
  private IWorkbenchAction helpSearch;
  private IWorkbenchAction helpDynamic;
  public ApplicationActionBarAdvisor(IActionBarConfigurer abc) {
    super(abc);
  }
  protected void makeActions(IWorkbenchWindow window) {
    helpContents = ActionFactory.HELP_CONTENTS.create(window);
    helpSearch = ActionFactory.HELP_SEARCH.create(window);
    helpDynamic = ActionFactory.DYNAMIC_HELP.create(window);
  }
  protected void fillMenuBar(IMenuManager menuBar) {
    MenuManager help = new MenuManager("Help", "help");
    help.add(helpContents);
    help.add(helpSearch);
    help.add(helpDynamic);
    menuBar.add(help);
  }
}
```

The `ApplicationBarAdvisor` class is typically hooked into the application at start-up time:

```
public class Application implements IApplication {
  public Object start(IApplicationContext ctx) throws Exception {
    Display display = PlatformUI.createDisplay();
    PlatformUI.createAndRunWorkbench(display,
      new ApplicationWorkbenchAdvisor());
    display.dispose();
  }
}
```

When the application starts up, the **Help** menu will be added, along with the **Display Help**, **Search**, and **Dynamic Help** menus.

Help and Eclipse 4.x

For Eclipse 4.x RCP applications, only the `org.eclipse.help.base` and `org.eclipse.help.webapp` dependencies are required (although there may be restrictions and warnings shown for the `base` plug-in). The reason for this is the Eclipse 3.x help system—particularly the dynamic help—is tightly integrated with the Eclipse 3.x UI components.

Since there is limited Eclipse 4.x support for dynamic help and the integrated search view, it is necessary to create a menu and handler in E4 explicitly for the **Help** menu, as follows:

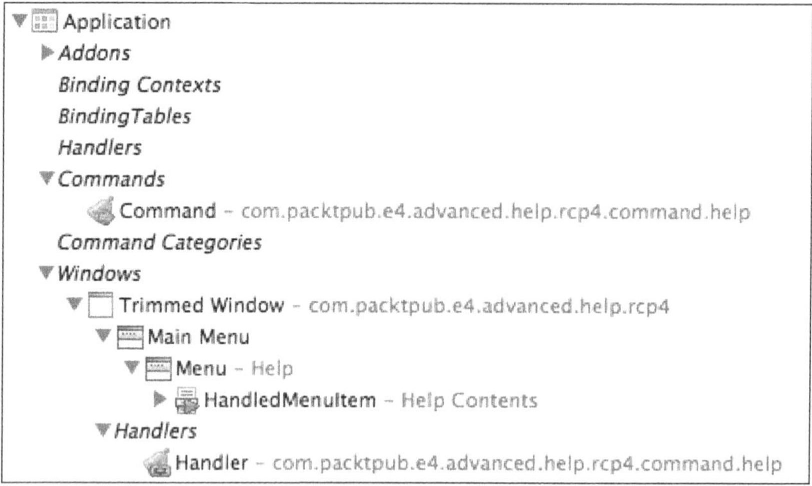

The handler class can use `BaseHelpSystem` to display the help page in an external browser. There are three modes that the help system can be launched in:

- `MODE_WORKBENCH`: This is integrated with the Eclipse 3.x workbench
- `MODE_STANDALONE`: This acts as a standalone SWT window
- `MODE_INFOCENTER`: This acts as an InfoCenter web application

The only one that works with Eclipse 4.x RCP is `MODE_INFOCENTER`; so this needs to be set on the base mode before launching the `help` option.

The E4 command will look like the following:

```
@SuppressWarnings("restriction")
public class HelpCommand {
  @Execute
  public void execute() {
    BaseHelpSystem.setMode(BaseHelpSystem.MODE_INFOCENTER);
    BaseHelpSystem.getHelpDisplay().displayHelp(true);
  }
}
```

Ensure that the Eclipse 4.x RCP product has the dependencies listed previously, as well as the `org.eclipse.equinox.http.jetty` bundle, along with optional dependencies. Now when the **Help** menu is chosen, the help page will be shown in an external browser.

To add search support, the `displaySearch` method can be used, possibly triggered by the selection that the user has made, or through an interactive dialog. One possible implementation would be as follows:

```
@SuppressWarnings("restriction")
public class SearchCommand {
  @Execute
  public void execute() throws UnsupportedEncodingException {
    BaseHelpSystem.setMode(BaseHelpSystem.MODE_INFOCENTER);
    InputDialog dialog = new InputDialog(null, "Search",
      "What do you want to search for?", null, null);
    if (Window.OK == dialog.open()) {
      String searchString = URLEncoder.encode(
       dialog.getValue(), "UTF-8");
      BaseHelpSystem.getHelpDisplay().displaySearch(
       "searchWord=" + searchString, "", true);
    }
  }
}
```

The `displaySearch` method allows arguments to be added to the search URL. This includes `searchWord` and `maxHits`. Since this is passed through to the browser directly, the `searchWord` should be validated and URI encoded; in other words, replacing non-ASCII characters with `%` values, as well as for control characters and characters requiring special treatment such as `&` and `+`.

Context-sensitive help is more difficult to implement in an E4 application. There are defined **contextId** names associated with views in Eclipse (such as `org.eclipse.jdt.ui.members_view_context`) that have a specific page associated with them. In a 3.x application, these contexts are associated with the view implementation themselves, and the help system wires up the content automatically.

To programmatically display help associated with a context from a given key, the following needs to be done:

```
@SuppressWarnings("restriction")
public class ShowContextHelpCommand {
  @Execute
  public void execute() {
    BaseHelpSystem.setMode(BaseHelpSystem.MODE_INFOCENTER);
    // obtain from UI in an appropriate means
    String helpContext="org.eclipse.jdt.ui.members_view_context";
    IContext context = HelpSystem.getContext(helpContext);
    if (context == null) {
      String message = "Cannot find help for context " + context;
      ErrorDialog.openError(null, "Cannot find help", message,
       new Status(Status.ERROR, "", message));
    } else {
      IHelpResource[] topics = context.getRelatedTopics();
      if (topics.length == 0) {
        String message = "No help topics for context " + context;
        ErrorDialog.openError(null, "Cannot find help", message,
         new Status(Status.ERROR, "", message));
      } else {
        // Display first topic; add UI if multiple are returned
        BaseHelpSystem.getHelpDisplay().displayHelp(context,
         context.getRelatedTopics()[0], true);
      }
    }
  }
}
```

The means that acquiring the help context from the given UI will be specific to how the Eclipse 4.x RCP is implemented. It could be stored as a context variable for example.

Running an InfoCenter standalone

The InfoCenter application can be launched from a standalone Eclipse installation. The `org.eclipse.help.base` plug-in provides an application that can be launched via the `eclipse` executable.

To launch a headless Eclipse instance with the InfoCenter, run the following from a command line:

```
$ eclipse -nosplash
 -application org.eclipse.help.base.infocenterApplication
 -vmargs -Dserver_port=5555
```

The help center will start and run on the port specified in the `-vmargs -Dserver _port` command-line option. If the port is not specified, it will start on a random port, which makes it more difficult to determine where the server is running.

Navigating to the root page will result in a "file not found" error:

```
http://localhost:5555/
```

Instead, navigate to `/help/index.jsp`:

```
http://localhost:5555/help/index.jsp
```

Cheat sheets

A **cheat sheet** is a guided set of steps that a user can perform. As well as being documentation, it can interactively launch specific operations in the Eclipse environment, so that the user not only achieves the task, but learns how to do it again in the future. Because of the tight integration with the UI, this is only possible in Eclipse 3.x applications and Eclipse 4.x with the 3.x workbench (in other words, not for Eclipse 4.x RCP applications as of Eclipse 4.4).

Creating a cheat sheet

A cheat sheet is an XML file that has a top-level `description` and a number of `item` elements that have a `title` and `description`. The idea is to provide a series of steps, like a bulleted list, to perform and in turn achieve a particular goal.

For example, a cheat sheet to create a Java project might start off by giving an introduction of what the cheat sheet is about with an initial step. The following can be saved in `cheatsheets/javaApplication.xml`:

```
<?xml version="1.0" encoding="UTF-8"?>
<cheatsheet title="Creating a Java application">
  <intro>
    <description>This cheat sheet shows how to create
     and run a simple Java application</description>
  </intro>
  <item title="Creating a new Java project">
    <description>Firstly, create a new Java project
     called &#x201C;HelloWorld&#x201D;</description>
  </item>
</cheatsheet>
```

> The XML file can only contain text; special characters such as `&`, `<`, and `>` need to be encoded as `&` `<` and `>`, respectively. HTML entities such as `“` are not understood, but Unicode characters can be inserted with `&#nnnn;` or `&#xnnn;` for decimal or hex values, respectively. Note that the cheat sheet also understands two specific elements: `<br/>` to create a new line break and `<b>...</b>` for bold text.

The cheat sheet is then referenced from the `plugin.xml` file:

```
<extension point="org.eclipse.ui.cheatsheets.cheatSheetContent">
  <cheatsheet composite="false"
   contentFile="cheatsheets/javaApplication.xml"
   id="com.packtpub.e4.advanced.doc.cheatsheet.javaApplication"
   name="Creating a Java application">
  </cheatsheet>
</extension>
```

Provided that the `cheatsheets` folder is included in the plug-in (via the `build.properties`), it should now be possible to open up an Eclipse instance, and navigate to **Help** | **Cheat Sheets...** to get the following dialog:

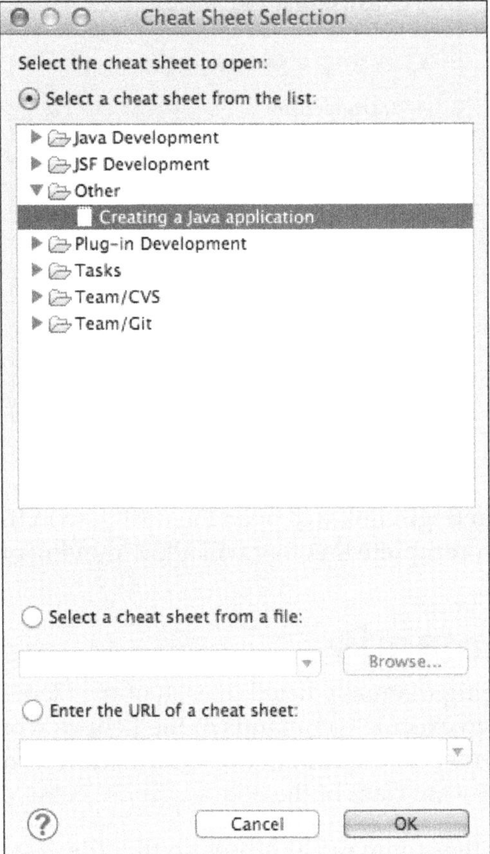

The cheat sheet will be in the **Other** category by default, unless `<category id="..." name="..."/>` is specified in the `plugin.xml` extension point.

When the cheat sheet is selected, it will open on the right-hand side of the Eclipse application with a window rendered from the content, as follows:

Clicking on the **Click to Begin** link will open the next item in the sequence. Each item will have a **Click when complete** link that will allow moving on to the next step.

Adding commands

As well as the steps being manually listed in each of the elements, it is also possible to provide hyperlinks to execute commands in the Eclipse workbench. The commands are represented in the **command serialization** format, which is defined in the `ParameterizedCommand` class of the `org.eclipse.core.commands` package.

The format represents the command as a pseudo function with hard-coded arguments. The function name is the command's ID, and the parameters are specified as comma-separated `key=value` pairs.

For example, to open the **New Java Project** wizard, the command is `org.eclipse.ui.newWizard`. This takes a parameter of `newWizardId`, which provides the wizard identifier to be used—in this case, `org.eclipse.jdt.ui.wizards.JavaProjectWizard`. Add the following to the cheat sheet:

```
<item title="Creating a new Java project">
  <description>Firstly, create a new Java project called
```

```
    &#x201C;<b>HelloWorld</b>&#x201D;, followed by pressing
    <b>Finish</b>
  </description>
  <command serialization="org.eclipse.ui.newWizard(
    newWizardId=org.eclipse.jdt.ui.wizards.JavaProjectWizard)"/>
</item>
```

If opening a modal dialog which may obscure the cheat sheet, ensure that the instructions indicate what to do to dismiss the dialog so that the user can return subsequently.

Optional steps

Not all commands or steps need to be performed. It is possible to mark an item as skippable, so that the user can elect to perform or skip the step. Without this, the user will be forced to follow each step in the sequence before they can make progress.

To recommend opening the **Java Browsing** perspective, the command is `org.eclipse.ui.perspectives.showPerspective`, and the argument is `org.eclipse.ui.perspectives.showPerspective.perspectiveId` with a value of `org.eclipse.jdt.ui.JavaBrowsingPerspective`. To make it optional, since not everyone likes the Java Browsing perspective, add the following to the cheat sheet:

```
<item title="Switch to the Java Browsing perspective" skip="true">
  <description>The Java Browsing perspective can be more efficient
   for navigating large projects, as it presents a logical view
   rather than a file-oriented view of the contents</description>
  <command
   serialization="org.eclipse.ui.perspectives.showPerspective(
    org.eclipse.ui.perspectives.showPerspective.perspectiveId
    =org.eclipse.jdt.ui.JavaBrowsingPerspective)"/>
</item>
```

Note that line breaks are not permitted in XML attributes, and the value has been split for typographical reasons. The whitespace inside the serialization attribute should not be added.

To find out what the command's arguments are, go to the **Plug-in Registry** view (which can be opened by navigating to **Window | Show View | Other ... | Plug-in Development | Plug-in Registry**) and search for the command ID. The `commandParameter` elements will be shown. These are the identifiers required to be added to the command itself:

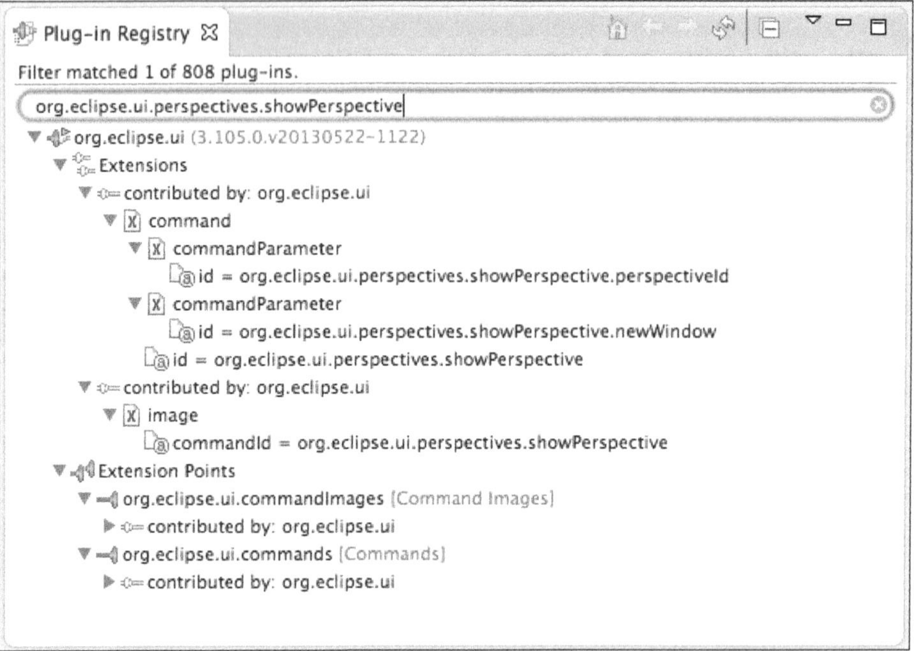

Responding to choice

Cheat sheets can be responsive to user input by prompting for choices during an operation. The result of the choice can be stored in a cheat sheet variable, and subsequent steps can be conditionally displayed based on the result of that choice.

The cheat sheet variable can be used during conditional command execution, allowing differing commands to be executed based on user choice. For example, to permit the user to choose either the **Java Perspective** or the **Java Browsing Perspective**, a dialog can be presented with these choices.

The `org.eclipse.ui.dialogs.openMessageDialog` command allows up to three buttons to be displayed to the user to perform an interactive choice. The text of the chosen button can be stored in a variable, and then subsequently used in later steps. Adding a `when` condition to the command and wrapping it in a `perform-when` block allows the value to be compared with a set of known values and the appropriate action to be taken:

```
<item title="Choose a perspective">
  <description>Choose your favourite perspective</description>
  <command returns="perspective"
   serialization="org.eclipse.ui.dialogs.openMessageDialog(
    title=Choose Perspective,
    message=Choose your favourite perspective,
    buttonLabel0=Java Perspective,
    buttonLabel1=Java Browsing Perspective)"/>
  <onCompletion>Your favourite perspective is the
   ${perspective}.
  </onCompletion>
</item>
<item title="Switch to the perspective" skip="true">
  <description>Switching to the appropriate perspective will
   facilitate working with Java projects.</description>
  <perform-when condition="${perspective}">
    <command when="Java Browsing Perspective"
     serialization="org.eclipse.ui.perspectives.showPerspective(
      org.eclipse.ui.perspectives.showPerspective.perspectiveId
      =org.eclipse.jdt.ui.JavaBrowsingPerspective)"/>
    <command when="Java Perspective"
     serialization="org.eclipse.ui.perspectives.showPerspective(
      org.eclipse.ui.perspectives.showPerspective.perspectiveId
      =org.eclipse.jdt.ui.JavaPerspective)"/>
  </perform-when>
</item>
```

Now when the cheat sheet is run, the user is asked for their preferred perspective, which is then opened. The perspective can be reused in later steps of the cheat sheet if necessary.

Note that the variable can only be used as the result of the `onCompletion` block, and also in the `perform-when` calculations. It cannot be used in the `title` or `description` of subsequent steps, because these are visible before the choice has been made.

The values shown must not include certain characters, such as percent (`%`), comma (`,`), or equals (`=`). Any such character must be escaped with a leading percent character, that is, `%%`, `%`, or `%=`.

Note that there is an editor for help context files. As long as the XML file starts with `<cheatsheet>`, the file can be double-clicked and opened in a cheat sheet editor, or via the context menu by navigating to **Open With | Simple Cheat Sheet Editor**. This is especially useful for commands, since the commands are shown in an easy-to-select drop-down list, along with the command parameters:

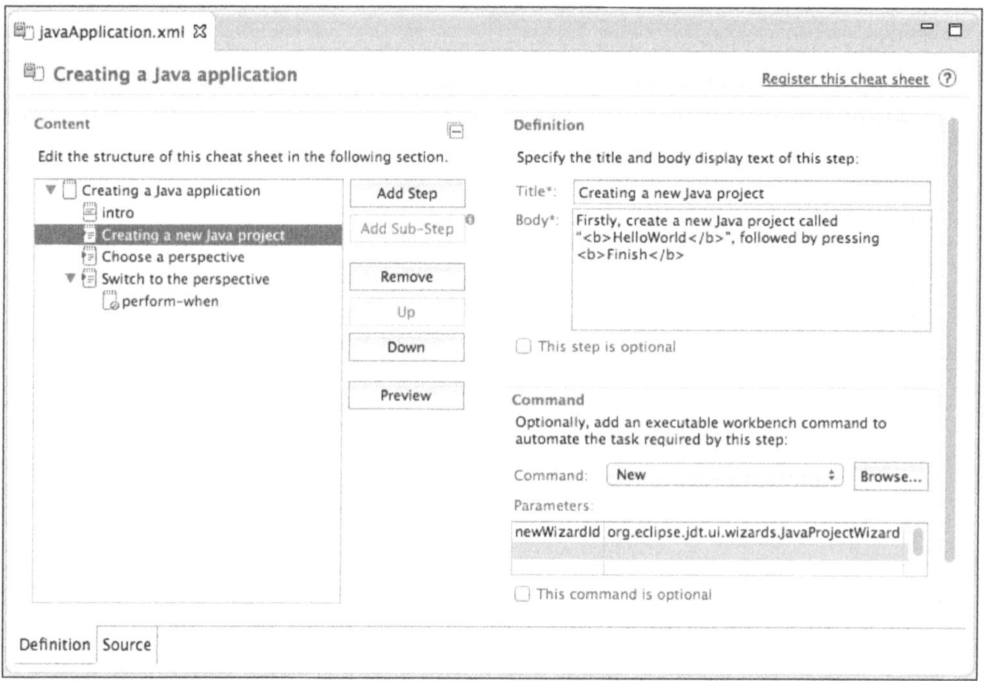

Composite cheat sheets

A composite cheat sheet allows several cheat sheets to be collected together and presented in a single sheet. This is useful if several smaller cheat sheets have been created previously but can be presented as a unified set.

A composite cheat sheet is specified in an XML file, with a `<compositeCheatsheet>` root element. This contains a `<taskGroup>`, which has an optional `<intro>` description, and then one or more `<task>` or `<taskGroup>` elements.

Each task has a name and refers to a cheat sheet, either by `path` to a reference in the current plug-in, or by its `id`. The cheat sheet can have its own `intro` and an `onCompletion` message, which is shown when the cheat sheet is complete.

A simple cheat sheet collection can be represented as follows:

```
<compositeCheatsheet name="A collection of cheat sheets">
  <taskGroup kind="choice" skip="false"
   name="Example Cheat Sheets Collection">
    <intro><b>Overview of cheat sheets</b></intro>
    <onCompletion>
      <b>Congratulations of completing the cheat sheets</b>
    </onCompletion>
    <task kind="cheatsheet" skip="false"
     name="Example Cheat Sheet">
      <intro>The cheat sheet provided in this plug-in</intro>
      <onCompletion>
        Congratulations, you have completed the tasks
      </onCompletion>
      <param name="path" value="javaApplication.xml"/>
    </task>
  </taskGroup>
</compositeCheatsheet>
```

The composite cheat sheet is referenced in the `plugin.xml` file, with the `composite="true"` attribute, along with an appropriate category:

```
<extension point="org.eclipse.ui.cheatsheets.cheatSheetContent">
  <category name="Example cheat sheets"
   id="com.packtpub.e4.advanced.doc.category"/>
  <cheatsheet name="Composite cheatsheets"
   contentFile="cheatsheets/composite.xml"
   id="com.packtpub.e4.advanced.doc.cheatsheet.composite"
   composite="true"/>
</extension>
```

When loaded in the runtime Eclipse, it will look like the following:

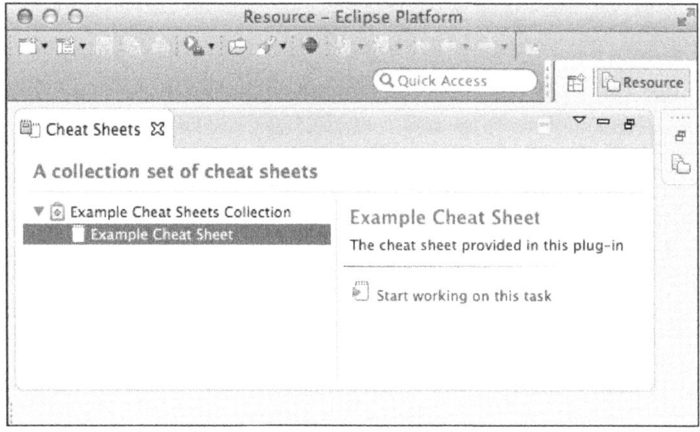

To refer to other cheat sheets, use the `id` that is defined in the extension point. For example, the standard JDT cheat sheets uses `org.eclipse.jdt.helloworld` and `org.eclipse.jdt.helloworld.swt` (that are visible from the extension point browser as well as the JDT `plugin.xml` file). These can be added as a task group in `composite.xml`:

```
<taskGroup kind="choice" name="JDT Cheat Sheets" skip="false">
  <intro>
    <b>Introduction</b>
    These are the cheat sheets provided by the JDT
  </intro>
  <onCompletion>
    Congratulations, you have completed the tasks
  </onCompletion>
  <task kind="cheatsheet" name="JDT Hello World" skip="false">
    <intro>Provides a simple Hello World project</intro>
    <onCompletion>Congratulations,
     you have completed the task</onCompletion>
    <param name="id" value="org.eclipse.jdt.helloworld"/>
  </task>
  <task kind="cheatsheet" name="SWT Hello World" skip="false">
    <intro>Provides a SWT hello world project</intro>
    <onCompletion>Congratulations,
     you have completed the task</onCompletion>
    <param name="id" value="org.eclipse.jdt.helloworld.swt"/>
  </task>
</taskGroup>
```

Now, when the composite sheet is shown, the JDT cheat sheets are shown as well:

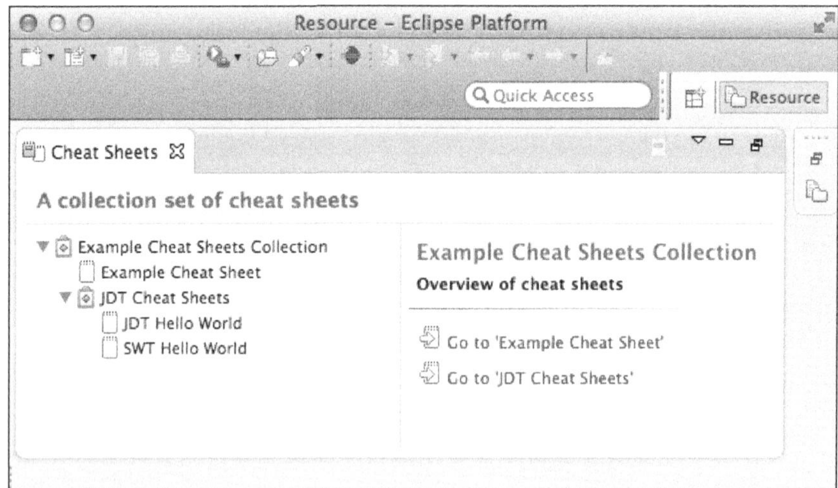

Summary

The user assistance support in Eclipse provides a way to inform and teach users about the user interface. Whether this is from standalone help documentation, if dynamic help is provided depending on the user's context, or the help documentation itself is interactive and allows the Eclipse user interface to be driven, it is possible to allow users to learn about the functionality of the product and allow it to be extended in a customizable way. Cheat sheets provide a set of recipes that can interact with the user allowing the experience to be self-driven, and a consistent set of help pages that offer one of the best documented open source projects.

Index

Symbols

A

B

C

F

G

H

I

J

K

L

M

N

O

P

Q

R

S

Thank you for buying
Mastering Eclipse Plug-in Development

About Packt Publishing

Packt, pronounced 'packed', published its first book "*Mastering phpMyAdmin for Effective MySQL Management*" in April 2004 and subsequently continued to specialize in publishing highly focused books on specific technologies and solutions.

Our books and publications share the experiences of your fellow IT professionals in adapting and customizing today's systems, applications, and frameworks. Our solution based books give you the knowledge and power to customize the software and technologies you're using to get the job done. Packt books are more specific and less general than the IT books you have seen in the past. Our unique business model allows us to bring you more focused information, giving you more of what you need to know, and less of what you don't.

Packt is a modern, yet unique publishing company, which focuses on producing quality, cutting-edge books for communities of developers, administrators, and newbies alike. For more information, please visit our website: `www.packtpub.com`.

About Packt Open Source

In 2010, Packt launched two new brands, Packt Open Source and Packt Enterprise, in order to continue its focus on specialization. This book is part of the Packt Open Source brand, home to books published on software built around Open Source licenses, and offering information to anybody from advanced developers to budding web designers. The Open Source brand also runs Packt's Open Source Royalty Scheme, by which Packt gives a royalty to each Open Source project about whose software a book is sold.

Writing for Packt

We welcome all inquiries from people who are interested in authoring. Book proposals should be sent to `author@packtpub.com`. If your book idea is still at an early stage and you would like to discuss it first before writing a formal book proposal, contact us; one of our commissioning editors will get in touch with you.

We're not just looking for published authors; if you have strong technical skills but no writing experience, our experienced editors can help you develop a writing career, or simply get some additional reward for your expertise.

Lightning Source UK Ltd.
Milton Keynes UK
UKOW07f1109150116

266406UK00001B/129/P